# Arrested Adulthood

# Arrested Adulthood

*The Changing Nature of*
*Maturity and Identity*

James E. Côté

NEW YORK UNIVERSITY PRESS
*New York and London*

NEW YORK UNIVERSITY PRESS
New York and London

Library of Congress Cataloging-in-Publication Data
Côté, James E.
Arrested adulthood : the changing nature of maturity and identity /
James E. Côté.
p.  cm.
Includes bibliographical references and index.
ISBN 0-8147-1598-2 (pbk. : acid-free paper) — ISBN 0-8147-1599-0
(cloth : acid-free paper)
1. Adulthood.  2. Emotional maturity.  3. Identity (Psychology)
4. Civilization, Modern—Psychological aspects.   I. Title.
HQ799.95 .C67 2000
305.24—dc21                              00-008435

New York University Press books are printed on acid-free paper,
and their binding materials are chosen for strength and durability.

Manufactured in the United States of America

10 9 8 7 6 5 4 3 2 1

*This book is dedicated to Dr. Arthur Yehle, my most significant and enduring adult role model and mentor, who has patiently taught me how to enjoy life while balancing key responsibilities.*
*Carpe Diem, Art*

# Contents

# Introduction

As strange as it may seem, my desire to write this book on adulthood springs from my previous research into the nature of adolescence. That research revealed two features of adolescence that are contrary to most people's commonsense conceptions of the period between childhood and adulthood: (1) adolescence takes different forms in different cultures and over time, and (2) adolescence is becoming longer and longer, especially in late modern societies. The second point led me to consider the possibility that for large numbers of people, prolonged adolescence—and more recently "youth"—now takes up much, if not all, of what in an earlier society would have been "adulthood." That is, although we now live much longer, it appears that an increasing number of people are not "growing up" in the traditional sense of the word, or at least in the way many people have understood it. The reasons for this are many, but my analysis of the issue suggests that social, economic, and technological changes have been making it increasingly difficult for people to become the type of adult that was characteristic of the past.

During a 1994 publicity tour for the book *Generation on Hold: Coming of Age in the Late Twentieth Century,* I found that the most frequently asked questions concerned what the future holds for young people today, given the numerous hazards and difficulties they face. These questions pointed to a gap in our understanding of contemporary life. When I turned my attention to this type of question and examined the life stage that supposedly follows adolescence, I realized that the concept of adulthood is as vague as the concept of adolescence. Moreover, adulthood is a hazardous and difficult journey for many people, not a destination of safety and security that is reached once and for all. In other words, like most people I had taken for granted the notion of adulthood as a reference point from which other life stages are judged, viewing it as a static time of security, at least from the point of view of human development.

Ironically, the idea of adulthood requires the idea of adolescence to make sense, for "maturity" implies a previous "immaturity," and being "grown up" implies having previously been childish or juvenile. It was only after the concept of adolescence took hold in the public mind that the notion of adulthood achieved any currency. Moreover, just as with the study of adolescence, two striking features are associated with adulthood: (1) it takes many different forms in different cultures and over time; and (2) it has increased in duration in industrial societies. In fact, "adulthood" now constitutes the longest, but the least understood, period of the life course.

These complexities piqued my interest in understanding better the ways people *experience* their adulthoods, along with the ways people *think* about adulthood in general (the two are linked). When contemporary Western adults are compared with adults from earlier centuries, remarkable differences are evident. For example, contemporary adults are on the frontier of a future for which there are few models and apparently infinite possibilities—certainly few of their forebears could have imagined what is now being experienced, or what will be experienced in the future.

Adults are responding in a variety of ways to this new world. The responses that initially caught my attention were those that seemingly involved preserving one's youth as long as possible, both in appearance and in behavior. Especially common is a desire to experience as much pleasure as possible and to avoid responsibilities indefinitely. But there are other responses as well.

In this book I explore the various responses in terms of how increasing numbers of people emerge from a vague and prolonged youth into a vague and prolonged adulthood. Moreover, I argue that this takes place in an apparently indeterminate "Brave New World." It is the desire to understand these "Brave New Adults," among whom I count myself, that compelled me to write this book.

## Plan of the Book

In order to achieve my goal for this book, which is to sort out the issues associated with maturity and identity on an ontological level (what is adulthood?), as well as in political-economic terms (how did it get this way, and whose interests are served?), I have chosen strategically what to mention and focus upon. Undoubtedly, those who view the world from one or more "isms" that differ from mine will find fault in what I write or do not write. I merely ask those readers who share an interest in the ontology and political economy of adulthood to consider what I have to say, taking into account my perspective.

The perspective I adopt can be described as a macro critical materialism informed by a micro developmental social psychology. However, my intention is not to promote that perspective per se. Instead, I attempt to keep it mostly in the background and use it to select the material and ideas that seem pertinent to understanding the nature of adulthood, historically and contemporarily. Moreover, I take the role of narrator in this book, walking the reader through those authors, theories, and studies that offer what I believe are the best explanations for what has happened and why it has happened. Of course, I cannot be a neutral narrator—that is impossible—but I can assist by drawing conclusions on those points most germane to the thesis of the book. I have therefore attempted to avoid getting bogged down in theoretical and ideological issues and disputes and rather to focus as much as possible on pragmatic issues: the things that matter in people's lives and that have practical consequences. There are two areas of dispute that are difficult to avoid, however: the disputes raised by postmodernism and feminism. Ironically, some of the issues raised by these two "isms" are related, although some of their proponents seem unaware of the interrelation. I find much of merit in these two perspectives, but in crucial ways they fail to provide sufficient insight into the problem at hand—the ontology and political economy of adulthood.

The thesis of this book is that the material conditions of existence have been continuously altered over the past few centuries as capitalism has intruded more and more into how people subsist and experience their worlds. These changes have been both positive and negative. The positive ones include improved nutrition, higher standards of living, a longer life span, and increased personal freedom. The negative ones include the loss of the structure and direction that once defined maturity and identity and a widespread psychological malaise for those people who have not been able to "capitalize" on the socioeconomic changes affecting the course of their lives, especially those that give them greater personal freedom. In addition, the transition to "adulthood" has become more prolonged and more difficult, and those who attempt to move into a "psychological adulthood" can find themselves in a new stage of "youthhood" with its own characteristics. This new stage has its own benefits and liabilities, but an important problem is emerging: youthhood is mistaken by a growing number of people as adulthood—as a final destination after adolescence. Instead, youthhood is more likely an additional step toward adulthood in an increasingly chaotic and confusing world.

But whether people's experiences are positive or negative, they appear to share a different experience of "adulthood," and a different transition to it, than that of their forebears. It is those historical differences and their implications that this book addresses.

My hope is to analyze the historical changes at a sufficient level of generality or abstractness to characterize the experiences of as many (Western) people as possible in the most parsimonious terms. I know that this approach goes against the current concern over documenting "differences" based on ethnicity, race, gender, class, and so forth, but I am targeting those experiences that people have most in common. It is worthwhile to focus on difference, but to do so to the exclusion of commonality can distort the "reality" of people's lives, such as their longer life spans, fewer children, and higher levels of consumption. Moreover, most everyone living in capitalist societies shares the same facts of life in that they must compete with one another for the price of their labor. I believe that this fundamental necessity to compete for resources promotes a false sense of difference that could easily be exaggerated and misunderstood if a social analysis, such as the present one, was to explicitly emphasize differences. I hope to help improve our sense of unity as a species, not worsen it. I am fully aware that this approach puts me at odds with currently popular perspectives such as postmodernism and feminism, but I explicitly address how these popular perspectives apply to the topic at hand and how they provide only limited accounts of it.

What has changed for people attempting to make the transition to adulthood? There is a consensus in the literature that adulthood has lost much of its role structure and traditional meaning and has become much more of a psychological phenomenon. The line between youth and adulthood is blurred for many people, especially those most affected by recent socioeconomic changes. In other words, the life course has been destructuring, and people have increasingly had to adapt by individualizing their lives—taking things into their own hands rather than relying on traditional institutions to provide structure for them.

This development has freed people to try to fully develop themselves and their potentials, and many people attempt to do so. However, there is evidence that a large number—perhaps the majority—are not taking advantage of the loosening of traditional constraints but instead passively allow themselves to be manipulated by the profit-based, "mass" structures that have arisen in place of traditional cultural institutions. Because this manipulation is largely based on hedonism and narcissism, there is reason to be concerned about how the future is being planned for, particularly how much care is given to generational replacement.

As we see, the science of adulthood is stymied by the lack of a clear definition of terms. I believe that deficit is directly attributable to the culturally induced ambiguities concerning the meanings of the various components of the life course. That is, the cultural confusion makes scientific precision difficult. I first examine expert opinion of the matter and then review evidence that has been gathered from those attempting to make the transition to adulthood. Again the ambiguities emerge, yet through it all there is an attempt to assert some certainty on the issue of what it means to be an adult. From this starting point, I review empirical evidence that reflects the current nature of adulthood and the world in which adults live, partly by their own creation. The review includes an examination of statistical evidence concerning the "state of the civilization" over the past few decades as well as the results of studies of adults' lifestyles and their values, attitudes, and opinions. It appears that systematic changes are under way that reflect mass phenomena, varying in degree by people's stations in life (i.e., class, race, gender, age). These data support the view that the transition to adulthood is becoming more hazardous and that the destination is becoming more difficult to reach. In this analysis I refer to data and opinions mostly from the United States, in part because that is where most of the data are available but also in part because the United States is a bellwether nation that either sets the trends by its sheer global influence or is emulated as a model of freedom and happiness.

Western societies have experienced a "massification" dating back to the nineteenth century. Theories of mass society once dominated in the social sciences, but they have been eclipsed by more recent perspectives such as postmodernism. I argue that many postmodernists have neglected the trends noted by mass-society theorists, who put the origins of our present concerns in a different time and place. Further, I contend that postmodernism as an "ism" is a symptom of mass society in its current late modern form and that "postmodernity" is an illusion created by the deleterious effects of "massification." This theoretical dialogue helps us to better understand how various social analysts—for the most part critical of how we have handled the changes and opportunities that capitalism has brought—have been attempting to comprehend what has happened to adulthood and why it has happened.

Even the nature of identity has undergone changes. I review those theorists who have attempted to understand the "normal" identity problems associated with contemporary society and then examine the more severe identity problems that have become so commonplace that many people now see them as "normal." With the decline of authority and structure, people have had to learn to live with psychological uncertainty. The confusion of identity that makes it difficult for people to find a place in this increasingly complex world has become a major impediment to truly benefiting from the affluence and technological sophistication that capitalism has brought us. Thus, many people now seem to find it difficult to get a grip even on themselves, let alone on this Brave New World. The literature that I refer to in this context focuses on more sociological understandings of identity problems, especially those that explicitly address the dual processes of individualization and cultural destructuring.

But what is this world to which so many people are having such a difficult time adjusting, and how did things get so confusing? I directly address these questions first by making comparisons between contemporary society and the world portrayed by Aldous Huxley in his book *Brave New World*. Though there are obviously key differences, there are also a number of uncanny similarities in how adulthood is structured in both societies, particularly with reference to the ongoing changes in adulthood. In order to understand how such a thing could have happened, I then undertake a historical analysis of the changing life course, focusing on the structure of youth and adolescence. The analysis shows how, as the period of youth has become increasingly prolonged, the period of adulthood has become increasingly destructured; indeed, the period of youth is encroaching on adulthood as more people stay "younger" longer. Moreover, the profit-driven industries of mass culture are more than willing to step in and provide the structure for people's lives that is now missing as the process of cultural destructuring continues.

Key problems, especially the problem of cultural narcissism, have been consistently cited in numerous analyses of contemporary life.

What can be done about those problems? Based on the components of adulthood that have emerged as Western institutions have been destructured, I suggest a typology that synthesizes significant elements of the lives of contemporary adults and differences among them. Nonetheless, there are persisting structural constraints and opportunities that are beyond the capacity of many individuals to deal with on their own. Since capitalism has solved many technical problems but has created more social problems, I retrace what has happened to direct Western values toward an extreme individualism, away from the collectivist values Western civilization once promoted. From this historical review, an idea emerges of the steps that need to be taken to unify concerns about justice and care, particularly when it comes to intergenerational relations and ensuring that the generations to come will have secure futures. It is perhaps only by accepting moral responsibility for our own actions and their impact on the future that we can hope to build a truly progressive society in which all members can develop their potentials, irrespective of what the money markets are doing. When both individuals and their polities follow these steps, we should have a clearer vision of what it means to be an adult.

# PART I

# The Changing Nature of Maturity

# 1

## Maturity Transformed
### The Rise of Psychological Adulthood

*Snapshots of Late Modern Society*

Luigi is a thirty-three-year-old man who lives with his parents in Naples, Italy. His mother does his laundry, and she cooks for him when he bothers to join his parents for meals. He pays neither room nor board but takes his casual girlfriends home when he needs a place to sleep with them. His parents do not mind any of this. They are glad to have their boy so close to them. An ad campaign in Italy refers to the 50% of Italian men between twenty-five and thirty-four years of age living with their parents as *mammoni,* or mama's boys. The campaign is intended to shame these men into getting their own apartments in order to reduce the high vacancy rates.[1]

Callie is a twenty-eight-year-old film director living in Chicago. She recently revealed to a journalist that the "last time I got mixed up with a casual partner—and it *will* be the last time!—he kept asking why I wasn't returning his frequent calls. I wanted to say, 'Why didn't I call? Because I'm making a goddamn film, that's why!" (14). Across town, Kate says: "When I wake up in the morning, I listen to NPR and read my e-mail and feed my cats and rattle the newspaper. Instead, I could be tiptoeing around trying not to awaken some guy whom I don't love and who doesn't love me—but frankly, I'd rather turn on *Morning Edition.* I have my life set up the way I want it" (17).[2] In England a twenty-eight-year-old journalist, Petronella Wyatt, proclaims in the *London Daily Telegraph*:

> Marriage offers dubious advantages for most women. . . . [She writes that] the failure of marriage to provide women with satisfaction is one of the most deep-rooted causes of discontent . . . in our age. . . . The single woman, providing she is not well below average intelligence and attractiveness, is now able to enjoy a thoroughly pleasant life. My contemporaries,

understandably, wish to prolong this state and most are either determined
not to marry or are delaying a decision until their 30s. (Reprinted in the
*London Free Press*, April 5, 1997, p. E5)

John is a twenty-six-year-old living with several of his mates in a flat
in downtown Manchester, England. He left school when he was sixteen
and has never had a full-time job. Instead, he alternates between government benefits and training programs. Although he is "trained" to
do a number of things, none of the training has led to permanent paid
employment. He spends his time with the lads, other men in the same
predicament, hanging around pubs and clubs when they can afford it.
They get "pissed up" when they can, and if no women are around, they
go looking for a fight, preferably with young visible minority men. He
and the lads also enjoy a good punch up with fans from competing
football (soccer) teams when matches are played in town.[3]

A recent incident in Troy, Ohio, contrasts with the free-for-all, me-
first undercurrent in the lives of the young adults glimpsed thus far,
none of whom have taken on committed family obligations. The contrast strikes at a key paradox of life in late-modern society—not because the character acted like a spoiled, indulged, or embittered child,
but because he acted like the type of adult found in many cultures who
believes he has responsibilities for others. In this case, according to an
article titled "Spanker Spanked" in Toronto's *Globe and Mail* of February 9, 1995, a thirty-three-year-old man was spanked by the police.
Why? Well, it appears that he bruised his ten-year-old son while spanking him with a wooden paddle. The incident was brought to the attention of the local police, who charged the father with domestic violence.
As part of a plea bargain, the police humiliated the father by spanking
*him* with the paddle and then destroying it. In the past—and in many
societies around the world today—the father's actions would have
drawn *praise*. Others would have seen him as meeting his obligations
as a strict but responsible parent. Certainly in the past the adage
"Spare the rod and spoil the child" governed child disciplining practices; no notion of impropriety would likely have been raised in this
case. In fact, not disciplining in such a manner was commonly considered morally negligent, because it was thought to leave the child's character unprepared for later life.

Although those stories contain elements of fiction and fact, they
should be familiar to all citizens of Western societies as snapshots of

"adult" life in late modern society. In each case there is something unique—and paradoxical—when it is compared with adult life in an earlier period. Yet, the youthful prerogative seen in each of these people and circumstances is "normal" now, in the sense of being commonplace. How did such a situation come about?

## A Brief History of Adulthood

Each of the stories in the previous section raises questions about what it means to be an adult today. In order to fully understand that, we need to learn what it meant to be an adult in the past and to compare that concept with what people now think it means to be an adult.

These may seem like odd issues to raise, especially if one simply accepts present Western culture as the model against which all others should be judged. However, when one takes off the rose-colored glasses provided by contemporary Western culture, these issues take on a different significance. The first revelation is that adulthood as we now know it is a cultural artifact. Its culturally relative nature can be illustrated by the fact that in most languages the idea is apparently not important enough for a word to have emerged to express it. Even among the European languages, according to Rogers (1982, 6–7), only English has a specific word for adulthood.

In tracing the etymology of the term *adult,* author Cheryl Merser (1987) notes that it first appeared in the Oxford English Dictionary (OED) in 1656. *Adulthood* did not appear until 1870. Thus, even in English, the word has a very short history. Moreover, when we examine the history of the term *adult,* we find that it follows a path similar to that of other terms that emerged to represent how we now describe the life course. Etymologically, according to the *Random House Webster Electronic Dictionary,* it is derived from the Latin *adolescent,* which is the present participle of *adolescere* (to grow up, mature). *Adolescere* is the inceptive verb of *adolere* (to make grow); *adultus* (grown) is the past participle. According to this source, *adolescent* was brought into English usage in the late 1400s, whereas the word *adult* did not come into usage for another half-century.

As this etymology illustrates, in the past people simply did not make the age distinctions that Anglophones, and increasingly others, do now. However, it is not simply a matter of how we speak about the life course. Beyond linguistic concerns, the reality experienced by the average person has changed dramatically in the past few centuries because of massive social, economic, and technological transformations that altered the institutional structures of modern societies. As the institutions changed, so did people's lives. Among other things, people's lives became longer, healthier, and less tied to raising offspring. These developments produced age groupings that grew internally homogeneous and externally distinct from one another. Consequently, people of different ages became more differentiated from one another in social roles and responsibilities as well as in expectations about the appropriateness of certain psychological attributes.

We can gain deeper insight into the cultural and historical variability of the notion of adulthood by reviewing a book written in 1987 by a person who was working through the complexities of her adulthood at the time. She describes some experiences that are increasingly common among "Brave New Adults."

### The Personal Testimony of a "Brave New Adult"

Cheryl Merser wrote *"Grown-ups": A Generation in Search of Adulthood* (1987) as part of her own struggle to understand why she and her friends did not feel like adults. She also wanted to provide insights for the general population into what have become "normal" problems for those now attempting to establish themselves as adults. Through her own experiences and generalizations from them, she explains how the Baby Boom generation had to deal with a highly ambiguous transition to adulthood—even when they were in their thirties, employed, and living away from their parents. A key problem, she writes, is that the traditional markers that defined adulthood for her parents' generation were either not applicable or were out of sync with their lives. These include the difficulties that go along with marriage, raising children, and maintaining a home. Concerning this problem, Merser asks her readers: "If we can't use the benchmarks of another generation to guide us through the life cycle, what benchmarks will we use instead?" (23). Complicating matters further, she adds, her parents belonged to an anomalous generation, especially in terms of their early age of first marriage.

Merser begins her exploration of the problem of what it means to be "grown up" by looking to psychological theories of "normal" development in adulthood. She is dismayed to find that these theories are geared to the (anomalous) generations of the first half of the twentieth century, when the life course was more predictable: people tended to do things more in unison, both in the options they followed and in the timing of them. For example, they tended to marry in their twenties and raise several children during their thirties. In contrast, a large proportion of the Baby Boomers spent their twenties gaining higher education credentials or attempting to establish a career, or both. She writes:

> Families? Children? Often cited statistics tell part of this story. Nearly a quarter of us in the postwar generation will not marry, and among those of us who do, about half will divorce. One-third of the women born in the 1950s will not have children, and not all by choice. . . . Among women professionals aged eighteen to forty-four, 48 percent are childless, as are 50 percent of those women with four or more years of college behind them. (1987, 41)

Merser argues that for the postwar cohorts, adulthood is becoming more a psychological process than a social one in the sense that more of what can be called "identity work" needs to be done. For Merser, adulthood is "about the capacity of the evolving self to make successive and successful connections to an unpredictable and changing world." But the world in which this must take place "is at the same time more or less unwelcoming to fledgling adults" (40). Much of the ambivalence toward the young is manifested economically, as the young are seen more and more as competitors of the older adults. Nonetheless, as the more "mature" adult world has become preoccupied with its material pursuits and problems, various traditions have been abandoned by adults. This has had a potentially positive effect, she argues, increasing the psychological and personal options for those seeking out an adulthood:

> Think of the range of choices we have today, choices that weren't so easy when our parents were young—to be single and still be "okay," to live openly with a lover (of either sex), to delight in our bodies and our extended youth, to enjoy real equal-partner marriages. . . . If we're up against limits, as all generations have been, we are also freer to make choices with those limits. (42)

Through her personal experiences, Merser uncovered the issue of the historical relativity of adulthood—namely, that adulthood is a period of the life course that takes different forms in different eras and in different cultures. She summarizes her research into this issue as follows:

> In preindustrial Western culture there was no such thing as adulthood. Strange as this may seem, there were no adults (nor were there such things as middle age or adolescence) . . . ; as an "official" stage of life, adulthood was simply never an issue as such. You were a man or a woman if you weren't a child, that's all, and the difference for men was one of size, age, and physical capacity; girls became women when they became fertile. Being adult had little to do with wisdom, opportunity, accountability, or a superior knowledge of the world, as it does now. The invention of adulthood is a recent one—and because its definition is still evolving (and will continue to do so) it's hard to know . . . when you've grown up "enough." Adulthood as we know it has its minimum requirements, but no end to possibilities. (52–53)

The recent appearance of a word to describe adulthood suggests to Merser that adulthood came to represent how people dealt with maturity in a world of increasing uncertainty but also of increasing possibility. The emergence of the word corresponds with early modernity, which is dated as beginning in the West during the seventeenth century. The rise of uncertainty and the consequent need to know more about the world gave new meaning to the notion of maturity and widened the gap between those with little experience (children) and those with more experience (adults). This process was hastened by the decline of absolute religious authority and the rise of secular authority. Increasingly, people became responsible for their own destinies: They could choose which authorities, morals, and values to accept.

A key point Merser makes is that because her parents' generation had experienced so much change themselves,

> there was no longer a culture to leave to us, and so what our parents unwittingly did was to leave us to ourselves. . . . [Consequently, by] the time we postwar kids were ready to leave home and in the absence of anything better, or anything else, youth—as a way of life, as a belief system, as a community, setting up traditions of its own—became the refuge, the religion of the young. (1987, 93)

To extend Merser's analysis, there is now a widespread view that in Western societies a "cult of youth" permeates many facets of experience. Adults learn from their children important lessons about this "new world" of continual change. But what we have seen in the intergenerational relations of the post–World War II period is that parents began imitating their children in certain ways, especially joining in on the hedonism that has become more widely acceptable. Meanwhile, many Baby Boomers did not want to face the responsibilities that they saw wear their parents down. Many asked, Why bother making sacrifices in a world that seems bent on its own destruction anyway? Why bring children into a world that seems to be going down the drain? These were common questions of the late sixties and early seventies.

A popular alternative was to enjoy life day by day—to be a free agent who never grows up. This philosophy involves a simple maximization of personal freedom and a minimization of personal responsibility. The problem with a life-for-the-moment philosophy is that the future is not taken care of. Eventually, the future catches up with those who follow the philosophy of immediate gratification. For example, a problem of identity eventually arises, because "identity" represents a continuity among the past, the present, and the future. A good part of this book is devoted to understanding the identity problems associated with rapid change and the loss of traditional markers.

## An Academic Search for Adulthood in America

Merser's book was written for the public, but much of what she says is supported by academics who have studied adulthood and maturity. In his essay "Searching for Adulthood in America," Winthrop Jordan (1978) provides an in-depth analysis that helps us answer questions about how adulthood has evolved. We also get a sense of what it meant to be an adult in the America of the past and what it means today. He begins by remarking:

> It is an interesting commentary on our culture that we find ourselves asking: What does adulthood mean? . . . what is arresting is that we [are] asking a question that would have made so little sense to our forebears. . . . Indeed, "adulthood," as we ordinarily think of it today, is largely an artifact of twentieth-century American culture. Historically that concept emerged by a process of exclusion, as a final product resulting from prior definitions of other stages in the human life cycle. (189)

In his search of the literature of the early New England settlers, Jordan saw little evidence of different stages of the life cycle; he found only references to patterns of the roles and duties assigned to husbands, wives, children, and servants. Within these patterns there was no reference to growth, maturing, or becoming a "psychological adult." Among the Puritans, at least, people were compelled to strive to know well their existing condition. They did not need to become something they were not already. Even religious conversion did not involve growth as we now think of it. Jordan traces the notion that psychological growth is a part of adulthood to the "Arminianization" of Puritanism. He uses the term *Arminianization* "as shorthand for that lengthy process by which Calvinist predestinarianism gave way to a theology that emphasized the individual's ability to gain salvation by means of his [or her] own efforts. . . . Only when the individual's own struggles were given far greater weight in the process of conversion would there be room for a process of reaching psychological maturity" (190).

Calvinist orthodoxy was slowly modified by Arminian beliefs, according to which all are eligible for salvation, not just a chosen elite.[4] The worldly struggles of all members of society thus became more important. Jordan also argues that what he calls the de-politicization of family made way for "notions about maturity and immaturity, mastery and dependence" (1978, 192). That is, two trends followed as the family unit and the polity became less patriarchal. One was that family members other than the dominant male gained status and rights. Consequently, people began to be defined less by their roles and duties and more as individuals with needs and potentials. The other trend was toward a more egalitarian democracy, with the extension of the vote from white male landowners to everyone over a certain age.

Before this period, Jordan says, concern over gender roles overrode interest in age roles. The conventional belief was that manhood and womanhood were distinct but complementary. Accordingly, it was more important to distinguish men from women than to distinguish children from adults. Over time, this has reversed; age roles and distinctions have become more important than gender distinctions in many respects. In early American history, it appears that women and men had more in common with those of the same sex regardless of age; now adult men and women seem to have more in common with each other than with children of the same sex.

Other developments contributed to the rise of "psychological adulthood," according to Jordan. For example, after the American Revolution there seems to have been a desire to ensure that those who were to become the citizens of this new country would be properly educated and properly raised. It was thought that this would make them suitable republicans. Such ideas contributed to support for compulsory education at the primary, and then the secondary, level, which began a process of segregation of children from older members of the republic. Simultaneously, the desire to protect young republicans led to child labor laws, which further excluded them from contact with older republicans. Since then, the age of exclusion has crept steadily higher and higher, contributing to the decline in the economic status of the young and the rise of increasingly distinct youth "cultures." Consequently, the original de jure logic for a point of exclusion based on age (e.g., sixteen years) became de facto for individuals beyond that age (e.g., late teens and early twenties) as people came to assume that the younger person could not perform production roles or was not entitled to them.

Complementing these trends was a reduction in both the fertility and the mortality rates. With fewer children to raise, parents could give each child more attention. At the same time, more parents lived to see their children leave their homes. Therefore, a new period of the life cycle, adulthood without dependent children, became more common, and people could turn more attention to themselves.

Finally, Jordan notes that the twentieth century saw the rise of the social sciences, one attribute of which is a tendency to develop a technical language that is used to document and create a sense of certainty about human behavior. This certainty was pursued with ideas that labeled life stages such as adolescence and adulthood. As Jordan argues, "the various segments of the life cycle were seen not merely as temporal stages but as descriptions of inner life and external behavior. Thus the 'oral stage' was not merely a temporal segment of the life cycle but a psychological syndrome" (1978, 196). Later in the twentieth century, these life cycle stages were increasingly taken for granted—reified—by most people in Western societies. During the postwar period, but especially since the sixties, preoccupations with inner life and its deficiencies have spread throughout the population. Most people are now expected to spend their adolescence and youth "finding themselves." An increasing number of adults continue this search, or engage in a series of searches, as they attempt to experience "self-actualization" in a widening variety of forms.

Jordan completes his analysis by noting that adulthood is now a social phenomenon in need of explanation:

If one had to plump for any single factor as being of central importance in this process, it might well be the actuality and expectation of rapid social change . . . . Technology, geographical and social mobility, and social pluralism have worked to speed up life so that we not only expect our children to lead different lives from ourselves, but we expect our lives to change, perhaps drastically through time. . . . We have moved, over the years, from condition to process. In our culture, adulthood as a condition used to be simply assumed; *as a process, it now seems to demand explanation.* (1978, 198, emphasis added)

This book attempts to provide an explanation for this process.

## Gender Divergence and Reconvergence

Some readers of these characterizations of the recent history of adulthood might question whether they accurately represent the experiences of both men and women, even though one was written by a woman and one by a man. There is reason to ask whether there might not be separate histories of adulthood for women and men (note the now popular term "herstory"). My answer to this is yes and no. The affirmative response is in recognition of the myriad specific conditions that have separated the experiences of men and women as they have performed different roles and have had different rights and privileges. The negative response is in reference to the most general nature of adulthood described by Merser and by Jordan, such as the decline in social markers and the rise in psychological requirements that characterize recent history. There is good reason to believe that at the most general ontological levels, these changes have affected men and women equally as groups (e.g., Arnett 1994; Levinson 1996). On balance, however, it is instructive to examine the specific circumstances that have distinguished the lives of individual women and men.

For example, when we look at the colonial history of the gendered division of labor with reference to its material basis, we find that most pioneering (European) men and women worked together in the same "sphere" of household production; men generally tended the fields and the barn, and women were "responsible for the house, dairy, and garden" (Pleck 1993, 1948). Sociologists of the family refer to this family form as a "household unit of production." In the earliest days of colonial settlement, there were few "middle-class" careers for which to compete, and only men from the few affluent families had a reasonable chance of obtaining them; indeed, there was little paid labor. There were also few products to be purchased and consumed. The economy was largely based on the production of necessities, with not much of what we currently call consumption.[5] Most of what was consumed was made by the family in the home, grown in the surrounding fields, or obtained through hunting and fishing. Under these conditions women and men shared the same superordinate goal, namely, survival. By most accounts women enjoyed a much higher status in this preindustrial setting than they did during the following industrial era, when men were drawn into the paid labor force and women were relegated to home and unpaid labor (Armstrong and Armstrong 1994).

Among the emerging middle class, participation in the growing paid labor force of the nineteenth century carried with it higher status and remuneration, and these bought privilege. On average, men's status increased, particularly the status of those who became part of the new middle and upper middle classes, while women's status decreased relative to their male equivalents. By the twentieth century, women's status had decreased primarily because their unpaid household labor was not seen as an essential and valid contribution to the industrial economy, and their role in providing a "home-as-retreat" was taken for granted (Pleck 1993). Among the emerging working class and the poor, "the doctrine of separate spheres" was slower to catch on, and it did so in part because of reform efforts by middle-class women (Pleck 1993). Eventually, the change in the status of children and teenagers affected the status of women. As children were increasingly viewed as "innocents" to be protected and educated, they were expected to contribute less and less to household maintenance, so the menial labor they once performed was largely taken up by their mothers. Women were charged with the sole task of "reproducing labor" for the industrial workplace. The rights of political and economic participation of the common woman did not increase in pace with those of the common man; instead, women found themselves performing essential labor for which they were neither paid nor fully recognized.

During the late nineteenth and early twentieth centuries, industrial capitalism radically transformed the family into a "household unit of consumption." Driven by the needs of the new industrial political economy, two increasingly separate spheres of labor emerged, the "private sphere" and the "public sphere." The arena of material production inexorably moved to the public sphere, while that of consumption emerged largely in the private sphere. Patricia Lengerman and Ruth Wallace define the public sphere as "the complex, bureaucratically organized institutions of modern life: the economy, the State, formal education, organized religion, the professions and unions, the mass media of communication and entertainment." The private sphere encompasses "the less formal, emotionally more open networks of social relationships that coexist with the public sphere: marriage, family, kin, neighborhood, community, friendship" (1985, 107). We can see how both spheres are multidimensional rather than homogeneous, in the sense that there are a variety of public arenas and multiple venues for private life. Although the two spheres overlap (cf. Eisenstein 1998), women still have restricted participation in the public sphere, and men have restricted participation in the private sphere. Certainly, much of the women's movement in Western societies has involved the effort to give women equal access to the public sphere, as well as to encourage men to take a more active role in the private one.

Accordingly, over the twentieth century, but especially in the last two decades of it, there were radical changes in these arrangements: women gained "considerable access to the public sphere," and there was "a searching and critical review of gender arrangements in the private sphere, and fairly energetic efforts to rework various of those arrangement" (Lengerman and Wallace 1985, 108). It follows that over this period, life opportunities and experiences have changed for both men and women, reflecting a reconvergence of the spheres separated by industrial capitalism. The reconvergence applies especially to those who are making the effort to cross spheres. Notably, in every Western country studied so far, women are doing more sphere-crossing than are men (see, e.g., Anderson 1991).[6]

I have dealt with these changes in detail elsewhere (Allahar and Côté 1998; Côté 1996b) so will not belabor the point here. However, it is useful to provide an example of the empirical support for the reconvergence thesis, which shows the gains women have made in the public sphere. Table 1.1 indicates the breakdown of women's proportional earnings by age and education for 1993 in Canada. It is apparent there that both age and education influence women's earning potential: younger women and those with more education tend to have the greatest earning power. Women from earlier cohorts still show strong effects of sphere divergence. Among the youngest cohort, university-educated women earn a full 84% of what men in the same category make. From

TABLE 1.1
*Percentage of Earnings of Canadian Women Working
Full-Time Compared with Earnings of Men,
by Education and Age, 1993*

| | Age Group | | |
|---|---|---|---|
| Level of Education | 25–34 | 35–44 | 45–54 |
| All women | 76 | 72 | 67 |
| Some secondary | 63 | 62 | 60 |
| High school diploma | 74 | 68 | 67 |
| Some postsecondary | 65 | 67 | 51 |
| Postsecondary diploma | 75 | 76 | 73 |
| University degree | 84 | 77 | 72 |

SOURCE: Adapted from Best 1995.

these figures it appears that progress has been made recently toward wage parity for younger, more educated women. The situation appears even better when hourly wages are the basis for gender comparisons. Wannell and Caron argue that previous estimates have been based on the erroneous assumption that annual wage estimates "adequately control for hours worked. The more recent surveys indicate that full-time men worked on average three to four hours more per week than full-time women." Wannell and Caron examined gaps in the annual salaries of Canadian university graduates from the class of 1990 and "found that female university graduates are rewarded slightly better than their male counterparts after controlling for experience, job tenure, education, and hours of work" (1994, 3). A similar situation can be found in Sweden, where only a small percentage of the pay differential between men and women cannot be explained by factors like age, occupation, hours worked, and education (*Equality* 1997). These Canadian and Swedish statistics might be a sign that other Western countries will soon arrive at this type of gender convergence, if they already have not done so.

Other, more general changes over the past several decades support the notion that a life-course convergence is occurring for younger men and women, especially those in the middle class (as was implicit in Merser's characterization). With each successive post–World War II cohort, the life courses of young women and men are increasingly resembling each other (cf. Furlong and Cartmel 1997, with respect to Europe). This is quite apparent for social markers like educational experiences and attainment, work and career opportunities,[7] and personal lifestyles. These are all increasingly matters of personal choice for both males and females. Particularly relevant is the choice women now exercise over their family lives[8] and alternative lifestyles; they base them more on affective ties than on parental arrangements and opt for dramatically lower birthrates. This reconvergence is also evident with psychological opportunities such as the increased possibilities available for identity formation (e.g., both women and men have the time to explore and develop their interests and greater freedom to base their commitments on personal choice) and personal fulfillment (e.g., more freedom to choose sexual partners and explore their sexuality, as well as to develop lifestyles suited to their talents and inner needs). When the matter is viewed in these ways, arguments that contemporary men and women live in separate worlds do not sustain scrutiny.

To put this another way, using a person's sex to predict a life course, and especially a lifestyle, is becoming less accurate, as more men and women face increasingly equal odds of various fortunes and misfortunes. This may sound like an obvious observation, but it has important implications regarding one's thinking about the intrinsic nature of gender differences: in terms of the most general parameters of adulthood, differences are role related, not essentialist or genetically predetermined, and are unrelated to the ontological nature of adulthood. In other words, the differences in the experience of adulthood discussed in this section depend on the roles one plays, not on one's genetic makeup. It is clear, however, that the legacy of the past separation of spheres persists for many women and men, especially for older women, those in less educated segments of society, and those in certain ethnic/racial groups.

The position I have adopted on this matter, which is based in part on years of teaching women's studies courses on gender roles and the sociology of the family, is shared by many others who have systematically examined the belief that there is a dichotomy between women's and men's experiences, with women being "essentially" more relational and men more autonomous.

Kathleen Day Hulbert cites the "self-in-relation model" as a "stream of feminist theory [that] proposes that a sense of connection to others is a central organizing element in women's lives, leading to a sense of responsibility for others and an ethic of care and justice . . . [whereby] women see their adult lives in terms of their networks of relationships and responsibilities." Hulbert goes on to note the weak empirical-evidential base for this model but acknowledges that it provides "an alternative framework for examining the lives and experiences of women . . . [that affirms] women's characteristics, *shaped through socialization,* as strengths" (1993, 421–422, emphasis added). However, she is critical that this model has not examined the (ostensibly different) nature of adulthood for women in terms of different stages or periods of adulthood, or "changing roles and relationships across the adult years." But, most germane to the central point of dispute in this area, she concludes that

> the conception of the "relational self," while it may describe how contemporary women arrange their responsibilities and organize their experiences within socially constrained expectations and limitations, does not necessarily represent a uniquely female perspective. . . . the self-in-relation model attributes differences in adult behavior to gender, without fully examining the extent to which historical, economic, and structural aspects of society constrain women. (422)

She warns that a belief in inherent difference between women's and men's experiences can inadvertently serve to perpetuate those conditions that create gender inequality, by reproducing "stereotypical and limiting views of each gender" (422). Indeed, it is easy to see how that belief can be used to perpetuate the private-public sphere separation of women and men, and how it can work against the convergence that has been taking place. This is a position shared by many feminists who do not accept the essentialist position on gender differences, including Carol Tavris, who wrote *The Mismeasure of Woman: Why Women Are Not the Better Sex, the Inferior Sex, or the Opposite Sex* (1992). In that book Tavris notes the lack of scientific support for the relational theory along with the misguided but strong lay support for the theory. In fact, there is no scientific evidence for gender differences in terms of most of the traits and abilities that are popularly believed to distinguish women and men, such as attachment and connection, nurturance, empathy, cognitive abilities (verbal, mathematical, etc.), emotions, moods and "moodiness," need for achievement, need for love, need for power, sexual capacity and desire, verbal aggressiveness, and so on (Tavris 1992, 296; see also Björkqvist and Niemelä 1992 for findings that females and males are equally aggressive when both psychological and physical aggression are examined; and Montgomery and Sorell 1997 for findings of no sex differences among adults in the matter of love attitudes affecting their approach to intimate relationships).

What the scientific evidence does show is that relational qualities are more often found among those performing subordinate roles (such as the roles encountered in the private sphere), whereas those in superordinate roles (such as those found in the public sphere) tend to show fewer of these qualities, regardless of gender. In light of that evidence, Tavris argues that "'women's intuition' should properly be called 'subordinates intuition'" (1992, 65). Nonetheless, the notion of essential differences between men and women is now part of a "popular bandwagon" that seems impervious to logical inquiry. Those who challenge this misguided but popular wisdom can find themselves dismissed as Philistines or even ostracized as "antifeminists" (a new term of exclusion). It appears instead that men and women have some different (not unequal) ways of relating and of maintaining their autonomy that are traceable to their differential socialization—a socialization affected by the legacy of segregation into separate spheres.

Daniel Levinson (1996) took up this issue in his *Seasons of a Woman's Life,* published shortly after his untimely death. He undertook this study and wrote the book in part to assess the validity of criticisms of his widely known book *The Seasons of a Man's Life,* published in 1978. His earlier book was criticized because he used only adult men in his first study and was therefore ostensibly androcentric (see, e.g., Gilligan 1982). On the issue of differences in the experiences of adulthood between men and women, Levinson drew a number of conclusions that support the notion that the most general "structure" of adulthood does not differ (on average), but the specific "content" can. He argued that this "perspective on the life cycle and adult development is like a navigational chart that gives latitude and longitude and certain features of the territory, without the geographical detail. It is not a blueprint for the concrete course of an individual life" (1996, 414).

We return to these issues in chapters 3 and 4, where we examine in more detail specific observations about the nature of contemporary adulthood. We see there that, although it is implausible that genetics is responsible for the segregation of men and women into separate spheres, the notion of human "relationality" is an important corrective to the strong impact of individualism in Western societies. In my view the problem is that the "blame" has been placed on men rather than on the history of capitalism.

## The Making and Unmaking of Adulthood in the Twentieth Century

As we have seen, there is a consensus in the literature that the adulthood characteristic of the early-twentieth-century Western societies and now taken for granted is not the historical norm. Not only was this an anomalous period, but also significant changes in adulthood occurred within the twentieth century. Adulthood became more rigidly structured in the first half of the twentieth century but underwent significant changes in the second half.

The social historian Tamara Hareven has extensively documented changes in the life course over the past few centuries in the United States. Hareven (1994) traces the gradual differentiation of the life course to the impact of industrialization and changing life expectancies associated with improved health. What became a "normal" life-course sequence in the early twentieth century, coupled with relatively late marriages and high mortality, had been experienced by only a minority of people in the nineteenth century. For example, the sequence for women—including marriage, a two-parent family, seeing the children off, and eventual widowhood—was experienced by less than one-half of those who were born in 1870 and who survived age fifteen. More than half never experienced such a pattern. Instead, they died young, never married, did not have children, or had a short marriage because of the death of their husband.

Hareven (1994) also argues that the timing of the major life-course transitions to adulthood underwent significant changes in the first part of the twentieth century. The major change was an increase in age uniformity in the timing of transitions, with those to adulthood becoming more uniform and orderly. In contrast, during most of the nineteenth century, life-course transitions were more gradual and less rigidly timed. The time range was wider for accomplishing transitions like starting work and getting married, and the sequence for them was not rigidly followed. In fact, the timing and sequence of life transitions followed family needs (economic and care-taking assistance to parents and kin) and obligations far more than specific age norms.

It was not until the early twentieth century that a widespread homogenization of life-course experiences was evident, but this homogenization appears to have lasted for only about three-quarters of the century. According to Hareven, by the 1980s there was a return to more erratic patterns in the timing of life-course transitions. For example, young adults now move in and out of the parental home in a less predictable fashion. However, they generally do so because of their own financial problems, and not in response to the needs of aging parents or younger siblings, as was the case in the nineteenth century. According to Hareven, we now have more erratic life courses, resembling those of the nineteenth century but for different reasons.

Other social historians agree with this portrayal of past and present trends. For example, writing in the *Encyclopedia of American Social History,* Steven Mintz (1993) traces the emergence of life stages. He argues that although life stages became more precisely defined and institutionally organized, the transition between them also became more disruptive and disjunctive. One reason for this is that people are increasingly leading lives based on individual preference, as opposed to family needs, thereby losing support in their lives. In addition, Americans (and those in other Western societies) have become more age conscious: "Not only are contemporary Americans more likely to organize activities and social institutions around discrete age groupings, they also are more likely to associate distinct biological and psychological traits and behavioral norms with specific ages" (2020).

The increase in age consciousness is attributed by Mintz to several of the factors already touched on: "the rise of new scientific and medical theories, which have linked certain physical and psychological characteristics and needs with specific ages; the creation of new social organizations, such as public schools and social welfare programs, which use age as an organizing principle; and the expansion of a consumer culture, which targets specific products and activities at discrete age groups and has helped disseminate age norms" (1993, 2020).

We see, then, that social historians concur that "the twentieth-century adult" was a historical anomaly and that the adult of the late twentieth century resembled "the nineteenth-century adult." However, I believe there is more to it than this and that the twenty-first century will most certainly be dramatically different from the nineteenth, in ways explored later in this book.

When we distill these social historical analyses, we can extract two factors that bear directly upon how adulthood is now experienced. The first is the decline of social markers associated with the transition to adulthood, and the second is the psychological adulthood that emerged, in part as a response to the decline in the markers. Furthermore, as observers like Merser and Jordan argued, changes in the life course reflect wider social and economic changes: the social change mirroring the decline of social markers is the general *destructuring* of forms of traditional culture with their civil and collective supports; the change mirroring the rise of psychological adulthood is the ascendance of the process of *individualization,* with associated pressures for each person to be a self-determining agent.

## The Blurred Line between Youth and Adulthood

A key sociological consequence of the recent historical trends examined in the previous section is the institutionalization of distinct life stages, which occurred as the life span of the twentieth-century adult increased. This greater longevity now includes childhood, a prolonged adolescence (which is increasing in duration with each successive cohort), a period of youth (for the more affluent or "unconventional"), and a long adulthood stretching through "middle age" and "old age." The new life course is characterized by several contradictory forces. It is dictated by conformity-producing age norms to a greater extent than in the past, yet it is also based more on individual preference for one lifestyle or another. In addition, age groups have been more segregated from each other, encouraging a homogenization within each group, yet there is considerable variation within each cohort. Finally, along with the variation within each life stage, there are serious disjunctures between stages, for example between youth and adulthood.

Sociologists refer to institutionalized processes like those as structural factors (cf. Giddens 1990, 1991; Hollinger 1994). More precisely, the institutional processes constitute *structuralization* when social patterns become stronger, more uniform, and more integrated, and *destructuralization* when they become less so.

The net result of those trends is that a greater onus is put on the individual, as opposed to the collective, to adjust to anomalous and contradictory social conditions. This process of individualization has helped shape the psychological adulthood that now characterizes many people's lives. But the fragmenting of the life course into segregated, preference-oriented, age-based stages has been accompanied by a loss of social markers, which in the past helped people to move between the stages with more certainty and more social support. Given the importance of these changes, it is useful to examine in more detail the decline of social markers in the transition to adulthood and the rise of psychological adulthood.

## Cultural Destructuring and the Decline of Social Markers

We have already reviewed some of the evidence regarding the decline of markers associated with the transition to adulthood. The decline has been a long, drawn-out process dating back to the Middle Ages. We revisit the historical significance of this issue later in the book when we consider the prolongation of youth and its implications in chapter 5. We also explore why this has happened in chapter 3. Here we focus on what is currently taking place in many Western countries.

By many accounts, major institutions in late modern societies have undergone transformations as a result of the more general process of cultural destructuring. This has occurred to varying but significant degrees, but it has diminished the normative patterns from which the bulk of the population derives meaning for their day-to-day lives. Among other effects, a "disorderly" timing of life-course events has emerged for much of the population. Some scholars call this a "de-coupling of the life course." People attempting to enter "adulthood," as well as "adults" themselves, find that they have fewer cultural restrictions on their choices than existed in the past, but they also have fewer cultural patterns to follow to govern their lives. The institutional and normative patterns that have undergone destructuring include gender relations, parent-child relations, ethnic/racial relations, and intergenerational obligations.[9] There has also been a decline in consensus regarding how to structure the institutions developed during the early modern and late modern periods, such as mass education. In addition, the premodern foundational institutions of the family and religion have lost their legitimacy among a sizable proportion of the population in many Western countries. The sociologist Claire Wallace (1995) describes this destructuring process in Europe:

> . . . age-status transitions have been de-structured. . . . Transitions are no longer associated with any particular age, or with each other. Youth has become more and more protracted with a long period of "post adolescence" at the upper end which is indeterminate. The outcomes of transitional phases are uncertain or risky—education is de-coupled from work, training is de-coupled from work, childbearing is de-coupled from mar-

riage, marriage is de-coupled from work, leaving home is decoupled from marriage and so on. People's options and identities are no longer fixed or certain and their futures can take a number of directions, the end point of which is not always clear. . . . Age-status transitions are open ended—they can go on for a long or a short time. (10)

Thus, in the late modern era, people increasingly find themselves forced to make life-altering choices whether they want to or not or are capable of doing so. Traditional markers have become vague and irrelevant for many people, and little has emerged to replace them. Many people are left in a limbo, as not quite adults and less than full citizens. This is a foundation upon which the late modern period of extended youth is based—a "generation on hold" without sufficient external guidance or internal resources with which to take stock and mature (Côté and Allahar 1996; Allahar and Côté 1998). Many people wallow in forms of immaturity characterized by partially formed ideals, identities, and skills.

This response pattern used to be an anomaly but is now so common that it is taken as unavoidable and normal. Consequently, few people sense that there might be something wrong, or they dismiss concerns such as those I have raised by claiming that this is part of a transitory stage in social evolution. In any event, partly because of destructuralization and partly in spite of it, the social process of individualization governs people's lives to an increasing degree, especially among those attempting to make the transition to adulthood. It is to this process that we now turn.

### Individualization and the Rise of Psychological Adulthood

As a result of the development in Western societies of conceptions of adulthood that involve age-based expectations governed by the process of individualization, people are expected to carve out major aspects of their own adulthoods by means of self-directed maturational processes. Consequently, in crucial respects adulthood is now more a psychological state than a social status. These expectations regarding individualization seem to have emerged as the social-institutional markers that once secured a recognized transition to adulthood have declined in importance and clarity. Simultaneously, opportunities for self-development have increased. There is also no simple definition of "the adult" or "adulthood." In a sense this should not surprise us, given that adulthood is now based more on individual preference than on social norms.

Marlis Buchmann (1989) has examined changes in the life course in the United States over the twentieth century, noting some of the trends I have discussed, including individualization. She argues that sociologically speaking, it is more useful to refer to "societal individualization" to characterize the "expansion of individual membership in modern society" (this especially distinguishes it from the more specific psychological process of "individuation," which we review in chapter 4). The process of societal individualization marks the "gradual release . . . in which the individual's linkages to traditional social collectivities (e.g., extended family, local community, status group) have tended to weaken" (21). In Buchmann's view, societal individualization is a twofold process: first the traditional constraints on individual freedom of action are loosened, and then mechanisms emerge to ensure continued conformity to (different) societal rules and obligations. One such mechanism was the "ideology of individualism."

According to Buchmann, the ideology of individualism in Western societies arose as political and economic structures underwent a process of rationalization. As authority slowly passed out of the hands of the elites during this process, it became vested in "the individual," which came to be seen as the basic unit of society. As basic units, individuals were defined as equal to one another, possessing certain inalienable rights of citizenship that the state could not violate. The individual was an economic agent of self-interest and a psychological entity "having a range of needs, motives, capacities, and competencies." Moreover, individuals were more commonly seen to have a schedule of development involving "a gradual unfolding of the potential to engage in purposive, responsible action," especially in managing their own economic efforts. At the same time, the increasingly rationalized state took on the obligation of regulating the psychological makeup of the *economic individual* "through appropriate socialization, which becomes institutionalized in the educational system" (1989, 23).

Buchmann's analysis parallels my discussion of the emergence of the "adult," particularly the psychological adult. Note, however, that she introduces the notion of social control via state intervention in the development and well-being of citizens. People are expected to care for themselves with minimal traditional collective support and to direct their own interests, but these expectations are delimited by the state and directed toward economic pursuits and purposive action. With the ideology of individualism, then, the person has an obligation to be instrumentally self-directed in relation to the (capitalist) economic system. In short, economic individualism is the standard of "rational" behavior to which people are held. Note also that the United States has led the way in its political history and that the ideology of individualism is probably strongest in America, although other countries are following suit as the globe has become increasingly Americanized.

The analysis so far has two general and related concepts: societal individualization, and individualization of the life course. The former pertains to the social forces that create the context for, and make possible, the latter: one is a sociological term and the other is a more social-psychological one. On the one hand, societal individualization symbolizes efforts of the state to restructure the minimal necessary collective support in the face of cultural destructuralization, especially through the formation of institutions like education and social welfare. On the other hand, individualization of the life course is a human developmental necessity made so because of the decline of traditional collective forms and the rise of psychological adulthood.

However, as we look into the matter more deeply, it becomes apparent that the individualization of the life course varies in a number of predictable ways. For example, at one extreme, people can pursue a life course totally devoid of traditional social markers without exerting much mental effort. They can do this by simply selecting a number of "default options" now available in the restructured consumer-corporate society and mass culture of late modernity. I refer to this type of individualization as *default individualization*, because it involves a life course dictated by circumstance and folly, with little agentic assertion on the part of the person. Alternatively, people can now pursue life courses based on extensive deliberation on the alternatives and opportunities available in late modern society, with its paucity of (stifling) social markers and its plethora of stimulating and liberating possibilities. I call this type of individualization *developmental individualization*, because it involves a life course of continual and deliberate growth.

I offer both concepts as a heuristic exercise, in order to determine whether these distinctions help clarify what is happening to adulthood in late modern societies. For present purposes, I treat them as two categories and recognize that within each there is variation by degree from low to high. However, I am not interested here in investigating the significance of this variation but rather in pioneering the concepts themselves. Moreover, I set aside for present purposes the complexities suggested by the concepts. For example, people's life courses likely mix these two types of individualization, perhaps pursuing one trajectory in various aspects of their personal lives and the other in various aspects of their professional or work lives. Accordingly, individualization is not a dichotomous process, but it is of heuristic value to speak of the "pure forms" or "ideal types" of individualization while recognizing the complexities of the processes in real life.

As I argue in chapter 5, consumer-corporate interests have capitalized on the default individualization trajectory by nurturing the notion of "individuality" and mass marketing it with the labels "cool" and "hip" (Frank 1997a, 1997b). Many westerners highly value individuality without really knowing what it means. Some people believe it can be achieved by selecting the right wardrobe or developing slight affectations in speech, behavior, or appearance. These constitute forms of "cultural capital" that are mass produced, but by definition cultural capital belongs to the elites, not the masses. Not coincidentally, these symbols of individuality are now the target of multibillion-dollar industries. The more such badges of individuality have been mass marketed by these various pop-culture industries and their ancillary mass media, the more popular they have become, not only among the youth segment but also among children and adults. However, instead of encouraging people to undertake the more difficult task of developmental individualization (which requires self-discipline, in order to develop advanced skills, aptitudes, and attitudes, as we see below), many people have undertaken the easier course of merely presenting themselves as "individuals." That option simply requires impression management skills in the presentation of self, using accoutrements of fashion and body sculpting made available by the multibillion-dollar industries of mass culture. The distinction between default and developmental individualization thus helps us understand how adolescents and adults can be misdirected to "paths of least resistance and effort" by the consumer-corporate interests of "mass society" (in chapter 3, I discuss theories of mass society, showing their contemporary relevance).

This mistaking of individuality (an impression management derived from mass culture) for developmental individualization (genuine intellectual and emotional growth) seems to be the crux of the problem many people face today in making a transition from youth to adulthood. It also may be at the base of the modernism-postmodernism controversy. It may be the crux of common personal problems because superficial displays of identity are situational, not developmental (i.e., they tend not to be growth-enhancing), so they do not prepare the person for the demands and opportunities of psychological adulthood. And it may be at the base of the modernism-postmodernism controversy because many postmodernists mistakenly regard these contemporary superficial behaviors as inevitable social adaptations rather than as the contrived and mass-marketed product of consumer-corporate efforts (Côté and Allahar 1996).

Simply put, there is a vast market in superficial, do-nothing forms of "individuality," but there is little quick profit in the genuine forms of growth-producing developmental individualization. Developmental individualization is a long-term process whereby people invest in themselves by first honing their aptitudes, skills, and personality resources and then trading these later in the various late modern marketplaces (see Côté 1996a, 1996b, 1997). Rewards accrue much more slowly from developmental individualization for the person and the society in which the person functions than when the emphasis is on mass displays of "individuality." Unfortunately, many young people *and adults* do not realize this, or they choose to ignore it.

The individualization process seems to have been taken for granted by American scholars, especially developmental psychologists, perhaps because of the longer tradition of economic individualism in the United States. Recent global changes, however, have made it apparent that economic individualism is being thrust on people around the world. Speaking of the European scene in general, Wallace (1995) writes that "late-modern trends are associated with 'individualization.' . . . This describes the tendency towards increasingly flexible self-awareness as the individual must make decisions and choose identities from among an increasingly complex array of options" (13).

In Denmark, as Sven Mørch (1995) observes, the period of youth has become ambiguously structured. People must not only pass through it; they must also master it in certain psychological ways if they are to become effective members of adult Danish society. The main requirement of "youthhood" involves successful individualization, that is, of negotiating the vagaries of Danish youth culture while preparing for a viable adulthood. But this is to be done largely on one's own, and the disjuncture between youthhood and adulthood is serious, with youthhood often involving antiadult socialization. A significant problem arises, then, for the growing population of immigrant youth in Denmark who are unprepared for the individualization challenge of Danish youthhood and who are not emotionally supported by their parents. Parents who are unsupportive often see this form of development as a threat to their more collective cultural identities and to their basic conceptions of adulthood as involving familial obligations. A key implication of Mørch's study is that individualization during youth and adolescence is crucial for a viable adulthood in a society that requires people to be psychologically self-directed and self-determined. Youth becomes a special preparation for adulthood in this respect. Those who do not undertake a self-directed trajectory of development in their youth are left unprepared for the full demands of adulthood in late modern societies like Denmark.

Britta Jonsson (1994) draws similar conclusions about Swedish society. She argues that youth must undertake their own "life projects" as part of the process of individualization because traditional life trajectories are of limited significance in late modern Swedish society. Young Swedes must now

> rely on themselves to a higher extent than any previous generation and on their own capacity of creating new structures of identity, moral and social life. In other words "life projects" are more than ever said to be left the individual's autonomous choices. As one consequence identity has become a problem, a life project in itself where young people continuously try new lifestyles and new experiences. (4)

Jonsson goes on to contrast individualization with collective forms of development, noting "a shift from solidarity with great collective projects to personal integrity and individual life projects" (4).

In study after study, then, the process of individualization emerges as a key global feature of late modern life. However, these studies, perhaps because of their sociological focus, have not distinguished between the two types of individualization I identified. I believe that distinction is necessary in order to appreciate the full gravity of the changes associated with late modern society. These changes are not all good, and they are not all bad, but which they are for each individual depends more than ever on what that individual makes of them. I believe that now, more than at any other time in history, the possibilities for self-development are enormous. Developmental individualization includes cognitive growth, identity formation, and emotional maturity, as well as finding and developing one's special skills, spiritual awareness, and so forth. The possibilities for a well-developed psychological adulthood increase as each traditional marker declines, taking with it old barriers and taboos.

There are vast subject areas within the field of developmental psychology in which the forms of development that could be used to illustrate developmental individualization are investigated. For the sake of brevity, I will review two areas, and in each area only one person's work.

Erik Erikson, a neo-Freudian who thought more in terms of human potential than human limitation, theorized extensively about identity formation. In his theory of the life cycle, the identity stage stands at the midpoint of eight stages. Because it has become so problematic for so many people in the modern era, Erikson focused on this stage more than on the other seven. But in his optimistic outlook, he saw the identity stage in modern societies as a time for healing old wounds, if necessary, and for building future strengths, if possible. These things became feasible because of the moratorium on community responsibilities that was available to adolescents. Rather than moving headlong into work and family duties, as in premodern societies, people have had more opportunity to participate in that moratorium. The identity moratorium originally emerged for upper-middle-class youth with the rise of higher education, but over time it has applied in various forms to those in the other social classes.

The identity moratorium can now last many years, during which people have the breathing space to rebuild deficient psychological attributes, explore their potentials in new areas, and accelerate the growth of previously identified potentials. Overall, for Erikson, the identity stage is potentially a time to enhance *ego capacities,* namely, the psychological abilities and strengths to master difficulties and obstacles presented by the social environment.

Apparently many people make use of the identity moratorium in these ways. As I have noted elsewhere, however, that is an ideal to which many—perhaps most—do not rise for reasons of discrimination, ignorance, and distraction to the paths of least resistance and effort (Côté and Allahar 1996). Erikson argued that a poor resolution of the identity stage means that the next stages (in adulthood) will be poorly resolved as well, and they will be fraught with unsettled identity issues.

If he was correct in his proposition, it would appear that many people will have persistent difficulties throughout their adult years with identity conflicts as they encounter issues associated with the stages that follow the identity stage (intimacy, generativity, and integrity).

Erikson wrote of various potentials associated with ego development during the identity stage. One of those is the potential to develop an ever broadening feeling of identity, such that more and more awareness is included in the sense of self and less is experienced as foreign to the self. Erikson called those levels of awareness the "value orientation stages" (see Côté and Levine 1987, 1989). What he meant was that with the longer period of identity formation now available, and the associated opportunities for ego growth, people should become less tied to parochial "moralisms" (the first stage) and "ideologies" (the second stage) and more aware of "universalistic ethics" (the third stage). This sense of ethics includes the knowledge that one is a member of the human species, not just a member of a small community, polity, or "tribe." Such an increased awareness of the importance of the world as a whole, and one's humble place in it, is possible when one defines one's self not against other people, but in terms of them. Thus, rather than finding emotional security by excluding others as part of one's self-definition ("I am who I am because of what I'm not"), one achieves emotional growth by including others in one's self-definition ("I am who I am because I am a part of a larger whole"). The person whose identity is based on an ethical awareness can move outside of his or her group of origin, becoming more a citizen of the world than a member of a small fearful or resentful group.

Erikson's schema of identity and ethics stands as an ideal to which many people subscribe in principle but few actually follow as a guiding principle in their lives. In a study I conducted among university students (undergraduate and graduate), I found only one person among 149 whom I could classify as exhibiting a full ethical awareness (Côté 1984). And she exhibited signs of severe strain in maintaining her ethical view of herself and the world. Most of the others were caught in a variety of parochial or single-issue ideologies that gave them security but made them fearful or resentful of others to some degree. I saw little hope that these others would do well in building the type of world community that Erikson envisioned.

Since the early 1980s, when I carried out that study, it seems that the world, including the university, has become less universalistic; there has been a rise in "parochial tribalism," often based on ethnicity or gender. People seek emotional security within their "tribe" in moralisms and ideologies that by definition work against the formation of a cohesive community (Elshtain 1993; Maffesoli 1996). To the extent that the majority of people live out their adult lives with moralist or ideological identities, the potential of the species is diminished. We can see this point more clearly and elaborately when we turn to Robert Kegan's cognitive theory.

Kegan's theory illustrates well the possibilities associated with developmental individualization. In his recent tome, *In over Our Heads: The Mental Demands of Modern Life*, Kegan (1994) presents an elaborate theory of cognitive potential. Following the Piagetian tradition, Kegan argues that humans have the potential to move through a series of "orders of consciousness" representing increasingly abstract and inclusive ways of understanding the world. He traces five orders of consciousness, the details of which are too extensive and complex to set forth in detail here. However, it is worth noting his postulation that few people move through the five orders of consciousness, even people from the educated elites of contemporary society. Instead, most people operate with a cognitive sophistication appropriate to earlier societies and are unable to fully comprehend and cope with the more complex demands of contemporary society.

Kegan builds this argument by noting that the first order of consciousness, representing childhood, is easy for most people to master, but many people get stuck at the second order, the level at which most adolescents understand the world. By implication, many adults go through life with an "adolescent" way of constructing reality. The third order involves the use of abstract reasoning; only about one-half of the "post-adolescent" population operate at this stage. These first three levels will be familiar to those who have studied Piaget's work (1954).

An insightful element is introduced into his theory when Kegan argues that the upper three orders of consciousness correspond with premodern, modern, and "postmodern" societies. Premodern societies require, in order to master the requirements and interrelations therein, the capacity to use logical abstract reasoning about one's self and to recognize similarities in others (the third order of consciousness). In modern societies mastery (at the fourth order of consciousness) requires the ability not only to reason abstractly about one's self (as subject) but also to reason abstractly about others (as objects).

This capacity allows for "self-authorship" along with an empathic intersubjectivity with others; one sees oneself as one element of larger complex systems based on mutualities of obligations and respect (cf. relational theory). Finally, in "postmodern" (or late modern) societies, the level of abstraction increases so that there is a consciousness of the interrelations of complex systems, within which one is a minor, but important, element subject to certain obligations (including self-authorship, self-regulation, self-formation, and the like).

Kegan submits that we can move to these higher orders through the "subject-object" dialectic that follows the Piagetian principle of assimilation and accommodation:

> "Object" refers to those elements of our knowing or organizing that we can reflect on, handle, look at, be responsible for, relate to each other, take control of, internalize, assimilate, or otherwise operate upon. . . . "Subject" refers to those elements of our knowing or organizing that we are identified with, tied to, fused with, or embedded in. We have objects; we are subjects. (1994, 32)

The good news is that human beings seem to be capable of growing through these levels of consciousness, coming to understand the world in more universalistic ways and from vantage points that give them a greater clarity of understanding of the vast worlds around them. The bad news from Kegan is that few people actually do so. He estimates that only about one-third of the (U.S.) population currently organizes reality at the fourth order of consciousness, although that is the level appropriate for modern life. In other words, the "mental burden of modern life" is the ability to operate cognitively at that level. Moreover, we are rapidly moving beyond modernity, into "postmodernity," where the mental demand is at the fifth order of consciousness. This is a level that few people are currently capable of sustaining, even many from the intellectual elites who call themselves "postmodernists," because they are "subjects" of postmodern thinking and cannot deal with these ideas in relation to themselves as objects.

I leave readers with this taste of Kegan's insightful theory in the hope that they will tackle his book themselves. When they do, much of what I am attempting to convey here will make more sense. So too will the work of other scholars such as Erikson, who tried to alert us to our higher-order capacities and the extent to which those potentials go undeveloped in societies that do not nurture them.

In the context of these developmental theories, we can understand how we have societies with such highly educated populations—unprecedented in history—that continue to live such undeveloped intellectual lives. The chief personal opportunities of advanced societies include cognitive and ethical growth, but this growth requires personal effort. The bulk of the population, including adults, seems to prefer the paths of least resistance and effort, perhaps because the educational structures channel most people in this way. We can appreciate the extent of this institutional channeling by comparing elite, private education with mass, public education. We can be sure that the elite forms of education are structured to foster developmental paths among their students, whereas the mass forms of education permit most students to take the default routes. It is not that mass educational systems explicitly discourage developmental individualization; rather, students must put forth considerable personal effort, in the absence of well-structured guidance, if they are to develop fully.

In any event, default individualization paths do not lead to higher orders of functioning but to lower ones, or to stagnation. I believe this is one of the greatest challenges facing the "Brave New Adult." On the one hand, adults can be content with the easily obtained pleasures and comforts that are virtually guaranteed by consumer-corporate societies. On the other hand, adults can set aside enough of these pleasures so that their energies and time can be devoted to the types of development charted by scholars such as Erikson and Kegan.

## More Freedom and Opportunity, but Who Will Take Care of the Children?

In the past, what we now call adulthood was characterized by an observance of strictly defined duties and an inflexible adherence to roles, particularly within the family and the immediate community. The duties and roles were often tied to a commitment to generational continuity and a "selfless," unquestioning devotion to raising children and tending to parents if necessary. The adult of the present era rides on the cusp of change, where there are great opportunities for personal growth, affluence, and experiencing the world. However, psychological adulthood, and its underlying process of individualization, is a double-edged sword. When it is undertaken, many potentials can be unlocked.

We have looked at just two: identity potentials that increase our ability to experience and appreciate the world, and cognitive potentials that increase our level of consciousness. But we know very little about how to guide people in developing these potentials. And the collective supports that might have provided this guidance have been undermined in part by the institutional destructuring associated with corporate-capitalist society. Consequently, psychological adulthood is increasingly a personal, individualized journey, and as such it has many pitfalls and many misdirected trajectories. It should not surprise us, then, that when we examine what contemporary adults are doing with their lives, it seems that only a small proportion are taking full advantage of the opportunities of developmental individualization.

What this analysis suggests is that partly because of the lack of guidance and the high failure rate, many people still follow easier paths in their life courses as opposed to pursuing trajectories that lead to higher levels of cognitive and identity development. The easier paths are based on the "pleasure principle"—the basic drive to avoid pain and seek pleasure. In its late modern form, this can involve undertaking a variety of unconventional and unplanned life courses, such as living from one moment to the next, balancing the avoidance of discomfort with the seeking of pleasure. Consequently, it appears that the paths of least resistance and least effort are increasingly taken instead of the more difficult paths that require some impulse restraint and the experience of discomfort in the service of growth. Currently there are few duties and roles tied to a commitment to generational continuity and a devotion to raising children. Instead, the focus is often on a selfishness that precludes any concern for the future of others.

At the same time, there are many people who are making the effort to develop themselves as part of the new psychological adulthood and in so doing contribute to a community in some form. Although it is difficult to estimate the proportion of the population doing so, these people are willing to restrain their impulses, postpone pleasures, and forgo many late modern forms of selfishness. They may do this not only for future personal gain but also out of a sense of civic and familial responsibility. They know that it is sometimes necessary to experience temporary discomforts in order to develop their skills and potentials (this used to be called character [Wheelis 1958]). However, many of these same people seem to suffer from the loss of social markers; in the past they would have taken strength from the structure associated with those markers. In the present they must personally compensate for the lack of guidance, and they do so in a variety of ways with varying degrees of success.

Nonetheless, there are great numbers of people who relish the demise of those social markers because of the potentially stifling and restrictive nature of traditional institutions. The people who by temperament do not respond well to social restraint constitute a significant group in any society. In addition, those whose sexual and lifestyle preferences had to be kept hidden in the past because of the dominance of those social markers can currently experience tremendous personal liberation. Both sets of people probably did not do well in the past in terms of experiencing a "rightness" in the world, but they have the opportunity to do so now.

I argue that it is not the increasing diversity of lifestyles that constitutes a problem in the present era (and in the future), and neither is it preference-based living. In my view, the problems lie with some new forms of adulthood that lack connection with a community through shared norms and common goals. Thus, it is the extreme form of psychological adult, cut off from significant ties and obligations, that is the greatest challenge—and threat—for civic society, because this type of person can be oblivious to, or even reckless with, community cohesiveness and generational continuity. And it is generational continuity that has allowed the human species to develop this world of potential. The problem is that this form of adult is found not only among the unconventional, path-of-least-resistance persons but also among those who are most successful in consumer-corporate society and are therefore making major decisions for the rest of us. Hence, we are left with the question, Who will take care of the children?

In this regard, remember the twenty-eight-year-old journalist, Petronella Wyatt, who was cited at the beginning of this chapter as proclaiming in the April 5, 1997, *London Free Press* that marriage "offers dubious advantages for most women." On the issue of children, she goes on to complain that they are part of a "prison" in which women risk losing their intelligence and looks, and besides "they leave home with greater frequency than husbands." She sees no way out of this "trap," because even "if you are rich enough not to do housework and cook family meals, you will be continually forced to think about your house, your children, husband and two sets of relations. Your world will inevitably become narrower." Her solution? She claims that it "is hard to think of a better [alternative to marriage] than work; the pleasure to be derived from professional success is one of the greatest life has to offer." This is but one snapshot of a growing number of Brave New Adults who apparently relish increased opportunities but seem oblivious to notions of community and cooperation. Or perhaps Wyatt thinks people who are "below average intelligence and attractiveness" will take care of the children. Aldous Huxley would be pleased with his powers of prediction but dismayed at how much his dystopia has taken shape within such a short period of time.

# 2

## The Science of Adulthood

*How Do I Know When I'm Grown Up?*
*Who's Going to Tell Me?*

*Examining the Evidence—In over Our Heads?*

The evidence regarding human development, some of which was reviewed in the first chapter, gives us two messages: (1) the rise of psychological adulthood has opened the door for a greater proportion of
the population to seek higher and more fulfilling forms of personal development, but (2) it does not appear that the bulk of the population is
doing so. Given that the adult populations of Western countries are
more highly educated than any previous citizenry, it is indeed a puzzle
why so few people are reaching the heights of personal development.
Robert Kegan titled his book *In over Our Heads: The Mental Demands
of Modern Life* (1994) to express his concern that so few adults are up
to the demands of contemporary society. He estimates that only about
one-third of American adults have a mental capacity that matches the
demands of "modernity." That estimate is even more alarming if one
accepts that we are rapidly moving beyond modernity to even more
complex social orders. An implication of the trend is that more and
more people will be left behind, or will find their lives suffering, because they do not have the cognitive wherewithal to function adequately (or fully) in the evolving social order.[1]

Kegan's concern is supported by the empirical findings generated by
other human development theories. As we saw in chapter 1, most people are likely functioning at an ideological "adolescent" level in terms
of Erikson's "value orientations" (the highest stage of which represents
an integrated and universalizing system of ethics). Research that parallels Kegan's and Erikson's tells the same story. For example, at best
only one-half of the adult population reaches, or uses on a regular
basis, the highest form of cognitive reasoning—formal operational

thought involving abstraction, complexity, and flexibility in dealing with ideas and situations (Crain 1992; Kuhn 1979; Rice 1998). Even educated, middle-class Americans employ abstract reasoning only some of the time, and even then mainly in relation to their special interests and abilities. This means that most adult Americans do not employ their highest cognitive potentials when it comes to extremely important civic responsibilities like electing politicians or raising their children. Similarly, most people do not reach the higher levels of moral development as laid out by Lawrence Kohlberg (1979). Instead, most adults reach only a "conventional" level characterized by an approval-seeking social conformity that is not concerned with universalizing principles of fairness and justice. Even by their mid-thirties, American adults employ a (stage 3) "good boy–nice girl" reasoning about 30% of the time and a (stage 4) "law and order" reasoning about 60% of the time. Only about 15% of reasoning reaches a (stage 5) "social contract" level, and almost none reaches a (stage 6) "principled" reasoning (Bee 1996). With respect to "identity formation," it appears that only a small proportion of adults (20–30%) reach what researchers believe is the optimal level of self-directed identity formation appropriate to the demands and opportunities of contemporary American society (Côté 1996b; Côté and Levine 1988; Pulkkinen and Kokko 1998).

One reaction to these findings is to say it is expecting too much of the average person to reach these higher potentials. But is that not what the whole ideology of individualism and self-fulfilment is about? Should not the most affluent and technologically sophisticated civilization in history expect its members to reach these higher potentials? I think so, but behind these figures reflecting arrested or incomplete development are the social changes associated with the cultural destructuring referred to in chapter 1. For instance, most people spend their childhood and youth in schools; yet in countries like the United States, many schools barely meet the standards of "education." Instead, much of what goes on involves crowd control and keeping students busy. Many schools do not stimulate and challenge students to attain these higher levels (Muuss 1996). Is this the schools' fault? To some extent, yes, but to avoid getting bogged down in the details of the debate about the specifics of education, I suggest that this situation reflects the current state of "adulthood." Adults are ostensibly in charge of things, so the responsibility ultimately lies with them. But which adults are responsible: the poor worker, who sees education as alien; those in the middle class, whose vote determines who is in political office; or those in the various business and political elites? Or is anyone ultimately responsible? The fact that there are no ready answers to these questions suggests that we are indeed in over our heads.

I attempt to answer these questions regarding responsibility in subsequent chapters; here I review evidence that helps us better understand what is happening to the notions of individual responsibility, accountability, and fulfillment in adulthood in late modern societies. Because the literature is vast, I have of course had to select a small part of it. And this primarily conceptual—rather than statistical—journey does not require a huge number of sources, given the meta-analyses available. Furthermore, I am limiting myself to research dealing with America, except where cross-cultural comparisons are revealing (as with different trajectories in the transition to adulthood). I do this, again, as a matter of necessity, since it would not be possible to treat all cultural variations. I do not believe this focus reflects an ethnocentrism because I am not an American, so the "centrism" has no ego-involved nationalism. America is my choice as a focus because the United States is the trend-setter in many respects, especially in the ideology of individualism (see chapter 1). Not only are people in many nations around the world emulating Americans and their lifestyles, but also the economics of the United States is being imposed on many of those nations. Thus, studies of the United States can help us understand where we are all headed, as Americanization shapes globalization.

From a more strictly empirical and scientific perspective, then, how has adulthood changed?

## The Social Science of Adulthood

A social science of adulthood has arisen in American academia. When a science emerges it usually means that there is a deficit of knowledge in an area and that there is a belief that greater knowledge of that area will be beneficial in some way. Both of these implications appear in the various textbooks that have been written for university courses on adulthood. Most striking in a review of the textbooks is that it is hard to find a simple definition for what is ostensibly the focus of this field of study. Yet, the whole point of the textbooks is to show how important it is to know about "it." Even under the heading "Scientific Study of Adulthood," we are told that this line of research "examines the physical, cognitive, personal, and social characteristics of humans throughout the course of adult life" (Turner 1996, 29). Turner notes that the study of adulthood is only a recent subdivision of developmental psychology. The reasons cited for a past neglect of the topic include the facts that a longer life span is quite recent and that in the past researchers focused on childhood and adolescence. In addition, during childhood and adolescence, developmental changes seem to be much more obvious and detectable, whereas during adulthood, changes are believed to be much slower. Importance is now accorded adulthood because it is the longest proportion of the life cycle, with about one-half of the U.S. population being between the ages of eighteen and sixty-four. However, we are never told what "it" (adulthood) is.

In a major textbook in this area, entitled *The Adult Years: An Introduction to Aging,* Dorothy Rogers (1982) pursues the elusive definition of adulthood in a section called "What Is an Adult?" But she admits that there is no definition and that the term has no definite meaning, either among the public or among social scientists. Instead, adulthood has a taken-for-granted quality that is based more on images than facts. Rogers notes that these images suggest processes rather than endpoints. To complicate matters further, the images vary by social class and ethnicity. Writing in the early eighties, Rogers predicted that "if the present trend toward increased ethnicity and diversity persists, we may not have an identifiable American adult, but instead diverse and inconsistent life styles and values representing the various subcultures" (7).

Instead of a straightforward definition, Rogers provides a set of factors that seem to characterize the adult years and variations during them. These include maturational, morale, physical, environmental, and pathogenic factors. But in characterizing adulthood this way, she refers to "aging." The problem with using the term *aging* to describe adult processes is that it suggests the field of gerontology, the study of the elderly (the terms *aging* and *gerontology* are now used interchangeably by social scientists). Rogers does divide the material in her textbook into three sections, describing "the young adult," "the middle-aged adult," and "older adults," but again, there is not simply an "adult."

P. B. Walsh (1983) takes a different approach in a textbook entitled *Growing through Time: An Introduction to Adult Development.* Adulthood is defined there in negation—in terms of what it is not. Walsh begins by arguing that current "American culture supports a vague but widespread myth of adulthood. The myth has two parts, both involved with a definition of adult as 'finished'" (3).

The first part of the myth contains the idea that childhood and adolescence represent periods of growth but that adulthood is an end of growth. Walsh argues that this might have been more accurate when there was a shorter life span and a more rigid society. However, Westerners can now expect to live at least a half-century beyond the commencement of legal adulthood: "Can you live 50 years without developing in some way? Definitions of *adult* that are based in completion, maturity, and being finished unfortunately imply that you can" (Walsh 1983, 3–4).

The second part of the myth, according to Walsh, is "that the only change to be expected in adult life is deterioration" (1983, 4); that is, adulthood simply involves losing one's youth and getting old. The contemporary "cult of youth" may be predicated on this part of the myth. To make matters worse, the media and mass marketers have exploited for profit this obsession with youth. Those who are susceptible to such influences have attempted to maintain their youth as dictated by the profiteers, with several adverse effects. First, any signs of nonyouthfulness have been stigmatized, and people needlessly try to hide natural features of human change. Of course, this is a losing proposition, with some perilous psychological consequences for those who take it too seriously. And second, realistic life planning is blocked for many people. Young people may believe that commitments and life decisions are traps and that they should avoid responsibilities associated with adulthood. But in doing so, they also forgo many opportunities.

Walsh concludes that a "contemporary definition of adult is an unfinished person, growing through time" (1983, 5) and accordingly argues that we need to take a life-span developmental approach and look for more gradual forms of complex growth. In addition, Walsh adopts a position compatible with Jordan's (see chapter 1) by stating that

the changes of adulthood may be largely under individual control. Many behavioral scientists view the events of adult life as the results of unconscious or conscious choices—in any case, our own choices. From this point of view, the directions of our development are a function of individual awareness: the more life choices we are aware of and the more thoroughly we understand them, the more appropriately we can choose. We live in a social setting that offers a wide range of alternatives in how to conduct our lives; and the options, too, are continuously changing. (6)

Viewing (American) adulthood as a largely psychologically based process, as Walsh and Winthrop Jordan recommend, opens up a number of avenues for investigation, because it becomes necessary to understand what might be changing as part of these psychological processes. Though developmental theories of adulthood are embryonic compared with theories of childhood and adolescence, several are taking shape. In his textbook, *Personality Development in Adulthood*, Lawrence Wrightsman (1988) outlines three perspectives that have emerged to account for changes that take place during the adult years. Each perspective focuses on, but provides different answers to, the following questions: "Do we simply unfold a scenario formed at an earlier age? Do changes reflect a smooth and seamless transition? Or are wrenching disjunctions and disruptive shifts inevitable?" (12).

The perspective Wrightsman calls "early formation theories" takes the view that the personality is basically formed in early childhood and normally remains stable throughout life. The second perspective, which he calls "stage theories of development," views the life course differently, as a set of predetermined phases of growth that build upon one another to produce a more complex and well-rounded person. Finally, Wrightsman's "dialectical approaches" look to tensions that individuals experience between various opposite influences, the resolution of which produces different outcomes. Still, however, we are not given a definition of adulthood.

If we follow the logic traced in chapter 1 regarding the changing nature of adulthood, the textbook treatments noted here of the topic are imprecise because the phenomenon to be studied is an abstraction and a cultural artifact. It appears that theories of adulthood do not provide us with a straightforward definition of adulthood either. Indeed, all of these sources beg the question of the ontological nature of adulthood. Definitions for terms like *adult* can be found in dictionaries and other scholarly publications. The problem with the dictionary definitions is that they do not take us much further because they are for the most part tautological, needlessly repeating the idea in different words. For example, according to the *Random House Webster's Electronic Dictionary,* an adult is "a person who is fully grown or developed or of age" or "a person who has attained the legal age of majority." There is no separate definition for "adulthood" in that source. These definitions tell us nothing about a possible *intrinsic nature* of adulthood. Instead, one definition reflects a legal conception that is an arbitrary standard set by social reformers who wished to establish age norms. The other, which refers to being "fully grown or developed," actually goes against the social-scientific characterizations that stress that we never stop growing or developing.

When we turn to the scholarly (nontextbook) literature for a more in-depth definition, we are still stymied in the search for precision. Instead of precise and simple *descriptions* of adulthood, we find *prescriptive* attempts to characterize it. That is, the "definitions" tend to tell people what they *ought to do* rather than depicting what all people actually do.

In the *Encyclopedia of Relationships across the Life Span,* we find an entry titled "Maturity during Adulthood," which gives the following criteria for the mature adult: "accurate self-concept, stable emotional behavior, a well-developed value system, and intellectual insight." In addition, mature adults are "realistic in their assessment of future goals, appreciate and respect others, and possess effective problem resolution skills" (Turner 1996, 27). These are clearly desirable characteristics, but they raise several questions.

The first question is, How widespread are these qualities in the "adult" population? Can we find them in most of the population, or only in a minority? Although the qualities that Turner cites may be widespread in some form, as we saw in the last section, the empirical research consistently shows that the highest levels of the more integrated qualities (such as reasoning abilities and moral development) are not found among the majority of legally recognized adults today.

Another question pertains to the tautology of trying to define *maturity* in relation to *adulthood.* The problem is that maturity simply means to be fully developed, which takes us back to the dictionary definition of adulthood but contradicts the social-scientific definition.

Granted, the author of this depiction of maturity stipulates that it "does not come automatically with adulthood." Rather, it is achieved gradually and in different areas. For example, a person can be intellectually mature but socially immaturity. Furthermore, maturity is an attribute that requires "work." If people do not work at it, they will tend to have shallow and superficial relationships with others. However, if they do work at it and "achieve" it, they can "discover the innermost and subjective aspects of [themselves] and significant others, such as a partner, friend, relative, or teacher" (Turner 1996, 27).

Again, these are certainly attributes that most people would agree are desirable. But the language used and the underlying assumptions suggest an underlying Arminianized Calvinism (see chapter 1). Together, these referents imply that people must achieve psychological adulthood on their own, through their own work and struggle. In other words, one wonders how much the notion of the Protestant work ethic is involved in this depiction of adult maturity. Although I do not disagree that people must now struggle on their own to achieve psychological adulthood, I do not believe that this is an optimal situation. Moreover, as I have argued, most people seem to be taking a path of least resistance and effort rather than engaging in that struggle. Instead, I believe that it is attendant on a civilized society to provide a certain amount of structure and guidance for those attempting to make the journey to, and through, adulthood.

To return, somewhat dissatisfied, to the social science of adulthood, what do we make of the efforts of social scientists who try to create a sense of certainty about adulthood? The primary goal of science is to study naturally occurring phenomena systematically with the intention of predicting and controlling them. However, making an *exact* science out of the study of human behavior is an elusive, and probably unachievable, goal for several reasons beyond the scope of this book. Besides, what if we could control human behavior in the same way that engineers can control matter and energy?

The scientific control of adult behavior is precisely the possibility that Aldous Huxley outlined in his book *Brave New World*. Huxley's book illustrates the ways in which human behavior, including adulthood, can be brought under more or less exact scientific control. In fact, as his title indicates, Huxley's book inspired a theme for the present book. In chapter 5 we consider in detail his work and its implications for contemporary adulthood. For now, we will leave the issue as follows: it is one thing to attempt to describe what is happening in a given society at a given time; it is another to use that description to make prescriptions regarding other societies and other times. And it is an intellectual failing to confuse the two or to be unaware of these issues.

Nevertheless, I do not believe it is helpful to abandon the scientific enterprise, because knowledge derived through the scientific method can have great prosocial value—it can be used to improve people's lives. When the focus of scientific inquiry is on carefully postulating and systematically testing falsifiable hypotheses, it is quite useful in resolving disputes. Without this means of arbitration, disputes over what constitutes valid knowledge (epistemology) can fester ideologically, driving otherwise like-minded people apart.

That seems to be what has happened in academia as a result of the growing popularity of some postmodern and feminist theories. We examine these theories in several places throughout the book, as they are relevant to the ontology and political economy of adulthood, but certain versions of them have taken stances that are either antiscientific or nonscientific. For example, some postmodernist theories are explicitly antimodernist; science and reason are identified as two of the "sins" of modernism (cf. Hollinger 1994). Once this stance is taken, unlimited claims may be made, with no objective means of testing them. In addition, some feminist theories reject quantitative testing of hypotheses as male biased (see, e.g., Judith Jordan 1997), choosing instead to start their empirical research with premises that actually constitute conclusions (there is then no chance that a hypothesis can be falsified as part of a study—a basic requirement of the scientific method). As we saw in chapter 1, when some of the claims regarding sex differences are tested scientifically, they turn out to be unsupported and are apparently based simply on stereotypes. Ironically, the extremely subjectivist approach of some feminist theories can simply perpetuate the stereotypes that divide men and women. At the very least, they abandon claims to scientific validity (see, e.g., Sprinthall and Collins 1995, 223).

Unfortunately, many of these academic disputes make it more difficult for us to understand the intrinsic nature of adulthood. I suggest, therefore, that we attempt not to lose sight of the fact that although adulthood now constitutes the longest period of the life course, it is the least understood. Adulthood also seems to be increasingly complex, not for the reasons that most people believe (e.g., because of technologies), but because of the vagaries associated with it (including confusions added by academics). At the highest level of analysis, these vagaries revolve around the processes of individualization and destructuralization, by which the onus is put on individuals to be agents of their own destinies in poorly structured contexts. Thus, the passage through adulthood becomes particularly difficult for women and men when certain resources for navigating it are deficient or absent. To further complicate matters, we are no longer sure of what many of these appropriate resources are.

## Going to the Source: Subjective Definitions of Adulthood

In spite of our best attempts, as we have seen, we cannot arrive at a precise, scientifically useful definition of adulthood, nor have we come to an agreed-upon way of studying it. Perhaps the problem is that these attempts have really been a form of armchair science. Several researchers have taken a more direct approach, asking those attempting the transition from "youth" to "adulthood" to define what they think the transition involves.

In a study published in the mid-1980s, Douglas Hardwick asked a group of second-year college students to write essays discussing their notions of adulthood. He was interested in whether the students possessed "the abstract, generic concept of adulthood advanced by social scientists." The essays addressed three questions. The first question was "What is an adult?" Six criteria emerged in the students' answers, with "social-emotional maturity" most frequently cited. The other criteria were, in order of importance, physical maturity, cognitive maturity, legal maturity, financial independence, and identity formation. In response to the question "How does one become an adult?" the most frequent response by far involved "learning experiences through social interaction." Three other responses were less important: completion of physical growth, attaining a certain age, and formal education. Responding to the question "How does one know when one is an adult?" about one-quarter of the students either could not provide an answer or said there was no way to know when one had become an adult. Among those who provided a response, self-reliance was the most frequently mentioned sign of adulthood, followed by completion of growth and conformity to social norms (1984, 967–968).

Hardwick notes that very few of the students mentioned identity issues. He concludes that their generic concept of adulthood is more limited than that advanced by social scientists. This again raises the question of just how prescriptive social scientists have been, as opposed to providing mere descriptions of adulthood.

Jeffrey Arnett (1994) conducted a similar study, in which he surveyed 346 college students at a large midwestern university regarding their conception of the transition to adulthood. Most were between eighteen and twenty-one, and there was an even gender split. A key question he asked them was "Do you think you have reached adulthood?" In response, 27% said yes, 10% said no, and 63% said "in some respects yes, in some respects no" (these categories were provided for them) (1994, 216). Viewed historically, the low number of self-identified adults in this sample would be surprising. Viewed in terms of how things have changed over the twentieth century, it is not surprising.

Arnett also provided the students with a series of items that measure perceptions of social markers as well as conceptions of psychological adulthood. Not surprisingly, he found that most of the students gave these markers little importance in determining what constitutes an adult. For example, completing education, entering the labor force, marriage, and parenthood all received low ratings as requirements for adulthood. Endorsements ranged from 12% for parenthood to 27% for full-time employment. Even marriage, a nearly universal cross-cultural marker, was endorsed by only 15% of the sample as a requirement (Schlegel and Barry 1991, 35, found that "marriage almost always marks the end of adolescence" in the 186 preindustrial societies they studied).

Psychological criteria received significantly higher endorsements. Arnett provided items that measured behavioral, emotional, cognitive, biological, legal/chronological, and gender-specific requirements. The three criteria receiving the highest endorsement were "'accept responsibility for the consequences of your actions' (92%), 'decide on beliefs and values independently of parents and other influences' (80%), and 'establish relationship with parents as an equal adult' (72%)" (1994, 222).

Other ratings suggest that neither biological nor legal/chronological markers were widely viewed as important. He notes that the requirements that are widely recognized were "all highly ambiguous, subjective, intangible criteria . . . and none of them lend themselves to a definite, measurable certainty that they have been achieved. None [are] marked by events; each is a process that may take many years" (1994, 222). Significantly, there are no differences between males and females in this sample regarding what constitutes adulthood (note the gender reconvergence thesis presented in chapter 1). Arnett concludes that the transition from adolescence to adulthood "is a process that may last many years, during which individualistic and intangible markers of adulthood . . . are gradually and incrementally pursued" (1994, 213). With respect to individualism, he notes that whereas accepting responsibility for one's actions received the highest endorsement, "making lifelong commitments to others" received a low endorsement (31%).

He interprets this to suggest that these students tend to understand a specific type of responsibility, namely, "responsibility for yourself more than responsibility to others" (1994, 222). Arnett views this as "a reflection of Western individualism, but not a rampant, unchecked individualism. A certain amount of impulse control and respect for the rights of others is also expected as part of becoming an adult" (1994, 223). However, that describes the views of only about 60% to 70% of his sample. A full 30% to 40% seem unconcerned about selfish behaviors such as petty crime, drunk driving, and using contraceptives if sexually active.

These findings suggest several questions that we will ponder throughout this book: What proportion of the population of contemporary Western societies are actually "adults?" Are fewer making the transition from youth than in the past? Are more recent cohorts less likely to make the transition, or are they likely to take much longer in doing so? Is a new type of adulthood emerging that will compete with or replace the life course experienced by the twentieth-century adult? Just what "space" has opened between adolescence and adulthood? Is it a space that some people may enter but never leave? For now, we turn to the question of the nature of adulthood in terms of what adults are actually doing and thinking about others and themselves, and what this says about the current state of adulthood in relation to the issues raised in chapter 1 about the forms that individualization is taking in an increasingly destructured society.

### The State of the Civilization: Are Americans Acting More, or Less, Grown Up?

It is one thing to view adulthood through a lense of scientific theory and systematic subjective appraisals, but it is another to take a hard look at the worlds that adults have created for themselves and how they have paved the way for the generations to follow them. In other words, it is telling to view just what adults actually do in their lives and how they structure the lives of their children and other wards. A focus on actual behavior, as opposed to mere attitudes and opinions, can be more revealing of underlying, long-term psychological character. Not only does this approach conform to common sense, but decades of social psychological research also confirm it (e.g., Michener and De-

Lamater 1999). In a sense, the "aggregate" behavioral manifestation of adults can illustrate how adults construct their adulthood. For example, these manifestations might help us understand the extent to which adults create their worlds in a "mature" manner, corresponding to the type of responsible, self-determining individualism that constitutes the basis of the contemporary liberal democracies ostensibly made possible by advanced forms of capitalism.

The world we will examine from the point of view of the behavioral parameters of adulthood (along with the transition to adulthood) is that of the average American, for reasons that have been discussed. The aggregate evidence we will examine reflects what these people do at crucial "decision points" in their lives. We will look for the consequences of the individualization and cultural destructuring processes discussed in chapter 1. With respect to individualization, we will look at statistics that reflect what people, or different types of people, do with their greater freedom of choice: do they tend to make choices that reflect developmental individualization, default individualization, or something in between? For cultural destructuring, we will examine statistics that reflect how adults meet each other in their "communities" and the extent to which these meetings are "nomic" experiences, supported by institutionalized "traditions," or less meaningful "anomic" experiences, for which there is little or no institutional precedence.

Figure 2.1 shows the logical outcomes of decision points that take a trajectory into either structured or destructured contexts. At the end of this chapter, we will take stock to see which of the four character outcomes represented by these possibilities are increasing and which are decreasing. With respect to figure 2.1, note that everyone making the transition to adulthood, and all of those ostensibly in adulthood, are continually confronted with decision points. As their decisions culminate in the various destinations, the destinations influence how subsequent decisions are made. Thus, developmental decisions can build a momentum toward subsequent character development; default decisions can do so toward passive forms of behavior associated with the paths of least resistance and effort. Common sense tells us that if we put the initial work and effort into developing a quality (such as a musical talent), the benefits accumulate later in terms of enjoyment, fulfillment, and monetary reward; but if we put off expending the effort to develop a quality, we face the same barrier of inadequate knowledge and preparation each time we are confronted with the

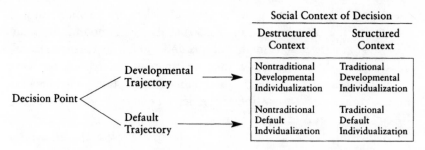

*Fig. 2.1.* Personal Decision Points and Character Outcomes

task. The learning and mastery of computers and the Internet is a common example with which most people can identify.

William J. Bennett recently published *The Index of Leading Cultural Indicators: Facts and Figures on the State of American Society* (1994), as part of an attempt to assess "the moral, social, and behavioral condition of modern American society" (7). He notes that since the early 1960s, an "index of leading economic indicators" has been published annually by the U.S. government, but nothing has been published regarding "cultural indicators." This suggests that the U.S. government has a greater concern for business interests than for the moral, social, and behavioral interests of average Americans. Bennett covers the thirty-year period from the 1960s to the 1990s, the same period in which tremendous changes in the nature of adulthood and the transition to it took place. He concludes that the United States has experienced a "substantial social regression" over that period, as "the forces of social decomposition . . . [have overtaken] the forces of social composition" (8). In effect, his report is about the cultural destructuring referred to in chapter 1.

Here are some of his findings: Although the population of the United States grew only 41% over that period, there was a more than fivefold increase in violent crime (total crimes tripled), a fourfold increase in births out of wedlock (a doubling of births to unmarried teens), a threefold increase in single-parent families and teenage suicide rates, a doubling of the divorce rate, and a drop of seventy-five points in SAT scores. In addition to these statistics, Bennett cites a number of disturbing anecdotes. Teenagers of the late 1980s were described as the first generation who were less healthy, less well cared for, and less prepared for life than their parents, with repercussions for their behavior (not their physical health, as in the past). In 1940 things like chewing gum, making noise, and talking out of turn were considered top problems by teachers. In 1990 teachers reported the top problems to be drug and alcohol abuse, pregnancy, suicide, rape, robbery, and assault. Have teenagers suddenly become afflicted with some genetic defect or biological epidemic? No, but the world that has been destructured for them by adults is different from the previous world. Bennett cites James Q. Wilson, who argues that young people "have embraced an ethos of self-expression over self-control." And he refers to the pollster Daniel Yankelovich, who claims that American society "now places less value than before on what we owe others as a matter of moral obligation; less value on sacrifice as a moral good; less value on social conformity, respectability, and observing the rules; and less value on correctness and restraint in matters of physical pleasure and sexuality" (Bennett 1994, 8).

Of course, not all of the figures reported by Bennett apply to all Americans, but the processes they represent do affect Americans' worlds and to some extent must be considered a product of it. Social class and race are reflected in these statistics independently and additively. For example, a young male from Harlem has less chance of seeing the age of forty than a young male from Bangladesh, one of the least developed nations in the world; about two-thirds of births are out of wedlock among African Americans, compared with one in five among whites; one in five American children lives in poverty, a 40% increase since 1970; one in eight children is being raised on government benefits (four times as many as thirty years ago), and 30% of child support payments go uncollected. As more and more children are brought up in poverty, Americans can expect more of the problems associated with insufficient resources to prepare children for the high-tech world of the future. As more and more children are brought up in single-parent families, Americans can expect more problems associated with these destructured families. And those two situations now combine, as Bennett notes:

> Poverty has historically been derived primarily from unemployment and low wages. Today it derives increasingly from family structure. In the 1980s, the United States experienced an important turning point: for the first time in recent history, a majority of all poor families were one-parent families. Single-parent families are six times more likely to be poor than married-couple families with children. (1994, 62)

Bennett also reports on changes in the ways Americans use time that have implications for the transition to, and nature of, adulthood. In 1960 the television in the average American household was on about five hours per day. In 1992 the figure was seven hours. Fifty-six percent of Americans believe that televison has the greatest effect on children's values (more than that of parents, teachers, and clergy combined), but only 2% think that this is right. In fact, according to Bennett, American teens now spend on average five minutes a day alone with their fathers and twenty minutes with their mothers, but three hours watching TV. And where do parents and their teens usually meet? In front of the TV. This is hardly an ideal situation for adults of one generation to guide and relate to the next generation.

Bennett's concern is reinforced by a recent research review article published in the medical journal *Pediatrics*. Victor Strasburger and Edward Donnerstein, a physician and a social psychologist, respectively, argue that "an increasing number of studies document that a serious problem exists" with respect to "children, adolescents, and the media." Part of their concern is over the expansion of the media into video games and videocassettes. When the time spent with these media is added to that occupied by television, some American teens spend as much as fifty-five hours per week in front of a cathode ray tube. The problem, Strasburger and Donnerstein believe, is that these media exert a "displacement effect" (1999, 129), which is both behavioral and psychological. Behaviorally, the time spent watching television takes away from other activities, such as physical exercise, reading, and socializing. Psychologically, the *content* of what is viewed affects the consciousness of the viewer, and the younger the viewer, the greater the effect. By consciousness, I mean what occupies a person's mind—what thoughts the person has access to. The more one is exposed to certain ideas or ways of thinking, the more likely they are to affect the choices one makes when crucial decision points arise, as suggested in figure 2.1.

With respect to violence, Strasburger and Donnerstein report that the most recent estimate is that young people view about 10,000 acts of violence per year. Sixty-one percent of television programming contains some form of violence. Children's viewing is the most violent, but between 20% and 25% of music videos, which are the domain of the adolescent, portray overt violence. Alongside the world of violence presented to American society's newest members is a world of sex. Teenagers view about 15,000 references to sex each year but only about 170 references to the responsibility and consequences of being sexually active. Sexual content has infiltrated the "so-called family hour. . . . [with] more than 8 sexual incidents per hour, more than four times as much as in 1976" (1999, 129). Sex and violence are the basest forms of image that are exploited by the various media because they "travel well" to audiences regardless of intelligence and literacy. Unfortunately, these images present role models for making choices based on the paths of least resistance, effort, or both.

Strasburger and Donnerstein conclude that there is now little question that there is a cause-and-effect relationship "between media violence and real-life aggression. . . . Taken together, the research data are persuasive that high levels of television viewing are causally related to aggressive behavior and the acceptance of aggressive attitudes. The correlations found are stable throughout time, place, and demographics" (1999, 130). Each successive cohort in America since the advent of television has been raised on an increasing diet of vicarious violence. Young children are the most likely to imitate what they see, and researchers concur that attitudes about violence learned in one's early years tend to be held throughout life. Hence, each successive cohort has been desensitized about violence and has seen it accepted as a solution for conflicts and problems, as well as a way to reach goals. So close are the most recent cohorts to television as a socializer that it and other media may now "function as a super peer in this respect" (1999, 130), reinforcing choices associated with aggression and violence.

Strasburger and Donnerstein extend their review of research to the role of the media in promoting irresponsible sexual activity, which can have dire consequences. They also argue that the advertizing of alcohol and tobacco has demonstrable consequences for the behavior of young people and that the eight billion dollars spent each year in the United States on advertising these products has a measurable statistical impact on consumption. Clearly, the statistical evidence is available for the deleterious effects of certain forms of media viewing. Yet, what is the adult community in America doing about it? The media are the creation of adults, adults specifically target groups such as the young with their programming and advertising, and adults buy television sets and related media for their offspring (more than half of American teens have TV sets in their bedrooms [1999, 133]). Is anyone willing to take full responsibility for these practices? Should adults blame young people for being self-indulgent, or should young people blame adults for exploiting them and leading them astray? Certainly everyone involved is exercising more freedom, but is there any widespread concern about the denial of responsibility for the consequences?

Strasburger and Donnerstein have a number of recommendations that include parents exercising control over what their children watch (most do not, at the present), health professionals becoming involved in educating parents and participating in programs to curb risk behaviors, schools promoting the responsible and prosocial use of the media, governments developing clear public policies, the entertainment industry stopping its denial response, and media advocacy. With respect to media advocacy, Strasburger and Donnerstein argue that these issues are often framed as issues of individual freedom and rights (i.e., as part of individualism); one way to deal with those who want to avoid their responsibilities is to reframe the issue. For example, simply classifying guns as consumer products would reframe how the government would deal with them and how people would think about them. Currently there are more regulations governing the making and distribution of teddy bears in the United States than there are for the making and distribution of guns. In this sense, "reframing involves exposing unethical industry practices rather than trying to improve individuals' behaviors by urging them to be healthier" (1999, 134). Strasburger and Donnerstein conclude their review of the literature with the following advice to American adults:

> What is needed is a virtual sea-change in attitude, from one of crass commercialism to one of respectful paternalism for the unique psychology and needs of young people. The American [adult] public is quick to criticize teenagers for their early sexual activity, drug-taking, or violent behavior; yet these youngsters are learning important behavioral cues from the media that surround them. . . . Children and teenagers comprise a captive audience for entertainment producers, but they also represent the next and only source of adults for American society. As such, they deserve far better that what they are being exposed to now. (137)

## Adults and Their Progeny: The Blind Leading the Blind?

The noted psychologist Urie Bronfenbrenner headed an interdisciplinary team of social scientists to produce *The State of Americans: This Generation and the Next* (1996), which speaks directly to the nature of contemporary adulthood and what is happening to those attempting to make the transition to adulthood. Bronfenbrenner and his coworkers look at the changing beliefs and behaviors of American youth and at crime trends, families, poverty and the next generation, and education. Their findings are prefaced by an expression of the alarm they felt after reviewing many of the changes that have taken place in the United States, beginning in the 1960s and 1970s. They believe that disruptive trends escalated and reinforced each other in the 1980s so much that these trends are now difficult to reverse. They further believe that we are in a critical stage because of the chaos and disarray that children and youth now experience as they grow up and that this chaos has spread throughout families, schools, neighborhoods, and communities. From the evidence they have reviewed, they conclude that "a history of growing up in such an environment has become one of the strongest predictors of the growing social problems confronting American society and of the accompanying decline in the competence of character of the next generation as we enter the twenty-first century" (ix).

With respect to the changing beliefs and behaviors of young Americans, this team of human development experts argues that there is "no more critical indicator of the future of a society than the character, competence, and integrity of its youth" (1996, 1). Yet they find strong evidence that these qualities are in decline among the most recent cohorts. For example, there has been a decline in the sense that others can be trusted: the proportion of high school seniors who believe that most people can be trusted has dropped from about 35% in the mid-1970s to 20% in the early 1990s, and the trend is on a downward slope; at the same time, the proportion who believe that "you can't be too careful in dealing with people" has increased from about 40% to 60%.

Hence, the majority of young Americans are now facing the transition to adulthood without a basic sense of trust in others. We can assume that this is a realistic response to the environment provided for them by the adults ostensibly in charge of that environment. At the same time, many young people seem to have become less trustworthy. From the late sixties to the late eighties, the percentage of high school students who admitted to cheating on a test doubled, from 34% to 68%. As of the late eighties, only 4% would report cheating (down from 12% in 1969), whereas almost all (98%) have let another student cheat off their work (up from 58% in 1969).

This change in the basic moral orientation of young Americans may be related to their declining participation in mainstream, "adult" institutions. Between the late 1960s and the late 1980s, the percentage of eligible and registered voters in presidential elections between eighteen and twenty-four years of age dropped from 51% to 36%. This is the only age group in which less than 50% vote. Interestingly, there was a comparable drop among "adult" voters (except for seniors, who increased their participation), but about two-thirds of adults still participate. Bronfenbrenner and coworkers also report a decline in the weekly religious attendance of high school seniors, from about 40% in the mid-1970s to about 30% in the late 1980s. And the sense of optimism that plans for the future will work out has declined (from 66% to 60% of high school seniors).

Bronfenbrenner and his team believe that these changes are mediated by family structure, with changes in the nuclear family structure compounding the effects. They compare two-parent, mother-headed, and "other" family structures. They find, for example, that teenagers in two-parent families have higher religious attendance and more trust in others. High school seniors from two-parent families achieve higher grades in school (and those with higher grades are less likely to cheat), are less likely to skip school, are less likely to use drugs, and are more optimistic about the future. There has been a decline in drug use from the mid-1970s to the mid-1990s, but this is attributed to concerted antidrug campaigns by adults—a model of action that Bronfenbrenner believes should be examined in relation to the negative trends that they report.

There is also strong evidence that high schools have become a source of serious difficulties for many students, especially because of the increase in violence. Data from the early 1990s show that one-third of the male students have taken a weapon to school with them (8% of the females have done so); almost half of the students are involved in a physical fight at school each year; and over half of them do not feel safe at school. These conditions pit student against student: 46% do not trust other students because of violence, and 34% see gangs and peers as the major source of violence at school. Indeed, young people have reason to be concerned. Those aged twelve through twenty-four are more likely than adults to be the victims of violent crimes and five times more likely than adults over fifty years of age.

Bronfenbrenner and coworkers suggest that young people are decreasingly regulated by their parents and other adults. This situation seems to be more pronounced in single-parent families and in many schools. They are concerned that the future competence of those making their way to adulthood may be adversely affected. They conclude that the studies they reviewed show "that beliefs and behaviors reflecting diminished self-regulation and expectations for the future, as well as disregard for rules, are evident among a significant proportion of today's youth" (1996, 19). They also note that although problematic behaviors are more common in single-parent families, many of the trends are paralleled in two-parent families. On the one hand, as the number of single-parent families increase, certain problematic behaviors should increase proportionately; on the other hand, given that two-parent families show the same, yet mitigated, trends, factors outside the family need to be examined, such as participation in, and guidance from, adult institutions. They reason that it is possible

> that youth are receiving less or less effective guidance from traditional, socializing institutions, such as their families or religion. Another possibility is that parents of teenagers (single parents, overworked parents) are not supervising them as closely as parents of previous generations did. The rising rate of poverty among children may also be implicated, through lack of opportunity, or increased exposure to physical threat and violence. (7)

The education system has taken on a more significant role in the lives of Americans over the last century, and the situation has been emulated in other Western nations. Schools have been designed by adults and are staffed by adults. They are the formal means by which American adults pass on their collective wisdom to subsequent generations. The schools' strengths and failings are thus the product of how several generations of adults have structured their worlds. The state of the schools therefore tells us something about that structuring process.

Bronfenbrenner and his team of researchers analyze the American public, or mass, system, finding numerous problems. They begin by noting that the much-discussed long-term decline in SAT scores that began in the 1960s has recently begun to reverse itself, although not to any great extent. On the positive side, the greatest turnabout has been among disadvantaged students. Nonetheless, one has to ask how the most affluent and powerful nation in the world could have let this happen. American students rank lower on most academic indices than many of America's trading partners; and these partners' students have recently improved their performances. In fact, "about half of all two-

and four-year college graduates operate at a fairly low level on tests of mathematical and verbal literacy" (1996, 186). Clearly, if other nations have attended to the quality of their educational systems, something could have been done to maintain standards in the American system. A 250% increase in spending over two decades did not correct the problem. Is this an example writ large of the tendency toward the paths of least resistance and effort? I think so.

The U.S. system of education has been one of the most successful in the world in getting students to attend and to complete high school. Almost nine out of ten will get their high school or equivalency diplomas by age thirty. Yet, Bronfenbrenner and coworkers emphasize that "there are areas of grave concern when we shift from measures of graduation and matriculation to measures of how much students are actually learning" (1996, 199). Even the top students in the United States are now mediocre in international terms. Bronfenbrenner's team searched for explanations, including the amount of television watched. American children are world leaders in this respect, with nine-year-olds now spending more time watching television during the weekdays than they do in school (over five hours per weekday). And when they are in school, they receive less instruction and guidance: up to 50% of grade-schoolers' time is spent in activities in which there is no direct guidance from teachers, leaving them to "spend far more of their school day in self-directed activities than in teacher-directed ones" (202). Moreover, teachers complain that much of the time they do spend with students is devoted to crowd control and keeping order in various ways.

The result at the higher levels of education is predictable. Bronfenbrenner and coworkers argue that college graduates

> no longer have the skills they were once assumed to possess. The achievement levels of college graduates . . . are embarrassingly low. In 1992, approximately half of all college graduates were classified as "level 3 or lower" on a survey of 26,000 adults who were asked to solve everyday problems, such as reading an editorial or answering questions. Levels 4 or 5 were not achieved by half of all graduates. These included such problems as calculating the amount of interest due on a loan. (1996, 203)

A reason for this low level of functioning at the college level may be the doubling during the 1980s in the number of low-achieving high school students who shifted out of vocational and general educational programs into college-preparation programs. Although their aspirations seemed have increased, their effort and abilities did not.

It is easy to understand why students would want more education; but the widespread inability to complete that education competently is telling, in terms of both the insufficient guidance and structure in the schools and the lack of effort put out by many students as part of any self-instruction or self-motivation. A U.S. college degree can mean lifetime earnings of some $800,000 more than one can expect with a high school diploma, which in turn can increase one's earnings by $200,000 over a high school dropout's earnings. Is the poor performance of American students the fault of the schools? The government? The students themselves? I would say yes in each case, but only to some extent. Bronfenbrenner and coworkers note that the only fiscally driven general solution that seems to make a difference is to reduce class sizes. But the problem is deeper and more profound than a change in fiscal policy, I believe. It has to do with (1) the changing nature of adulthood and how seriously people take the late modern requirement that they be self-determining agents and (2) the extent to which we collectively structure (or do not) the contexts in which we meet each other as we attempt to be self-determining, choice-making agents. These are the issues of individualization and cultural destructuring and of the tendencies of people (administrators, teachers, parents, and students) to choose the paths of least resistance and effort under current conditions.

Bronfenbrenner and his researchers conclude their review of economic and cultural indicators by noting the two reasons that have been given for the above trends. One is economic, yet in the 1990s, the American economy performed extremely well in overall terms (although the wealthy benefited from this much more than the less wealthy). The other explanation has been the rather vague notion of a "decline of values." They note that many people sense that something is "terribly wrong" and that there is an "unraveling of the moral fabric" but that little consensus has emerged about the nature of this problem. Bronfenbrenner and coworkers also argue that there has been a "seismic shift . . . in the beliefs and values in this country, particularly those endorsed by the nation's youth." And though some changes have been positive, especially those that have helped women and minorities participate (read individualize), they state that many have not been positive, including a decline in allegiance to values associated with

> honesty, a sense of personal responsibility, respect for others anchored in a sense of the dignity and worth of every individual, and a willingness to give a helping hand to those who have suffered misfortune through no fault of their own. Something has gone wrong, many now argue, in a society in which more and more teenagers are becoming unwed mothers, in which teenagers murder teenagers with impunity, in which civility, community, and safety are fast disappearing in many urban centers. (1996, 260)

One comparison that the Bronfenbrenner group did not make pertains to spending in the United States on buildings for higher educational institutions as opposed to prisons. Astonishingly, the amount of money spent building prisons has surpassed that spent on building colleges and universities. Nationwide, between the mid-1980s and the mid-1990s, spending on prisons increased by 30% while that on colleges declined by 18%, according to CNN, reporting statistics from the Justice Policy Institute on February 24, 1997. In California the prison population grew by about 400% between 1970 and 1995, while school funding dropped precipitously (from a rank among the states of about fifth to fortieth [Males 1996, 5]). These figures reveal something about the priorities in the United States assigned to providing structure and guidance for those attempting to make the transition to adulthood. The trend is clearly toward a withdrawal of benign guidance and the imposition of oppressive structures as part of an overall decline in the sense of community shared by all in that society.

### The Decline of Civil Society: Cultural Destructuring and Default Individualization

Another revealing perspective from which to view recent changes in American society has been provided by Robert Putnam, a political scientist and the director of the Center for International Affairs at Harvard University. Putnam has been studying the relationship between good government, economic well-being, and well-functioning communities for several decades. On the basis of his examination of these qualities in various countries, but especially in the United States, he has concluded that the key element binding these three elements together is "social capital." Social capital fosters civic engagement by enhancing the "level of engagement, trust and reciprocity" that exists in a given concrete community (1996, 28). Putnam defines social capital more specifically as those "features of social life—networks, norms, and trust—that enable participants to act together more effectively to pursue their shared objectives" (Putnam, 1995a, 664–665). The more these "bridging" qualities exist in a community to span underlying cleavages, the greater its economic prosperity and civic vibrancy. Communities with higher levels of social capital have more people who subscribe to a "norm of reciprocity" that helps create a "dense civic fabric" in which people connect with their neighbors and community institutions. In short, social capital represents the sort of "win-win" situations in which everyone who participates benefits from "social connections and the attendant norms and trust" (665). Putnam has found, however, that many of those things that represent and build social capital have been in decline in the United States and in many other Western nations for the past few decades, especially since the 1960s.

Putnam's evidence for this decline in civic society and social capital is alarming, but it is consistent with the evidence we have reviewed so far. In the United States the following trends are evident.

*The Decline in Trust.* In the 1950s and 1960s, 75% of adults trusted their government "to do what is right most of the time" (Putnam 1996, 29). By the 1990s that percentage had dropped steadily to 20%, and it was not contingent on which party was in power. Moreover, there has been a parallel decrease in the sense of trust in most major institutions, such as religion, medicine, business, and education. In the 1950s almost 60% of adult Americans said they believed people could be generally trusted, but by the mid-1990s the figure was down to about one-third (Putnam 1995b, 72). The decline in trust occurred for all educational groups. Putnam emphasizes that "because social trust is also correlated with education and because educational levels have risen sharply, the overall decrease in social trust is even more apparent if we control for education" (72).

*Civic Disengagement.* The psychological withdrawal in terms of trust is paralleled by a behavioral withdrawal of civic duties and responsibilities. Voting is down about 25% over the thirty-year period between the 1960s and the 1990s (Putnam 1996, 29), attendance at political rallies and speeches is down 36%, and the number of people who have worked for political parties is down 56% (Putnam 1995a, 666). In 1995 one-third of American adults did not know about the upcoming 1996 elections, and 50% said they did not care about the outcome, according to R. Grossman and C. Leroux in the *London Free Press* of February 3, 1996. Putnam concludes from his research that American adults are not only voting less but that they also "are exchanging ideas with one another less about public affairs" (1996, 29). This disengagement of adults is not limited to politics. It extends to all forms of participation in community organizations, for example the PTA, the Masons, the Shriners, the Boy Scouts, the Red Cross, labor unions, and even bowling, where participation has declined between 25% and 50% (Putnam 1995a, 666).

The disengagement also applies to participation in mainstream religions. Surveys show a 20–25% decline in the number of Americans "who say that they went to church last Sunday" (Putnam 1996, 30). But there is more to the story than these simple numbers. Many studies have suggested that the United States has bucked the almost universal secular trend among Western nations whereby religious observance has dropped off sharply over the past thirty years (e.g., Bibby 1993), yet there have been rather inconsistent estimates given regarding participation. For example, Chadwick and coworkers (1994, 198) note that there are "contradictory findings about Church attendance" in the United States. The Catholics surveyed between the 1960s and the 1990s admitted to lower attendance per week, from 74% to 46%. The Protestants surveyed admitted to no such decline in attendance over this thirty-year period, and surveys show about a 40% weekly attendance rate for the entire thirty-year period. Putnam provides some insight into this apparent anomaly between changing Catholic and Protestant attendance rates—many (Protestant) Americans apparently lie about how often they go to church! Studies that have investigated whether those who said they went to church actually did so have found that only about half as many actually went to church regularly as claimed to. In fact, only evangelical denominations can claim any growth in attendance over this period (and some of these effected the increase by making attendance more "fun" [Brady 1991]), but their growth is not enough to offset the overall decline among American adults in their religious participation, as well as their participation in the volunteer organizations associated with religions (Putnam 1996, 30).

But note the implication here—a significant proportion of Americans apparently lie about their church attendance (about 20% of those who self-identify as Protestants). Little wonder, then, that trust levels have declined. It appears that religion in America has also been affected by the individualization process, as it has in other Western countries. Most Americans will say that they believe in a god and that they have certain beliefs, but generally their beliefs have been fashioned (often in cafeteria style) independently, not by a mainstream religion that has tradition and collective structures. We can also surmise that some of this individualization follows a default pattern, whereby some people may say they believe certain things because they want to avoid being stigmatized as "atheists." Nonetheless, we can also assume that some of the new religious or spiritual proclamations follow a developmental individualization pattern, signifying a certain amount of cognitive, emotional, and spiritual growth. What does appear to be distinctive about the American religious scene is the history and extent of religious "entrepreneurship" and the connections that are often made between economic individualism and religious freedom (see, e.g., Bibby 1993).

*Atomization.* Putnam also notes trends in "social decapitalization" with respect to the family and association with neighbors. He writes that "the massive evidence of the loosening of bonds within the family (both extended and nuclear) is well known" (1995b, 73), and ample evidence for this has been examined thus far in this book. However, the decline in informal social capital is less widely recognized. According to the evidence that Putnam cites, Americans "are spending about 25 percent less time in ordinary conversation with other people and about 50 percent less time . . . in organizational meetings. [They also know their] neighbors less well. Over the past 20 or 25 years, the number people who say they never spend a social evening with a neighbor has doubled" (1996, 31). We can add to Putnam's analysis the statistic that one-quarter of Americans now live alone, up from one in twelve in 1940 (Fishman 1997). The trend toward social atomization, by which people are separated into their own individual lives and "cubicles" seems pervasive; it picks up on longer-term trends associated with "mass society" that we explore in the next chapter.

*The Prime Suspect?* Why has this social decapitalization (or cultural destructuring) occurred in the United States, and why in the recent past? Putnam has reviewed all of the explanations that he (and others) could imagine (e.g., work and time pressure, mobility and suburbanization, and the rise of the welfare state—none of which are candidates) and has arrived at an answer that partially explains this trend: "the technological transformation of leisure" (1995b, 74). Here is how he explains this transformation:

> There is reason to believe that deep-seated technological trends are radically "privatizing" or "individualizing" our use of leisure time and thus disrupting many opportunities for social-capital formation. The most obvious and probably the most powerful instrument of this revolution is television. Time budget studies in the 1960s showed that the growth in time spent watching television dwarfed all other changes in the way Americans passed their days and nights. Television has made our communities (or, rather, what we experience as our communities) wider and shallower. In the language of economics, electronic technology enables individual tastes to be satisfied more fully, but at the cost of the positive social externalities associated with more primitive forms of entertainment. (1995b, 74)

Given these apparently inexorable trends toward atomized forms of destructured individualization, should we be concerned with the technological transformations of culture, and should we attempt to exercise some form of (adult) control and responsibility over them? If we follow Putnam's argument, the answer to both questions is yes. Here is a short statement from him concerning why we should be concerned about our stock of social capital:

> For a variety reasons, life is easier in a community blessed with a substantial stock of social capital. In the first place, networks of civil engagement foster sturdy norms of generalized reciprocity and encourage the emergence of social trust. Such networks facilitate coordination and communication, amplify reputations, and thus allow dilemmas of collective action to be resolved. When economic and political negotiation is embedded in dense networks of social interaction, incentives for opportunism are reduced. At the same time, networks of civic engagement embody past success at collaboration, which can serve as a cultural template for future collaboration. Finally, dense networks of interaction probably broaden the participants' sense of self, developing the "I" into the "we," or . . . enhancing the participants' "taste" for collective benefits. (1995b, 66)

Putnam emphasizes that he is not simply blaming television or the other media technologies. A number of demographic transitions that have altered family life since the 1960s also seem to be implicated, such as "fewer marriages, more divorces, fewer children, lower real wages, and so on." In addition, economic factors can be cited, for instance "the replacement of the corner grocery store by the supermarket and now perhaps of the supermarket by electronic shopping at home, or the replacement of community-based enterprises by outposts of distant multinational firms—may perhaps have undermined the material and even the physical basis of civic engagement" (1995b, 75).

Along with these other factors, it is worth taking a look at television, an influence that has been repeatedly cited, for example by Bronfenbrenner and his coworkers. Putnam argues that television is an obvious culprit in the decline of social capital for several reasons. First, the introduction of television coincides with the decline of civic society. In the early 1950s, only one in ten American homes had a television set, but by the late 1950s nine in ten had a set. Over this period, viewing steadily increased, by about 20% in the 1960s and almost 10% in the 1970s. By the mid-1990s Americans viewed 50% more television than they did in the 1950s. According to Robinson the leisure time available to Americans increased by 5.5 hours per week during the same period, but this extra time has been taken up by passive television viewing (about a 4.5-hour increase) rather than by more active forms of engagement (1990b, 24). Robinson reports that 40% of an American adult's free time is taken up by television. If we add secondary and tertiary viewing (the TV is on but not receiving full attention), television takes up more than half of the American adult's free time.

Television has clearly revolutionized the way people spend their time. For example, fewer people are reading, and when they do read, it is for shorter periods. According to Robinson (1990a, 6) the percentage of American adults who read newspapers on a daily basis dropped steadily from 85% in 1946 to 55% in 1985. Every hour spent watching television means less time doing other things, such as reading (a displacement effect of television). But the link to social capital is that people who read the newspaper more are also more involved in, and imbued with, social capital. For example, those who read daily but view television lightly are 55% more trusting of others than those who view heavily and read lightly (Putnam 1995a, 678). With respect to membership in civic organizations, the difference is 76%. Based on his review of the literature, Putnam concludes that "for every hour you spend reading a newspaper you are substantially more likely to vote, more likely to trust others, more likely to join a group. For every hour you spend in front of the television you are, statistically, substantially less likely to vote, less likely to join a group, and less likely to trust other people" (1996, 34).

The link with a sense of trust points to the "cultivation effect" of television viewing, which includes among other things a more fearful view of the world among adult heavy viewers (the "mean world effect" suggested by Gerbner et al. 1980). We also now have cohort after cohort "raised" on a steady and increasing diet of television—some forty hours per week for young children (Putnam 1995a, 679). Setting aside the obvious psychological and attitudinal effects that this level of exposure (to anything) must have (though "deniers" are not hard to find), this amount of television viewing takes up as much time as all other childhood play activities, wherein children actually learn how to socialize with others (i.e., how to cooperate with and trust others, how to be involved in networks). In this literal sense, television is now the greatest single socialization influence on children. Television therefore must have some impact on the formative years and how people eventually make their way to adulthood, by encouraging passive forms of socialization and by displacing more active socialization.

Children are not the only ones vulnerable to the potential negative effects of this passive, displacing, cultivating medium. To the extent that people get their information from television (a passive medium) and not from newspapers (an active medium), they are probably less informed factually; furthermore, they are likely to have less well developed and integrated cognitive mechanisms with which to analyze the world on their own, without the colorful images and sound bites. According to Taras, a person who watches a television news program can only spontaneously remember 5% of what he or she viewed. Even with prompting, only 50% can be remembered on average. Taras argues that television viewing has become "dead time," a time to "veg out" and escape from day-to-day pressures. As people retreat from the pressures of contemporary life, rather than engaging themselves in it, televised images "wash over" them, "leaving them with few traces of thought or information" (1999, 34).

Putnam (1996, 34) summarizes the effect of television on our lives and communities as follows:

The main effect of the introduction of the television—and this, by the way, is not unique to the United States—has been to make us more home-bodies and more isolated. Whereas in the very first period all the family was sitting around the hearths watching television together, now with the number of multi-set homes skyrocketing, we are just watching alone. And what we are watching is simulated social capital. (1996, 34)

In the make-believe worlds of television, characters and communities try to make us feel at one with them.

## The Adult of Mass Society

In this chapter we have taken a quick tour through a vast amount of literature, in order to gain a better sense of what contemporary American adults (as trend-setters in the bellwether nation of the world) are doing and thinking, both to provide structure and guidance for generations to come and to improve themselves in a society rife with opportunities to do so. The verdict is mixed, but on the whole it would appear that the tendency toward default forms of individualization is stronger than the tendency toward developmental forms of individualization (fig. 2.1). I believe there is sufficient evidence to conclude that at the aggregate level the "adult population" of the United States is on balance choosing more passive than active forms of engagement. At the individual level, it makes more sense to group people by the choices they make in a society undergoing cultural destructuring (or social decapitalization, as Putnam describes the most recent phase of this). For the time being, then, we will stay with the four categories of individuals represented in figure 2.1 and pursue the hypothesis that the groups represented by a trajectory toward default individualization are increasing in prevalence while those groups representing developmental individualization outcomes are decreasing in prevalence.

The most common factor that emerged in the studies examined in this chapter—television—offers a way to estimate the relative trends toward default or developmental individualization, namely the decision to watch television or to do something that requires more active participation. I propose that that decision constitutes one of the key decision points (mentioned earlier in the chapter) that moves a person toward undertaking developmental individualization or default individualization, with the decision to watch television usually leading to default forms of individualization. In fact, the correlates of television viewing suggest that it is a passive and default form of experience. Thus, the amount of television a person chooses to watch can be used as an indicator of how much he or she follows a default individualization trajectory; conversely, how much a person chooses more active forms of engagement can be used as an indicator of the extent to which she or he follows a developmental individualization trajectory. More active forms of engagement include reading, studying, undertaking educational programs, and involving oneself in athletic, musical, intellectual, artistic, and other forms of mentally challenging activities (these would also include mechanical or construction activities and craft or hobby endeavors).

Americans have been able to enjoy increased leisure over the last thirty years, from 34.5 hours per week in 1965 to 40.1 hours in 1985, according to Cutler's research (1990, 38). The question is, Have Americans put this to "good use"? Cutler's results suggest not, on the whole—of this 5.6 hours per week of extra spare time, 4.6 hours have been taken up by television viewing. American adults also spend more time in conversation (1.7 hours in 1985), traveling (.4 hour), in sports and outdoor activities (.3 hour), in hobby activities (.1 hour), in adult education (.6 hour), and in thinking and relaxing (.5 hour). The amounts of time given to these more engaging activities can be used as rough estimates of the extent to which people undertake developmental individualization trajectories (3.6 hours in total, but if we subtract the time for talking and relaxing, we are left with 1.4 hours per week). Decreased engagement in more traditional forms of developmental individualization is evident. Americans now spend less time visiting neighbors and relatives (1.7 hours), reading (.9 hour), engaging in religious activities (.1 hour), participating in cultural events (.3 hour), and being involved in clubs and organizations (.3 hour), for a total of 3.3 hours. In a sense, then, the increases in activities that (loosely) represent newer forms of developmental individualization have been at the expense of activities that represent more traditional forms of developmental individualization, so a zero-sum situation may have resulted where old and new forms of developmental individualization cancel each other but where the new, more passive forms of default individualization have grown, signaling at best a stagnation and at worst a regression.

As valuable as the studies examined in this chapter have been, they all lack an overarching theoretical or conceptual framework within which the various findings can be organized, made sense of, used to suggest solutions to the problems identified. For example, although "adults" are the focus of these studies, either directly in terms of their behaviors and attitudes or indirectly in terms of the way they raise their children, the whole question of adulthood itself is avoided. Thus, the questions Putnam raises about social capital and civil society could be reframed, as I did in chapter 1, to ask how the ontology and political economy of adulthood has changed as a result of the decline of social markers and the rise of psychological adulthood.

The reader will recall that the forces altering adulthood predate the twentieth century and the rise of mass technologies. In other words, the destructuring and individualization that have been picked up by these studies (initiated three to four decades ago, when social scientists took notice) began before the most recent decline in civil society. In fact, Putnam (1996) acknowledges that the late nineteenth century had much in common with the late twentieth century in terms of the social disorganization and anomic conditions associated with capitalism (the late nineteenth century was the heyday of industrial capitalism). Many of the civic organizations he studied have their roots in the late nineteenth and early twentieth centuries, when people took the initiative to re-stock social capital. Actually, the roots of many of these periods of social disorganization can be traced to the rise and spread of capitalism in its various stages, but particularly in the stage of industrial capitalism during the nineteenth century. What we are witnessing now is the most recent manifestation of capitalism's conquest of American culture—this time by corporate capitalism. With this conquest, capitalism has altered the ontology and political economy of adulthood, creating new forms of identity (loss) and (im)maturity.

The fact is that an overarching framework has been available for some time, but most contemporary academics have either forgotten it or never learned of it, perhaps being exposed to more contemporary variants of it. I am referring here to the concept of mass society and the various theories associated with that concept. The forms of theorizing currently called "postmodern" are very much replicates of mass-society theory, like old wine in new bottles. Curiously, most postmodernists do not acknowledge this intellectual heritage. But unlike much postmodern theorizing, theories of mass society are quite straightforward and easy to understand.

Just why these theories are no longer recognized is an interesting question. Daniel Bell (1961) dismissed them for a number of reasons that seemed sensible in the 1950s, when things seemed to going so well in the United States. Since then, though, much of what mass-society theorists forecasted has come true, as the studies considered in this chapter reveal. The sequence of events that has brought us to the current state of affairs is simple enough: through much effort by industrial capitalists over several generations, industrial capitalism has brought about a society in which mass production and mass consumption prevail, in turn creating segmented (largely by age), undifferentiated, but atomized "masses" in the population that maintain the system of mass production-consumption. While this was happening, aspects of "traditional" culture have been manipulated or destroyed in the effort to develop a compliant labor force and a population of willing consumers. The decline of social markers and the rise of psychological adulthood noted in the first chapter have followed. Now we are deep into a society dominated by a mass culture (or mass cultures, differentiated by birth cohort), of which TV is but one important part, that caters to people's lower and lazier natures, enticing them to choose forms of default individualization over the more demanding and difficult forms of developmental individualization. What we need to do next, therefore, is to examine the notion of mass society, and its relation to the mass culture that is taking over the social landscape and increasingly penetrating people's lives and communities.

# 3

## The Brave New Adult
### Models of Maturity for Mass Society

### Problems Faced by the Adult of Mass Society

In chapter 1 we saw that not only is adulthood a vague concept, but many people's experience of it is now fraught with vagaries as well. It appears, further, that not only is guidance for the passage *into* adulthood deficient or absent for many people, but there is even less guidance *through* adulthood. It became evident in chapter 2 that an increasing number of people are left to their own wits to define what it means to be an adult; during their deliberations they are enticed to take various paths of least resistance and effort. Adults as a group appear to be on a downward slope with regard to self-betterment, in spite of all of the opportunities made available by industrialization and the rapid advance of technologies that make the physical-survival aspects of life easier. Many people now seem to have more trouble with the psychological-survival aspects of life.

Certainly, a good proportion of people seem capable of making their way from childhood into their adult years in a effective manner; but more and more seem not capable of doing so, I believe in part because of a lack of guidance from the generations now in their adult years. In this chapter we consult observers of mid- and late-twentieth-century adulthood and its concomitants to see what they believe the dominant trends have been. First, however, we pause to consider a sociological understanding regarding the historical context in which adulthood has been changing.

### Mass Society

Given the uncharted nature of this territory, it is helpful to consult some available "maps" to continue our search for the contemporary adult begun in chapter 1. There are a variety of maps, or social analyses, being offered these days about the nature of contemporary and future society, but virtually none touches on the intrinsic nature of adulthood. Instead, for the most part the underlying assumptions in these analyses concerning adulthood must be inferred, and the terrain they map is only roughly outlined. The most common analysis is of the "postmodern" variety. Such analyses are useful to some degree, as we see later in this chapter, but my feeling is that they are often misleading in the "headings" they provide and their definitions of the immediate "landscape." Specifically, postmodern analyses often miss the history of the "mass" nature of Western societies and recommend that we go in directions that may make what is problematic about mass society a permanent heading.

At midtwentieth century, theories of mass society were considered to be the most influential social theories in the Western world (Bell 1961). The term *mass society* originated in the early part of the century to describe what was believed to be a dehumanization of life in modern society. Theories of mass society reached their peak in the 1950s through the efforts of people like Hannah Arendt, Ortega y Gasset, Karl Jaspers, Emil Lederer, Gabriel Marcel, and Paul Tillich. Although these theorists varied in their conceptions of the causes and ills of mass society, common to all was the notion that modern societies had grown in size and complexity as a result of industrial capitalism. Through the process of industrialization, many traditions were eradicated, leaving industrial workers and their families (the "masses") alienated from each other, themselves, and their cultures. Cut away from their traditional sources of meaning, modern populations were targeted by industrial capitalists, who produced segmented (e.g., by social class) but internally undifferentiated, masses that were prone to mass manipulation and mass hysteria; at the same time, modern societies became bureaucratized, mechanized, and atomized.

By midtwentieth century, then, many social theorists said that in Western societies—especially American society—people (1) were locked into a subjective sense of the present, with few ties to the past emotionally (kinship and bonds) or intellectually (knowledge of their lineage, culture, and history); (2) were exposed to sets of common influences that attempted to manipulate them and produce a standardized result (mass production, mass consumption, homogeneous beliefs and habits); (3) had a sense of connection with others based on mutual self-interest rather than emotional or unconditional bonds; and (4) experienced themselves as fragmented and in flux, with little attachment to the past. In short, in the early twentieth century, the American population was characterized as having a narrow consciousness of the present that was continually manipulated by others, either remotely or immediately, and a myopic sense of the future. The average American was also thought to have a problematic sense of identity, made so by the alienating social structures to which he or she was exposed. It was feared that citizens of mass society would be easily swayed by shifts in values, mass movements, and trends; and lacking a deep sense of tradition, loyalty, and commitment to community, "mass man" was prone to mass manipulation by unscrupulous politicians and capitalists.

These theories are rarely referred to today. Instead, we hear much about theories of postmodern society; the postmodern theories, however, are now making many of the same claims as did mass-society theories (cf. Meštrović 1997). In this respect many postmodern theories are historically myopic. Granted, it is a centuries-old feature of social commentary to claim that a given society is in a precipitous moral decline. Yet many postmodern theorists, apparently incompletely schooled in social theory, seem to believe that "declines" of this sort are recent phenomena associated with the advent of high technology, as opposed to being associated with longer-term effects of capitalism in its various forms (cf. Stafseng 1994). If this is true, much of postmodern theory is simply the product of a new generation of academics who use new jargon to describe old problems that they think are new because of their personal and intellectual inexperience. For this reason I believe it is useful to go back to the original theories of mass society to try to determine more clearly the "prepostmodern" effects of industrial capitalism.

To understand theories of mass society, we need to take a longer view of economic changes. When we do so, we find that the history of capitalism accounts for much of the change that has taken place in the name of "progress." Five hundred years of capitalism have introduced remarkable technological advances. Few would argue with that. Many have argued, however, that social advances have not kept pace with these technological changes. In fact, it is an old argument that societies have not moved as fast as their machines. The theory of cultural lag dates back to the early 1950s, when it was first noticed that although life was getting easier because of mass-produced labor-saving devices, many people were not becoming happier, more fulfilled, or more advanced morally, ethically, or intellectually. We return to this issue in the final chapter when we take a longer view of the impact of capitalism.

For now it will suffice to point out that the earlier mercantile capitalism made possible an accumulation of capital to stimulate industrial capitalism, which has given rise most recently to corporate capitalism. Corporate capitalism, through monopolies, transnational expansions, political leveraging, and the manipulation of consumption patterns, now prevails as a new global political system. According to Eisenstein (1998), more than half of the world's largest economies are corporations rather than countries, and five hundred corporations account for 70% of the trade around the world. The largest transnational corporations have far more wealth than most governments have. For the most part, they answer to no government. In fact, these corporations now exercise control over nation-states in a number of strong-arm and subtle ways. The strong-arm tactics include control of money markets or buying a country's national debt; the subtle tactics include donations to political parties, public relations campaigns, and interlocking corporate directorates where ex-politicians are given lucrative positions.

One does not actually need to be aware of this critical-materialist argument to recognize the impact of the capitalist economy on cultural change. Some of the greatest benefits of capitalism have long-term effects that we are not coping with well. For example, increased affluence means that the population is better fed, so the life span is longer. Technological advances pursued out of a desire for profit and capital accumulation have also led to medical advances that have increased the life span and reduced infant mortality. A direct consequence of industrial capitalism, therefore, was dramatic population growth and societies with greater numbers of people. In these large societies, goods could be mass produced, wiping out whole categories of skilled trades. The techniques of mass production were essentially mastered in the first half of the twentieth century, Henry Ford being their "poster boy."

But the system of mass production faltered because capitalists had not yet developed effective means of convincing people to become mass consumers. To create a mass of compliant consumers, the mass media were exploited in a search for more effective ways of delivering information to the masses (see, e.g., Caldicott 1992; Rifkin 1995). The sciences of mass persuasion, now known as public relations and mass marketing, got their foothold in the 1920s during the heyday of mass production. These techniques are now so commonplace that people not only consider them normal, but many people also consider them indispensable (especially via television and the Internet).

The technologies have also affected intergenerational relations. For example, the availability of the automobile contributed to a loss of parents' control over their offspring's dating behavior, and music reproduction gave corporate interests a direct connection to the emotional "core" of the young, driving a wedge between offspring and their parents by creating separate cultures. To the extent that mass consumption plays on people's desire for pleasure and thrills, social institutions that once required obligations, attachment, and commitment have been undermined and are being replaced by those catering to individual wants and needs.

Thus, many of the trends beginning in the 1960s that Putnam documented regarding the decline of social capital (see chapter 2) were really part of a second wave in the twentieth century of the penetration by capitalist-produced technology into people's lives. The first wave occurred around the 1920s. In effect, then, we have moved further and further into the mass society described by early theorists like Ortega and Arendt. In my view we are not moving into a new era, as some postmodernists would have it, but rather are simply witnessing continuing trends begun centuries ago by which capitalists have searched for more effective ways of penetrating cultures and the daily lives of people in the search for profit (a "heightened modernity" as Anthony Giddens [1990, 1991] puts it, although he would not consider himself a mass-society theorist). In the early part of the twentieth century, capitalists mastered mass production; in the latter part of the twentieth century they mastered mass consumption. In overcoming this latest challenge, capitalists have built on mass society and have created a fully elaborated mass culture (cf. Cadello 1990). We explore this mass culture and its ramifications for adulthood throughout the remainder of this book.

When the history of the situation facing us is framed in this manner, several things take on a clarity that is missing in postmodern analyses. First, celebrations of the confusions introduced into people's lives by mass society, and more recently mass culture, suggest that the social change "headings" offered by postmodernists are misguided. In my view the confusions of self that postmodernists point to are symptomatic of how corporate-capitalist interests have penetrated public institutions and personal lives. To celebrate these confusions is to play into those amoral and ultimately self-destructive interests. And to think the disruptive influence of capitalism is new is to ignore five centuries during which community after community has been stripped of its traditional foundations in the name of "progress." Capitalists today have simply perfected the techniques and speed with which they can convince people to become emotionally and materially dependent upon them.

Second, the notions of mass society and mass culture maintain commonsense grips on the material conditions governing social and economic change and do not surrender a sense of reality to "idealist" explanations that may be lacking in their connection with the "real world." There is a value in simple and straightforward explanations; overly complex and convoluted explanations may not help resolve the sorts of problems we now face because they miss the mark. For example, in a recently syndicated article titled "It's a PoMo PoMo PoMo world," in Toronto's *Globe and Mail* of June 5, 1999, Richard Nilsen gives an account of "postmodernism" (PoMo) that can more accurately be termed a description of mass culture. He defines postmodernism as "a trend in culture at large: a self-conscious awareness of ourselves as playing parts, and a blurring of the lines between genres, and between media and life." But he then writes:

> In a PoMo world, everything is marketing, and consumers not only recognize the fact, they eagerly participate in it. We wear billboards on our baseball caps and T-shirts. We look for the swooshes on jogging shoes. It doesn't strike anyone under 40 as odd that we should name a stadium after a snack food or a long-distance telephone company. And even TV commercials are likely to be about making TV commercials: A chameleon puts out a contract on a Budweiser frog. This is not about beer, it is about media.

Clearly, an awareness of the history of capitalism would rescue the illusion that these media trends have "just happened" or that they are something to celebrate as a cultural breakthrough.

Third, there is a consensus among most social theories that people in contemporary Western societies have increasing problems in establishing stable and viable adult identities based on commitments embedded in a community of others (see, e.g., Gergen 1991; Giddens 1991). The disagreement is mainly about the roots of these problems.

Rather than to delve into the details of this dispute here, I simply provide a framework that helps us understand the historical conditions that have contributed to the current problems associated with psychological, as opposed to physical, survival. This framework of "societal stages" contrasts premodern and modern societies in terms of the widely accepted sociological distinction between folk and urban society, a distinction that parallels other typologies such as agrarian versus industrial, folk versus urban, or gemeinschaft versus gesellschaft (see, e.g., Tönnies 1980; Wirth 1938). In most Western societies, the transformation from premodern to modern was largely completed during the nineteenth century (the final phase was the transition from household production to factory production, noted in chapter 1, that resulted in the emergence of separate private and public spheres for women and men). Since then, it is widely believed among sociologists, modern societies have undergone significant changes, so much so that it is possible to contrast early modern and late modern societies.

The distinction between early modern and late modern makes sense if the early modern is defined as a period of "modernism" in which mass production was a defining feature of social relations. Over the twentieth century, however, mass consumption increased in importance as a defining feature of social relations and identity, with production declining in relative importance as technology supplanted labor. Postmodernists prefer the term *postmodern* to *late modern*, but I have several reservations about using *postmodern*. My main reservation stems from the fact that the transformation from premodern to modern was on a scale far greater than the transition from the modern to the so-called postmodern era. That is, with the transition to modern society there was a shift in the basis of social solidarity from one of primary-group relations to one of secondary-group relations. With the spread of secondary-group relations, social bonds became more voluntary and based more on rational self-interest than on collective familial and intergenerational obligation. I do not think that a transition of such a magnitude took place in the twentieth century. Instead, during the twentieth century, secondary relations evolved toward greater self-interest, but the basis of social solidarity was essentially the same (i.e., contractual).

Simply put, I do not believe we are "post" anything (cf. Furlong and Cartmel 1997). Note, however, that late modern society is structured to a great degree with reference to the problems of consumption—how to entice the "masses" to center their lives around consumption. Note as well that it is dominated by the mass culture or cultures that have been created to institutionalize these mass consumption patterns. Thus, the late modern position shares certain concerns with the postmodern one, but the former sees different roots and consequences of the ongoing social changes.

We return to these sociological concerns in the conclusion of this chapter after reviewing several characterizations of what constitutes "normality" and "maturity" among late modern adults. We also revisit them in chapter 4, where the late modern paradigm is reviewed more thoroughly.

## Observations from the Midtwentieth Century

Two highly influential observers writing about twentieth-century conditions provide frameworks that complement the premodern-modern distinction discussed in the previous section. Their frameworks also complement each other's, even though they wrote at different times and from different disciplines. Perhaps not coincidentally, both observers found it useful to distinguish among three periods of social change. The two observers I refer to are Margaret Mead and David Riesman. The correlation of their frameworks with the three periods of change is illustrated in figure 3.1.

### Mead's *Culture and Commitment*

Margaret Mead, the best-known anthropologist of the twentieth century, studied a variety of cultures, especially non-Western ones, over about a half-century. She often focused on the lives of the young in a community and the relations of the young with older members. Toward the end of her career, she wrote a short, insightful book that integrated her insights concerning those cultures. There, she laid out a theory of how cultural change affects relations between generations.

In Mead's book, *Culture and Commitment: A Study of the Generation Gap,* she postulated a theory of intergenerational relations that reflects three stages in the cultural configuration of socializing institutions: "postfigurative, in which children learn primarily from their forebears, cofigurative, in which both children and adults learn from their peers, and the prefigurative, in which adults learn also from their children" (1970, 1).[1]

Mead's theory of changing intergenerational relations is straightforward yet profound because it encapsulates what appears to have hap-

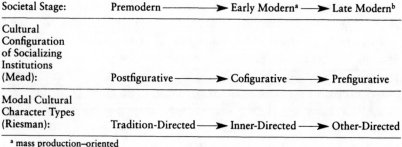

*Fig. 3.1.* The Culture-Identity Link: Cultural Concepts

pened in most world cultures in recent history. Mead was fascinated with how preliterate (or "primitive") societies are affected by contact with advanced technological societies. She noted how deep these effects ran, down to the day-to-day relations between children and adults, as both attempted to make sense out of their changing worlds. The reader can see at a glance in figure 3.1 how Mead's theory of intergenerational relations parallels the typology of societal stages set forth in the previous pages.

In postfigurative cultures the relations between parents and their offspring are governed by traditional norms that are beyond questioning by either parent or child. Certainly, child-disciplining practices are long established and not open to discussion. The postfigurative culture is stabilized by the coresidence of three generations and the ascription of most social roles. Consequently, change is slow and intergenerational continuity great, even revered. Included among postfigurative cultures are those that engage in ancestor worship and have a sense of responsibility for descendants. Some cultures teach their young that they are responsible for many generations to come, up to seven generations. Postfigurative cultures bear clear similarities to premodern societies.

In cofigurative cultures, the intergenerational linkage becomes tenuous because of social change brought on by technological advancement, economic transformation, immigration, war, and so forth. One or more of such forces affects the culture, giving children a different set of experiences than their parents had, if only for a brief time. Consequently, to some extent offspring look to nontraditional sources for components of their sense of meaning, particularly to their contemporaries. There is a fundamental change in the relations between parents and children, whereby the authority of the parent can be questioned and the child can actually give direction to the parent in certain instances. As a result, the eventual adult roles of the offspring are no longer taken for granted by either parent or child as much as they were in the past. However, the schism between parent and child is limited because the offspring are obliged to observe and respect significant elements of the traditional culture shared with their parents. Cofigurative cultures bear clear similarities to early modern societies.

Prefigurative cultures are characterized by rapid and massive social change and bear clear similarities to late modern societies. Because of the extent of social change, parents have little conception of what the future holds for their offspring; their past life experiences are therefore of little use to offspring with respect to the offspring's present sense of meaning and future roles. As a result parental guidance is not well regarded by offspring. Moreover, parental belief systems (and traditional culture, if applicable) are often dismissed as invalid by offspring. Mead argued that in cofigurative cultures the young can actually teach their parents about the ongoing social changes, or achieve a level of social status, to the point where parents can become subservient to their offspring in various ways. Hence, the gap between parents and offspring that opens in the cofigurative culture is widened in the prefigurative one. Consistent with her generally liberal outlook, Mead saw much that was positive in prefigurative societies. In view of what we have examined thus far in this book, however, it would appear that there are many hazards associated with a society in which parents are unable to guide their children into adulthood. And many other observers are not so sanguine about the consequences of prefigurative-type societies.

Mead's theory sheds light on a number of issues. For example, with her theory we can make better sense of the incident mentioned at the beginning of chapter 1 that involved a father's being spanked by the police for spanking his child too hard. Clearly, the authority of the parent to discipline a child would not be questioned in this way in a postfigurative society, and child discipline is often severe in that type of society. In fact, in premodern Western societies, *not* disciplining a child in a strict manner was often seen as cruel and negligent. In an increasingly prefigurative society such as the United States, we are witnessing a reversal of that view, in which the act of physical discipline is viewed as negatively as was not disciplining in the past. Parents now do not have as much authority rooted in tradition; and there is less faith that they possess sufficient wisdom of their own to properly raise their children.

In short, the well-being of the current and future generations of children has been largely divorced from past practices. Consequently, there is great confusion about how to effectively raise children. There is even more bewilderment about what the future holds for generations brought up with very little discipline, physical or otherwise. Mead would not be surprised to hear that in the 1990s these issues were of increasing concern. As Underwood wrote in an article in Toronto's *Globe and Mail* of April 17, 1999, titled "Parent Trap: Are Your Kids Driving You Crazy?," "Somewhere along the line, things got little off track. . . . [Parents] began to let their youngsters call the shots. Children today are not only seen and heard, they expect to be obeyed: their war cry, 'You are not the boss of me!' is ringing out across the continent" (D1). In response to this increasing tyranny of childhood, bewildered and frustrated parents are looking for help. Their children, by the standards of virtually all known societies, are behaving like spoiled brats who cannot control their impulses, take responsibility for their actions, or empathize with others. The help being offered, however, is mainly from conservatives who cannot see beyond the so-called liberalism of the sixties as the source of these problems. Underwood cites books like *Who's in Charge?* and *I'll Be the Parent, You Be the Kid* that offer advice to beleaguered parents, telling them to forget ideas associated with sixties liberalism and the self-esteem movement and instead to look to good, old-fashioned family values. Although there may be some merit in this remedy, such prescriptions are historically myopic, as are many of the remedies we have examined that do not look back far enough in time to see why things are the way they are (or were the way they were in the sixties).

### Riesman's *Lonely Crowd*

Although Riesman's sociological classic *The Lonely Crowd: A Study of the Changing American Character* (1950) predated Mead's book by twenty years, his conception of the relevance of social change affecting Western societies is complementary to Mead's. In figure 3.1 we can see how Riesman's schema of modal character types—represented by three complementary concepts—parallels Mead's model of the changing cultural configuration of socializing institutions.

Riesman argues that a "tradition-directed" character type characterizes premodern societies (Mead's postfigurative society). In such societies the "important relationships of life [are] . . . controlled by careful and rigid etiquette, learned by the young during the years of intensive socialization that end with initiation into full adult membership" (1950, 11). This character type is heteronomous, in part because "the range of choice . . . is minimal[; thus] the apparent social need for an individuated type of character is minimal" (12).

In societies that parallel cofigurative cultures, Riesman argues that "inner-directed" character types emerge as "the principal mode of securing conformity" (1950, 14). To counteract the disruptive influences of early industrialization (associated with geographical mobility, urbanization, capital accumulation, and mass production), individuals are socialized with a metaphorical "gyroscope," which "is implanted early in life by the elders and directed toward generalized but nonetheless inescapably destined goals" (15). Accordingly, parents come to see their offspring as "individuals with careers to make" (17). In this context inner-directed persons exercise choice and initiative, but the general heading and pattern of acceptable behavior is set before they embark upon their careers. The resulting individuality is not a threat to the social and economic order because the person is self-governing, equipped with this gyroscope (or superego, in Freudian terms).

The third character type arises under conditions that resemble prefigurative cultures. As the means of mass production become mastered and abundance becomes more taken for granted, the "scarcity psychology" of the inner-directed character is supplanted by an "abundance psychology" that gives rise to what Riesman calls the "other-directed" character type. Hence, in late modern society, the overproduction that results from technological advances is met with heightened consumerism. That is, with production problems mastered, a late modern society needs consumption on a large scale; otherwise capital accumulation suffers.

Complementary to mass consumption are mass insecurities regarding whether the "right" things are done and said. For the population to engage in mass consumption, mass insecurities are necessary, since consumption promises to alleviate anxiety if the "right" things are consumed. Now, according to Riesman, "other people are the problem, not the material environment" (1950, 8), and consumption emerges as a way of identifying one's loyalties and relationships. Consequently, the other-directed character is highly sensitive to others—to their opinions and their approval. Riesman uses the metaphor of radar to characterize this orientation; individuals are taught early in life to constantly monitor the social environment to ensure that their consumption patterns (especially in appearance and behavior) conform to whatever are the accepted standards of the time and place. The other-directed person strives to meet goals, but those goals can shift, and it is staying in tune with the shifts that is of paramount importance to this character type.

It is easy to see how the prefigurative socialization mechanisms that Mead postulated can contribute to other-directedness. When parents provide less guidance and have less influence over their children's identity formation, the children naturally turn to others for direction. To the extent that this becomes part of the cultural conditioning, it should contribute to the character development for individuals in that culture.

Riesman's schema is well known in sociological circles but little referenced elsewhere. One exception is the Merser book, reviewed in chapter 1. Merser extended Riesman's midcentury analysis to argue that many people in the postwar cohorts became other-directed, as Riesman predicted: they became increasingly susceptible to influence by their peers, but also to the media and everything the media represent, such as consumerism and narcissism. For Merser, the problem with the other-directed character is that the person lives in a sand castle—in a world of constantly shifting demands and standards. People do not have the security of a "tradition-directed" character or the strength of an "inner-directed" character. Instead, they are at the mercy of their peers, their coworkers, and strangers, who commonly have self-interested agendas. Consequently, the "relationship" becomes an important element of self-definition. However, as Merser notes,

> to take stock of who we are through these external relationships still gets us only partway to a definition of the self: Relationships are fluid, volatile, dependent on outside circumstances, while the "who am I" kind of identity . . . [that we grope for] is an inner self . . . that is fixed, dependable, and strong enough to see you through the failure or disruption of any of these outside relations. (1987, 134)

It appears, then, that people are becoming more and more susceptible to the opinions of others, for good or bad. The good side of this may be that people are more sensitive to others' rights and feelings; the bad side is that if "sensitivity" is all there is, people will not reflect fully on the implications of their own actions. In theory, greater sensitivity should reduce prejudice and stereotypes, but often it does not. Indeed, there is little evidence that Western societies are any less prejudiced; the prejudices seem to have simply shifted. For example, for some people gays are now good, but heterosexuals are bad; for others, women are now superior, but men are inferior (Tavris 1992). The net result is an equal amount of prejudice: it has simply shifted to safer targets—safer in the sense of interpersonal censure from others. What we seem to be left with is a population with a large number of confused people who have little knowledge of the past, a hedonistic or instrumental orientation to the present, and little sense of the future (Cadello 1990). These confused people are often "ethical" only in terms of the politically correct "issue of the week" as delivered to them by the media or their reference group, but they give little deep thought to the implications of their ethics (Meštrović 1997). Indeed, media packaged and delivered ethics gives little insight into serious moral-ethical issues such as the universal application of a principle (cf. Taras 1999), as opposed to a single-issue application or an application only to the "correct" group (in contrast, recall Erikson's and Kegan's formulations from chapter 1). It is unsettling just how easily influenced the other-directed person is when one compares current mass behaviors with those from the past, such as the Nazi movement and the ensuing Holocaust. But these were the types of things that mass-society theorists of the early part of the twentieth century feared.

## Contemporary Observations

### The Sense of Entitlement in *The Culture of Narcissism*

One of the most widely read social observers of the second half of the twentieth century to comment on the changing nature of the adult character was Christopher Lasch (1979). Lasch argued in *The Culture of Narcissism* that Western "character" has come to involve an array of personalities that range from "normal" to pathological self-absorption. In fact, he argues that a high level of "normal" narcissism is an asset for those in pursuit of successful careers, because of the degree of self-absorption necessary to focus on those careers.

Lasch asserts that people have always had the potential for selfishness and greed and that many people have been selfish and greedy in the past; but it is only recently that a culture has emerged that facilitates and glorifies these traits. Hence, he uses narcissism not as a strictly psychological concept but as a way of understanding the psychological impact of recent cultural change. In other words, social conditions bring out narcissistic traits that are latent in everyone, and "cultural narcissism" represents a effective way of coping with the demands and anxieties of modern life.

Lasch provides a sketch of the personality qualities associated with cultural narcissism. People who are well-functioning cultural narcissists are good at managing the impressions they project in social situations, they crave admiration but are contemptuous of those who provide it, they have an insatiable desire for emotional experiences with which to fill their inner void, and they are petrified of aging and death.

In his view this form of "psychological man" has replaced the "economic man" of earlier capitalism when "bourgeois individualism" prevailed. For Lasch, cultural narcissists are "haunted not by guilt but by anxiety." The modern-day narcissist is liberated "from the superstitions of the past, [but] doubts even the reality of his or her own experience." His or her sexual permissiveness is an emancipation from puritanical taboos but "brings no sexual peace." This personality type is highly competitive so long as the competitiveness leads to approval and acclaim but experiences rage when it does not. Cooperation and teamwork are but means to personal ends, and rules are insisted upon but do not apply if one personally gets caught breaking them. Everyone is a "rival for the favors conferred by a paternalistic state." The craving to acquire material goods is not for future security so much as for immediate gratification. Consequently, the cultural narcissist "lives in a state of restless, perpetually unsatisfied desire" (Lasch 1979, 22–23).

Lasch does not offer an estimate of how pervasive he believes this personality type to be. He does, however, give a concrete example of the adaptive utility of the narcissistic personality in managing large-scale organizational machinery:

The narcissist comes to the attention of psychiatrists for the same reasons he rises to positions of prominence not only in awareness movements and other cults but in business corporations, political organizations, and government bureaucracies. For all his inner suffering, the narcissist has many traits that make for success in bureaucratic institutions, which put a premium on the manipulation of interpersonal relations, discourage the formation of deep personal attachments, and at the same time provide the narcissist with the approval he needs in order to validate his self-esteem. . . . The management of personal impressions comes naturally to him, and his mastery of its intricacies serves him well in political and business organizations where performance now counts less than "visibility," "momentum," and a winning record. (1979, 91–92)

In Lasch's view this personality type is a logical outcome of "bureaucracy, the proliferation of images, therapeutic ideologies, the rationalization of inner life, the cult of consumption, and . . . [of] changes in family life and . . . changing patterns of socialization" (74). In other words, Lasch's argument is compatible with the observations of others that we have reviewed, in the sense that this personality type might be a product of conditions associated with mass society and more recently late modern society. The cultural narcissist is certainly at home in an other-directed society (Riesman's term) with a gap between parents' and children's experiences (as in Mead's analysis).

Lasch bases his contentions on observations of the 1960s and 1970s. If he is right, the "culture of narcissism" must have had a frightening momentum by the 1990s. If large-scale organizations were controlled by narcissists at midcentury (and demanded narcissistic behavior among their upper ranks), there is little reason to believe that such control has abated. Nothing we have examined thus far suggests that cultural narcissism has diminished. Just the opposite seems to be true, as the evidence reviewed in chapter 2 suggests. But add to this picture the possible encroachment of narcissism into the basic unit of the society—the family—and we can see how it may have insidiously spread throughout the social fabric.

According to Lasch, the family has been affected by many of the same developments affecting the larger society (e.g., technologies that capture the self in its various manifestations, the therapeutic ideology of "a normative schedule of psychosocial growth," the cult of self-actualization, and so forth). Lasch considers that the family has become historically dislocated and self-absorbed; increasingly, it has been cut off from the past, and parents have little sense of the future. Consequently, the focus in families is more and more on the present and what the present can offer. Because the family "shapes the underlying structure of the personality," Lasch argues, this is "a good prescription for a narcissistic personality structure." As each successive cohort is brought up by, and composed of, an increasing number of narcissistic parents, we see less and less attention given to the next generation, let alone the many generations that will follow the next. Lasch summarizes the poor conditions for socializing new members of the society as follows: "The modern parent's attempt to make children feel loved and wanted does not conceal an underlying coolness—the remoteness of those who have little to pass on to the next generation and who in any case give priority to their own right to self-fulfilment" (1979, 101–102).

As hyperbolic as Lasch's analysis might seem, it is entirely compatible with most of what we have examined thus far. Certainly the conditions of mass society have made possible the germination of this cultural character type, as have more recent changes associated with the proliferation of mass culture in late modern society. It is also undisputed that each successive generation of the twentieth century pushed the boundaries of permissible behavior out further and further from that of their parents' generation. If the parents of Baby Boomers produced a generation of more extreme cultural narcissists (than their own generation) through their permissive child-rearing techniques, one has to wonder what personality characteristics Baby Boomers as parents have nurtured in their children. Thus, the sense of entitlement that seems to have grown with each cohort over the twentieth century makes perfect sense within Lasch's analysis; even if he overestimated the extent of the sense of narcissistic entitlement when he wrote in the 1970s, it is less likely that his analysis did not apply by the 1990s.

Another way to assess the claim that narcissism is an insidious force in contemporary society is to consult *The Diagnostic and Statistical Manual,* fourth edition (*DSM*-IV), the official manual of the American Psychiatric Association (1994). We find there that it is estimated that only 1% of the general population can be characterized as having a personality disorder constellated around these qualities (the prevalence is estimated at somewhere between 2% and 16% of the clinical population). However, the *DSM*-IV also supports Lasch's claim that those who are most successful in late modern society exhibit these traits: "Many highly successful individuals display personality traits that might be considered narcissistic. Only when these traits are inflexible, maladaptive, and persisting and cause significant functional impairment or subjective distress do they constitute Narcissistic Personality Disorder" (661).

These words may be reassuring, but they do not resolve the rather blurry line between the normal and the pathological that Lasch explored. One way to read that passage is to see that narcissistic traits are only pathological when they control the person instead of the person controlling them. In other words, it is all right to *have* these traits but not to be *had by them* (cf. Kreisman and Straus 1989). It seems that if one can use the traits of narcissism in a flexible, adaptive, and situational manner *and be successful*, one escapes psychiatric classification.

Indeed, a case can be made that in late modern society (with its various institutionalized excesses) one is not likely to experience distress or to exhibit functional impairment if one is successful at one's career. Moreover, there is a cause-and-effect problem here—if for some reason one fails, subjective distress is a normal reaction *and* others are likely to view the failure as a result of functional impairment. Based on the theories we have viewed thus far, then, if one is other-directed and narcissistic, it seems that one is more likely to do well in organizations of late modern society because other-directedness entails being flexible, adaptive, and situational. However, it is likely that if one is inner-directed, or even tradition-directed, and therefore lacking the flexibility, the adaptiveness, or the impression-management skills necessary for late modern organizational life, these narcissistic traits are more likely to cause functional impairment or subjective distress. For one, I am not comforted by the possibility that our business and political leaders escape the distress of their narcissism because they are other-directed in their narcissism.

One also has to question the *DSM-IV*'s 1% prevalence for the narcissistic personality disorder. Normally these rates are based on reported cases that come to clinical attention, but in a society so conducive to and inviting of these traits, one has to wonder how much goes unreported, even if a person experiences distress. In fact, many highly narcissistic people experiencing distress may well be seeking nonmainstream help such as spiritual advisors, psychics, and the like, or seeking comfort in the "cafeteria" of New Age and spiritual therapies now available. To illustrate, review the following list of symptoms of the narcissistic personality disorder and then consider (1) how many people in your personal and public or work life have *in some degree* some of the symptoms (either latently or manifestly) and (2) how many role models currently featured by the media *exemplify* these traits and therefore are likely spawning them in the general population.

A pervasive pattern of grandiosity (in fantasy or behavior), need for admiration, and lack of empathy, beginning in early adulthood and present in a variety of contexts, as indicated by five (or more) of the following:

(1) has a grandiose sense of self-importance (e.g., exaggerates achievements and talents, expects to be recognized as superior without commensurate achievements)

(2) is preoccupied with fantasies of unlimited success, power, brilliance, beauty, or ideal love

(3) believes that he or she is "special" and unique and can only be understood by, or should associate with, other special or high-status people (or institutions)

(4) requires excessive admiration

(5) has a sense of entitlement, i.e., unreasonable expectations of especially favorable treatment or automatic compliance with his or her expectations

(6) is interpersonally exploitative, i.e., takes advantage of others to achieve his or her ends

(7) lacks empathy: is unwilling to recognize or identify with the feelings and needs of others

(8) is often envious of others or believes that others are envious of him or her

(9) shows arrogant, haughty behaviors or attitudes (*DSM-IV* 1994, 661)

## The Half-Adult of *The Sibling Society*

The writer and poet Robert Bly (1996) recently published a scathing critique of consumer-corporate society in his *Sibling Society: An Impassioned Call for the Rediscovery of Adulthood*. Although he does not explicitly cite their writings, Lasch's culture of narcissism, Mead's prefigurative culture,[2] and Riesman's other-directed society[3] all leap from the pages of Bly's book. We also see how the negative trends about which mass-society theorists alerted us in the early twentieth century have likely worsened. Moreover, we see in Bly's book how much prefigurative, other-directed society has inculcated forms of narcissism so that now virtually everyone is affected by it in some way. Indeed, Bly argues that the sibling society gives "permission for narcissism" (48). He submits that one-third of population is "there," and the rest are on the way (viii). "There" refers to the "sibling society" populated by "half-adults." In generational terms, he believes that most "adults are about one-third of the way into the sibling society. Children are two-thirds of the way in" (139).

Bly uses the phrase "sibling society" metaphorically to provide a "lens" with which to examine a culture where adults "regress toward adolescence; and adolescents—seeing that—have no desire to become adults. Few are able to imagine any genuine life coming from . . . tradition, religion, devotion" (viii). He argues that this society has already taken shape and assumed as much coherence as its predecessor, patriarchal society. In fact, the sibling society can be understood as a widespread rejection of "the father," including a desire among some people to "kill" the father in all of his symbolic forms. The following principles constitute the internal logic of the sibling society:

> The teaching that no one is superior to anyone else; high culture is to be destroyed, and business leaders look sideways to other business leaders. The sibling society prizes a state of half-adulthood, in which repression, discipline, and the Indo-European, Islamic, Hebraic impulse-control system are jettisoned. The parents regress to become more like children, and the children, through abandonment, are forced to become adults too soon, and never quite make it. There's an impulse to set children adrift on their own. The old . . . are thrown away, and the young . . . are thrown away. (Bly 1996, 132)

Bly believes that the past several cohorts of children and adolescents have been given less structure and guidance, especially since the Second World War. Accordingly, each cohort has received less and less parenting in the traditional sense of the term. Now many of these "unparented" persons have become parents themselves, or at least have entered what used to be the well-defined and well-structured period of adulthood. But they do not have adult role models to follow, and they do not see a "dignified adult life. . . . [Instead] they see incoherent emptiness and chaos" (133). This has created a sense of rage in many, so much so that if we take a step back to look through Bly's lens, we see a society very much like a household of children screaming at each other about perceived injustices and entitlements, but this household has no parents in sight. In the sibling society, as in the unparented home, there are no authorities that command enough respect to settle disputes to everyone's satisfaction or to tell people they are not entitled to everything they want on a whim.

How does Bly believe this came about? In part, we are in the ruins of a patriarchal society that was dismantled with no foresight. We are experiencing the type of anarchy that follows the fall of a government or ensues after a war. But there are no "adults" to assume the leadership necessary to restore a type of order that is considered fair to all citizens; instead, leadership comes from "big money"—from corporate interests. Consumer capitalism has hijacked Western culture, in Bly's view, by "stimulating greed and desirousness" (1996, xiii). Money has been "domesticated" by siblings to suit their self-interests, and what has replaced patriarchal society is no more compassionate or fair when administered by half-adults: "The sibling society is shaping up as a place where business finds few forces that hold it accountable. . . . The defeat of unions by corporations in recent times and the replacement of working-class intent and austerity by consumerism are trends that probably cannot be reversed. . . . acquisitive capitalism has won, more completely than in any other complicated culture on earth" (148).

Bly states in a chilling fashion what many educated people sense and what my analysis here thus far strongly suggests—that we are on the verge of being enveloped in a Brave New World analogous to what Huxley warned us about: "It is no surprise to anyone to say that business has effectively become our government, and now rules American life on all levels. The long battle [dating back to the Renaissance] that Catholic thinkers, Humanist scholars, and ordinary people instituted against expansive capitalism has been won, and the newly quiet battlefield is called the sibling society" (Bly 1996, 158)

Bly is adamant that we are in a period that can be described as "opportunities lost," in which the best of Western civilization has been reduced to ruins by greedy and shortsighted business people and politicians who have taken advantage of the "sibling house" for which they were supposed to take some responsibility. Echoing the evidence and commentaries we examined in chapter 2, Bly believes that much of the damage has been done through media technologies such as television. Not only have they contributed to illiteracy, but they have also been used to shape the consciousness of the population, especially the young, increasingly so with each successive cohort. Bly believes that even brain functioning has been impaired by overexposure to these technologies. With decreased intellectual capacities to understand the world around them, young people have been even more susceptible to mass-cultural influences that entice them into mindless consumerism, as part of a conditioned conformity to the whims of corporate capitalists. Politicians themselves have not escaped, as they have "bought" the message of corporate capitalists and have undertaken the dismantling of the social safety net that was built to ease the transition out of patriarchal society. Now, according to Bly, we all stand "in the rubble of a destroyed literate society, looking at the ruins of education, family, and child protection." He characterizes the lost potentials of Western civilization in contrast with immediate prospects:

> Technology has destroyed interrelations in the human community that have taken centuries to develop. The breaking of human beings' connection to land has harmed everyone. We are drowning in uncontrollable floods of information. We are living among dispirited and agonized teenagers who can't find any hope. Genuine work is disappearing, and we are becoming aware of a persistent infantilizing of men and women, a process already far advanced. (169–170)

As patriarchal structures declined in dominance, there was little to replace them to give meaning and direction to people's lives. Instead, according to Bly, those "devoted to the bottom line have effectively interposed themselves between the father and the family. Part of the effort has been to get at the children more easily. The more the parents' dignity and strength are damaged, the more open children are to persuasion" (1996, 230).

Bly laments the decline in the legitimacy of the father as a significant adult social role for a number of reasons, foremost among them the negative impact on young men. That impact includes not only the obvious loss of respectable role models during childhood, but also the loss of mentors later in life, the sense of isolation in relation to other males, and the actual vilification of the male, all of which he believes has contributed to a loss of "identity" for a generation of men.

*The Sibling Society* does not provide a typology that might be used to characterize different Brave New Adults of late modern society. Bly's distinction instead is between the half-adult (one-third of the "adult" population) and the other two-thirds, who attempt to resist the social and economic conditions that would rob them of their maturity and sense of responsibility for their actions. Bly argues that "hope lies in the longing we have to be adults," particularly in guiding and mentoring the young (1996, 237). If enough people take this seriously and live it, then adulthood and parenthood may regain some respectability in the eyes of the young. However, in the sibling society, Bly submits, few adults are available as public role models, so few children and adolescents see positive adult role models, either in their day-to-day lives or through the media. Indeed, Bly acknowledges that "the very idea of the adult has fallen into confusion" (238). He can only express it in vague and metaphorical terms, but I will attempt to convey more specifically what I believe are his intentions.

For Bly, an adult is someone who is not governed by a need for immediate pleasure, comfort, and excitement. An adult can establish order in his or her life along with a sense of biography and future. Adults understand that their lives are a minor part of a long chain of accomplishments and that the future belongs to their children, their children's children, their children's children's children, and so forth. Believing that one has the wisdom to change everything for the better in one's lifetime is arrogant and insulting to one's ancestors and descendants. Adults are able to maintain their age-appropriate vigor and to engage the vigor of those in younger cohorts. And adults are willing to assume the responsibilities of elders as they age; they have the courage to renounce instead of merely complying with the latest social or economic fad. Bly believes that Native American cultures can provide a model for restoring the legitimacy of the elder, especially those that hold a sense of responsibility for the next several generations.

Some readers may feel that Bly's case is overstated, and maybe it is. But what if it is not? He certainly takes seriously what he says, and he admits to being overwhelmed by the implications of what he uncovered as he explored the nature of contemporary adulthood. I leave it to readers to engage themselves further in Bly's rich text and illustrations and then to consider his question of how in such a brief time we have gone from being "a moderately disciplined, moderately respectful culture to a culture in which twelve-year-olds shoot each other, [and] Calvin Klein uses children for sexually explicit advertisements" (1996, 28). One may not agree with his explanation, but it is hard to dismiss the possibility that there are serious problems facing many people of all ages today—not only half-adults but also those attempting to maintain some semblance of maturity and responsibility for their actions.

### The "Relational Self" of Postmodern Society

The psychologist Kenneth Gergen has an entirely different take on the events associated with late modern society, or postmodern society, as he and other postmodernists call it. Gergen does not share the alarm of analysts such as Lasch or Bly; they are dismissed as "romantics" or "modernists." In fact, Gergen celebrates the changes we have been examining as being of "Copernican magnitude" (1996, 135), paving the way for a new "oceanic" states (1991, 74). What people must do, according to Gergen, is to fully embrace the technological influences that increasingly "saturate" their "consciousness" (television, the Internet, high-speed travel, etc.). As they do, he promises, their "selves" will become increasingly "relational" and supposedly open to the raptures of postmodern society.

It is instructive to examine Gergen's argument because it represents the stance that most of the social changes we have been examining should not be interpreted in a negative light; rather, he believes they represent an opportunity for the species to adopt higher forms of "consciousness." Moreover, Gergen lays out stages by which he believes the adult can move toward this higher consciousness.

Gergen presents these ideas in his book *The Saturated Self: Dilemmas of Identity in Contemporary Life* (1991). He argues that as Western societies are moving into the era of postmodernity, beliefs in a stable inner character and reason-governed behavior are being abandoned in favor of an externally oriented "relational self," shaped by "socializing technologies" that increasingly mediate our relationships with others. Immediate face-to-face encounters are becoming rarer, as we find more and more ways to interact with others through, or aided by, various technologies. That is, interaction is increasingly mediated by technologies such as the Internet and is aided by other technologies, for example air travel. As a result, says Gergen, the postmodern self is free to slide from image to image and to eschew substance in favor of superficiality. Images are presented according to the whim of the moment with identities constructed from fashions, cosmetics, and the like. Thus, the postmodern self comes to exist only in relation to external images conveyed to, reflected upon, and received from others. Where there might have been an inner core earlier, the "interior" self is now "populated" by others and their images.

Gergen proposes that the transition to the "postmodernist self" follows three stages of development, from the strategic manipulator, to the pastiche personality, to the relational self. According to this framework, adults came under siege in the late twentieth century as a result of the saturation of self and relationships engendered by the technologies that increasingly dominate the social and occupational landscape. Those who experience social saturation can pass through these three stages of reaction until there is "no self at all" (1991, 7).

> Emerging technologies saturate us with the voices of humankind—both harmonious and alien. As we absorb their varied rhymes and reasons, they become part of us and we of them. Social saturation furnished us with a multiplicity of incoherent and unrelated languages of the self. For everything we "know to be true" about ourselves, other voices within respond with doubt and even derision. This fragmentation of self-conception corresponds to a multiplicity of incoherent and disconnected relationships. These relationships pull us in myriad directions, inviting us to play such a variety of roles that the very concept of an "authentic self" with knowable characteristics recedes from view. (6–7)

The first reaction to "the forces of social saturation," according to Gergen, is to experience oneself as a strategic manipulator. Those who are at this stage experience a sense of alienation from their beliefs, opinions, and conscious intentions and lose faith in the predictability, honesty, and sincerity of self and others, as well as in the validity of social institutions. There is a sense that life is simply a set of roles played for social gain. Instead of experiencing a face-to-face validation from others, the strategic manipulator feels overwhelmed by the sheer number of relationships with others intruding into everyday life via various technologies. Contact with others expands exponentially but assumes a superficial nature. As a result there is an unreliability in identity confirmation and little upon which to maintain a sense of authenticity.

Without a comfortable niche in which to function, the person experiences superficiality and meaninglessness in the actions of self and others. Daily life becomes a matter of impression management, of trying to get the best out of encounters with others who are doing the same. As people become distressed and unhappy about these circumstances, Gergen advises that they let themselves move to the next stage of postmodern personality development.

This next stage is to adopt a pastiche personality: "The individual experiences a form of liberation from essence, and learns to derive joy from the many forms of self-expression now permitted" (1991, 147). At this stage the search for a real self is not an issue. The feeling that there is no core identity is embraced: there is no authenticity, no sincerity, no guilt, and no superficiality. There just "is," without conscious judgment. The pastiche personality is thus a social chameleon who cobbles together elements of identity from available sources, changing as the situation dictates. Those who are good social chameleons can derive substantial rewards in the "devotion of one's intimates, happy children, professional success, the achievement of community goals, personal popularity, and so on." If one avoids attempting to locate or build an inner character, according to Gergen, and acts in terms of the impulses and demands of the present, one can escape the debilitating sense of "multiphrenia—the sense of superficiality, the guilt at not measuring up to multiple criteria," and experience a sense of tremendous possibility. The world of the pastiche personality constantly expands socially and geographically: "Life becomes a candy store for one's developing appetites" (150).

Gergen argues that the pastiche personality is most commonly constructed through fashion. People literally believe that they are what they wear, and social relationships are opportunities to act out whimsical identities: "The boundary between the real and the presented self—between substance and style—is erased" (1991, 155). But what motivates this type of person? Gergen is vague on this issue, although he does acknowledge that the pastiche personality involves "a form of narcissism . . . [where] life becomes suffused with the search for self-gratification. Others merely become the implements by which impulses are served" (154).

As one continues "to experience the raptures of the pastiche personality," Gergen contends that the relational self grows, based on a "reality of relatedness—or the transformation of 'you' and 'I' to 'us'" (1991, 156). Individuals supposedly give up their self-centeredness and recognize that they are nothing without others. Their beliefs, attitudes, intentions are no longer their private domain but the product of their encounters with others. With belief in a "real self" gone, people turn to a belief in a relational self. All is played out in relation to others, even the construction of one's identity—indeed everything about the world and existence. Persons at this stage of postmodern development accept that they are mere participants in social processes, which eclipse their own personal being; they come to understand that their potentials are realized only in relation to others; and they accept that their identity is possible only through the social rituals and "broader games of society" (156–157).

Gergen is obviously idealistic about "postmodernist" forms of consciousness and is enthusiastic in his endorsement of them. I am sure that many readers of his work share his idealism, believing that identities based on "sameness" rather than "difference" are preferable for a variety of reasons (e.g., those who define themselves in terms of their similarities with others should be more communal, ethical and prosocial, for example). Gergen does admit, though, that it is "foolish to propose that a consciousness of relational selves is widely shared in Western culture" (1991, 157). He provides no evidence that even a small proportion of the population actually live a life dictated by this relational consciousness. Moreover, the anecdotal evidence he cites for it can be more easily characterized as updated manifestations of Riesman's other-directed person (e.g., Gergen cites dressing for dinner and being disappointed that the restaurant is empty as evidence for the pastiche personality). Thus, it appears that Gergen has taken us on a conceptual journey through "postmodernity," only to bring us back to where Riesman began in 1950 with *The Lonely Crowd* (cf. Meštrović 1997).

What do we gain from Gergen's analysis, then? I believe he is correct in his identification of the pervasive effects of advanced technologies on social relationships and people's experiences (and the empirical evidence reviewed in chapter 2 supports this). However, I disagree that the Garden of Eden lies at the end of the postmodern path that he and others glorify. In fact, a psychiatrist viewing the behavior patterns of the first two types of postmodern adults would likely find elements of personality disorders. If Gergen is correct that people are increasingly experiencing these things, this is not a reason to celebrate, in my view. Rather, it signals that these disorders, or milder forms of them, are becoming widespread. As I indicated at the beginning of this chapter, this is one striking way in which postmodernist analyses, and the mentality they breed, are symptomatic of the ills and confusions of late modern society (in which corporate-driven mass culture is dominating), not routes to higher forms of consciousness.

We explore identity disorders in chapter 4, where we find that the primary symptoms of the borderline personality disorder include identity disturbance, with an unstable self-image, unstable relationships, and chronic feelings of emptiness. As we saw, the narcissistic personality disorder involves a grandiose sense of importance and of being special, a sense of entitlement, and having fantasies of success, while at the same time the person is interpersonally exploitative and nonempathetic (according to the *DSM*-IV, the narcissistic and borderline disorders can overlap). Gergen describes the postmodern person as attempting to escape feelings of not having a stable inner core and as having a highly changeable, fragile, and elusive sense of self-definition, while being a consummate manager of impressions for personal gain and pleasure. More specifically, the strategic manipulator is distressed by feelings of emptiness around role playing but manipulates others nonetheless; and the pastiche personality is without guilt over manipulating others through chameleon performances, including the self-indulgent use of fashion and personal fronts. The pastiche personality apparently seeks self-gratification and impulse release based on entirely situated, contrived selves. Neither seems to experience the strength derived from the sense of temporal-spatial continuity of an inner self that has characterized the experience of identity before the so-called postmodern era, as we see in chapter 4 (cf. Cadello 1990).

I do not doubt that these personality attributes are reasonably common today, nor that numerous people have forged an identity around them. However, I do doubt that these are positive developments or that passing through the stages Gergen postulates will deliver one to a relational, communal self. The egocentric and self-indulgent behavior patterns represented by his stages are more likely to create persistent disruption in people's lives as they pattern their behavior around the paths of least resistance and effort. Rather than creating a more communal-relational community, which requires a citizenry with integrity and inner strength, such chameleon-like behaviors are more likely to further deteriorate those forms of cooperative community that have survived five centuries of capitalism. Clearly, Putnam's research (discussed in chapter 2) shows that the technologies that Gergen cites as the means to move us forward toward more community actually diminish community through "social decapitalization." Accordingly, we must seriously consider that to celebrate "social saturation" as a route to salvation is irresponsible and without regard for the history and future of the communities about which Gergen writes. In effect, Gergen may be celebrating the growing pathologies of Western societies and recommending that we all join in, based on some millennial promise of rapture and bliss. I, for one, do not buy it, and I am sure many others do not, especially those who are concerned about the sibling society and the culture of narcissism we are creating. Moreover, as we see in chapter 5, Gergen is recommending much of what Huxley warned about in *Brave New World*.

In sum, even though I do not agree with Gergen's underlying argument, there is some merit to it. He makes a good case for the overwhelming psychological effects of media technologies, but so do many others such as Putnam and Bly. Indeed, the saturation processes to which he refers seem to be increasing as more and more people increasingly embed themselves in these technologies (see Côté and Allahar 1996 for a similar argument). However, he makes a weak case, in my view, that "inner resources" are no longer relevant (for example, ego strength and cognitive abilities). He mocks the notion that people can direct their behavior using their ethical and intellectual faculties. His position appears to be an antimodernist version of antiestablishment sentiments: that anything a "mainstream" produces must be wrong (cf. Smart 1993). Yet he provides no evidence that people are so helpless in the face of external influence, and he treats those social scientific traditions that provide this evidence in a "straw" fashion (i.e., he describes them in a such a weak fashion that they are easily knocked down). And though he mocks reason as an Enlightenment illusion, he provides a *carefully reasoned argument* in support of welcoming "postmodernity."

These and other contradictions in Gergen's work deserve a careful critical appraisal, but this book is not the appropriate venue for it. However, I return to his celebratory position concerning postmodernity in chapter 5. There I expose it as a call for people to surrender to a Brave New World that awaits us if we do not we use our inner resources, including our reasoning powers and common sense.

## The "Relational Voice" from Patriarchal Society

The theorists we have reviewed in this chapter do not make explicit distinctions between the psychological adulthoods faced by men and women. Some feminist scholars object to that lack of attention to the differences in experiences of men and women. Judith Jordan, for example, contends that much of our understanding of adult development is really an understanding of men's development. She portrays what she sees to be a bias in the social scientific understanding of adulthood in the following way:

> In traditional Western psychological theories of development, the "self" has long been viewed as the primary reality and unit of study. Typically, the self has been seen as separated from its context, a bounded, contained entity that has both object and subject qualities. Clinical and developmental theories generally have emphasized the growth of an autonomous, individuated self. Increasing self-control, a sense of self as origin of action and intentions, an increasing capacity to use abstract logic, and a movement toward self-sufficiency characterize the maturation of the ideal Western self. (1997, 9)

Jordan believes that this model of development has a "limited applicability to the psychology of women." Instead, she believes in an alternative that she calls the "relational self" or the "being in relation" model (1997, 9).

Jordan's work is based largely on that of Carol Gilligan, which emphasizes the ethic of care-taking and relationship in women's lives. Jordan argues that her relational model "emphasizes relationship and connection. Rather than a primary perspective based on the formed and contained self, this model stresses the importance of the intersubjective, relationally emergent nature of human experience. While there is still a 'felt sense of self,' . . . it is a 'self inseparable from a dynamic interaction.'" Jordan goes on to note that the relational model "goes beyond saying that women value relationships; we are suggesting that the deepest sense of one's being is continuously formed in connection with others and is inextricably tied to relational movement. The primary feature, rather than structure marked by separateness and autonomy, is increasing empathetic responsiveness in the context of interpersonal mutuality" (1997, 15).

Thus, Jordan and others working from the relational perspective believe that there are "primary" differences between men and women in their senses of separateness and relation. Relational theorists argue that men tend to construct boundaries that protect and define themselves and, in contrast, that women are more contextual and intersubjective in their relations with others, creating more flexible and fluid boundaries. Thus, women are seen to be more embedded in context, more concerned with those in their immediate presence, and more able to establish mutual relationships. According to relational theorists, women are more concerned with care-taking and the empowerment of others, whereas men are more concerned with power-based dominance patterns, abstract and universal principles, and self-empowerment.

As discussed in chapter 1, it is unclear from this sort of model just how much of this difference is supposed to be a product of nature and how much is supposed to be a product of nurture, for both elements seem to be mixed in the explanations of why women and men are different. Certainly the tendency to dichotomize men and women is a widespread one, especially in the popular literature and in pop culture, as anyone who has visited a bookstore or watched a television talk show will know. But when these ideas are scrutinized from a more scholarly and social-scientific point of view, what was first intuitively pleasing becomes intellectually slippery. For example, the model tends to caricature men and women: the language used implies, for example, that all women are weak psychologically but strong interpersonally, whereas all men are strong psychologically but interpersonal opportunists. Thus, there is little room for nontraditional women who have the supposedly masculine tendencies, and there is little room for nontraditional men who have the ostensibly feminine tendencies.

This formulation has much in common with the postmodern view of self examined in the previous section, where a relational mode of being is highly idealized and recommendations are made that we abandon the notion of a strong inner self. To make matters worse, many of those working from the relational model dismiss scientific discourse as a way of resolving disputes. For Jordan, scientific "inquiry itself has aimed toward 'objective truth,' mastery over nature; as such, it represents a masculine ideal" (1997, 21). With such statements, there appears to be little reason to attempt to find common ground—relational theory insists on a subjectivist, antiscientific grounding and will likely remain part of a pop psychology, feel-good alternative to trying to develop a dialogue about the nature of society (including adulthood) and the direction of social change. In refusing to enter into such a dialogue with "men," this model is ironically "antirelational" and curiously juvenile.

Surely, however, there are merits in both categories, "being" and "knowing," and the same criticisms can be directed toward the feminist relational model as toward the postmodern relational model. Not only do they focus on a highly idealized state of being, but also, upon reflection it may not be a wholly desirable state of being as a permanent stance in life. For example, having flexible boundaries in relation to others can leave one exceedingly disorganized and open to manipulation. In fact, being uncritically open to mass manipulation is one of the primary problems of modern societies to which mass-society theorists alerted us. In conjunction with an unformulated sense of self, people can simply drift along through life, not attending to their own needs for security and survival, let alone those needs in others. There are also elements of the path of least resistance and effort, which can lead to default forms of individualization. Moreover, it is not as if most people any longer can decide against an individualized life course. As a result of five centuries of disruption by capitalism—in which traditional, *communal* forms of community have been dislocated and dismantled—there are few options now for most women, or men, involving a predetermined, well-structured life course. The question now is whether people do a responsible, forward-looking job of individualization or simply let themselves be passively manipulated. To do a good job of it requires the development of inner strengths and potentials to take into our relations with others (proximal and distal) in order to combat the deleterious effects of mass society and mass culture.

Moreover, as I argue in chapter 1, the distinction between the relational and the autonomous self parallels the distinction between the private and the public spheres. As a matter of functional adaptation within the present corporate-consumer system, those who function in the private sphere will tend to be more relational (or care dominant), and those who function in the public sphere will tend to be more autonomous. Over the past couple of centuries, more women have been socialized to function in the private sphere; hence, we expect them to display more relational behavior. During the same period more men have been socialized to function in the public sphere, so we would expect them to display more autonomous behavior. There is no reason to believe that these constitute "essential" (biological) differences between men and women.

When this position regarding socialization is adopted, behaviors among men and women that do not conform to the stereotypical dichotomy offered by Jordan and others make more sense. We would expect women who move into the public sphere to exhibit characteristics of the autonomous self, and there is strong evidence that they do so (see, e.g., Hulbert 1993; Tavris 1992). Likewise, men who move into the private sphere exhibit the nurturance and empathy associated with the relational self. In fact, it appears that people can adopt the characteristics demanded by these different roles rather quickly regardless of sex or gender (Tavris 1992).

But when we turn to the primary source, Gilligan's *In a Different Voice* (1982), that provided much of the impetus for the development of the relational model, we find the ingredients for more complex formulations than the simple male-female dichotomy. We see there the makings of a model of maturity for which we have been searching. Ironically, this more complex model of maturity combines the dichotomous elements of relation and autonomy into a more sophisticated model of adulthood that promises to take us beyond the pitfalls and liabilities that we have noted thus far among the Brave New Adults of late modern society.

In Gilligan's book we find the rhetoric of the relational model, including the critique of conceptions of development that emphasize "separation," but we can also discover a synthesis of ideas associated with separation and attachment. Gilligan starts with the assumption that because females are more (socialized to be) oriented toward relationships, their moral reasoning will be more focused on issues of care, sensitivity to the feelings of others, and responsibility to others, as opposed to the "male" concern with abstract principles of justice. She argues that we need to think, therefore, in terms of two voices: one focusing on rights, rules, and principles (justice), and another expressing concern for others, sensitivity, and attachments (care). Rather than holding these as incompatible opposites, as some do, Gilligan argues for higher levels of maturity in adulthood that integrate the moralities of justice and care in a sense of rights and responsibilities. In this way, implicit in Gilligan's argument is a call to reunite the moralities of the private and public spheres separated by industrial capitalism.

In a model that parallels previous models of (ostensibly male) development postulated by Jean Piaget and Lawrence Kohlberg, Gilligan proposes three levels (or stages) of development toward maturity. At the first level, characteristic of childhood, the primary concern is for oneself and one's own survival. There is a preoccupation with one's own needs, along with an egocentricity tied to self-interest. Gradually, an awareness emerges of the difference between want and obligation, between self-interest and responsibility, along with the realization that what one ought to do is not necessarily what one wants to do. That awareness of conflicting pressures can push the person toward the second level, where concern for one's responsibilities overrides self-interest in significant ways.

The egocentricity of the first level gives way to a social perspective-taking (seeing things from others' points of view). According to Gilligan's model, individuals at this level develop a need to please others by engaging in forms of self-sacrifice and caring-giving; self-assertion can be threatening because of a fear of criticism or abandonment. Thus, there is an imbalance in the sense of a dependent relationality. Over time, a person at this level can begin to question his or her emotional dependency and the appropriateness of tending more to others than to oneself. This conflict can lead to the third level, where the emphasis shifts back to the self but in a more balanced manner in which compromises are sought between self-needs and the needs of others. At this point, which Gilligan claims most people never reach, one incorporates a concern for responsibilities to others *and* to oneself, in which self and others become interdependent but not merged. The tendency to see oneself as powerless and submissive gives way to active decision making (agency), with a moral concern about the implications of the decisions for self and others. What was defined at level two as selfishness becomes redefined as self-assertion; what was defined as self-sacrifice becomes sensitivity to others.

Although Gilligan originally proposed that this developmental scheme pertained mainly to women, subsequent research (involving dozens of studies) has found that it applies equally to men and women with regard to their capacity to reason out issues (for reviews, see Muuss 1996; Sprinthall and Collins 1995). Moreover, subsequent research found that the scheme Gilligan critiqued as being androcentric applies equally well to men and women, when all things are considered (e.g., educational level). More noteworthy is that this research suggests that both male and female African Americans, and members of other subordinated minority groups, emphasize a care orientation. A conclusion that has been drawn is that a care-dominated orientation can reflect subordinate status in a social hierarchy (Tavris 1992). Those who are in subordinate statuses tend to focus on the immediacy of daily living more than on abstract, remote circumstances. Accordingly, interpersonal relationships take on more importance, as does gratification from those relationships, and subordinates will tend to look out for each other because of their common plight. In light of these findings, we should not be surprised that people whose daily lives are spent in the private sphere, as is the case for many women in capitalist societies, will emphasize relationships and interdependence, whereas those in the public sphere will be oriented toward self-sufficiency and abstract principles of universal justice (wherein their right to participate in the public sphere is more or less guaranteed). But that does not mean that they are incapable of reasoning in terms of both orientations.

The point here is that, on the whole, it does not matter what the sex of the person is in the private or public sphere, because men in the private sphere adopt the consciousness associated with that sphere and women in the public sphere adopt the consciousness of that sphere. Obviously there will be exceptions to this rule when we look at individual differences, but the empirical research does not support essentialist claims about why there are relational-separation differences in consciousness. Instead, the research strongly argues that the differences are the result of socialization into private or public and/or subordinate or superordinate roles, some of which can be found in childhood and some of which can be seen in adulthood as individuals attempt to exercise choice and control over their lives. Thus, although Gilligan's work does not differentiate women and men in the way she thought it did, her model suggests that two paths to moral maturity may exist and that the most advanced forms of maturity involve a synthesis of those two paths (cf. Conger and Galambos 1997). We return to this point in chapter 6, where we conclude our search for models of maturity to take with us into the future.

## Transitions to Adulthood in the Late Modern Cafeteria

We have reviewed a variety of opinion and conjecture in this chapter, some of which can be supported with empirical research and some of which lies somewhere between pop psychology and wishful thinking. Some of the sources add to our understanding of the fundamental nature of adulthood and help us locate adulthood sociohistorically. The frameworks of Mead and Riesman provide clear foundations on both counts. Figure 3.1 confirms the compatibility of these frameworks. The works of Lasch and Bly add to the foundation, but primarily for late modern societies. Gergen's postmodern framework seems to get the symptoms right but the illness wrong. Indeed, it appears that his celebration of the illness is symptomatic of problems central to our current sociohistorical location. And the feminist relational model seems to misdiagnose both the symptoms and the illness. It mistakenly contends that it is only men who have been socialized into the ethos of individualism, whereas both men and women have been affected by five centuries of capitalism. The result is that both sexes have adopted this ethos but within separate spheres. Gilligan has the ingredients for a cure, but we must get past the misunderstandings surrounding her work in order to benefit from it.

In considering the fact that both the postmodern and the feminist views reviewed here hinge a good part of their platforms on the notion of relationalism, one would think that they would have developed a relationship in which their similar terminologies are compared in terms of potential mutualities. This appears not to have happened, however, and their frameworks remain separate and autonomous. In his *Saturated Self*, Gergen simply writes that Gilligan's framework "can be extended to form the basis for a postmodern relational view of morality, in which moral decisions are viewed not as products of individual minds, but the outcome of interchange among persons" (1991, 168). But he goes on to say that "a fully developed theory of relational morality has yet to appear" (169). In a later work, Gergen dismisses feminist efforts such as Gilligan's as unable "to break with the explanatory fulcrum of the individual mind" (1994, 215), and he states that he is not interested in "championing an 'ethic of care'" because of its "universalist intimations" (109). Readers can see from this intellectual chasm how little unity there is among "relationalists." Instead, relationalism appears to have taken on cultlike characteristics with small pockets of ideologically driven supporters who would rather adhere to a "cause" than to engage in an intellectual discourse that attempts to reach a consensus about the nature of the realities affecting everyone.

Within the context of capitalism's conquest of Western civilization and the rise of, first, mass society and then mass culture, we can appreciate the merits of the "best" of the analyses considered. The cultural change at the level of socializing institutions appears to have been accurately described by Mead, with her "figurative" model of change. We appear to be in the early stages of prefigurative culture, where the gulf between parent and offspring is wide and getting wider. Now, with so many technological advances and so much affluence, capitalist societies do not need the productive labor of their entire populations, especially the youth segments (Côté and Allahar 1996). With no threat to survival needs and with no need to engage in so much productive labor, Western populations have taken advantage of what the affluence has to offer largely in terms of self-interested pursuits, as Riesman foresaw. This means that the citizenry of Western nations increasingly resembles a prototypical composite of the sketches provided in this chapter, namely, a person who has no sense of inner identity rooted in traditional meaning, who is in habitual conflict with his or her parents; inhabiting a sibling house with other confused and angry half-adults; socialized to be other-directed; prone to narcissism and excessive pleasure-seeking; skilled at impression management and chameleonlike identity changes but unable to make a passage from youth to adulthood and therefore unable to find a direction in life that would lead to maturity.

PART II

# The Changing Nature
# of Identity

# 4

## Identity Transformed
### *The Decline of Authority and Structure*

*How Has Identity Been Transformed by Mass Society?*

Thus far we have seen how the changes associated with various phases in the rise of capitalism have made "identity" more problematic. This is most evident in the consequences of mass society during early modernity and more recently in the effects of mass culture during late modernity. However, we have not specifically examined how the psychological and social components of identity have been affected, nor have we examined the ramifications of a society in which the bulk of the population experiences these components of their identities as problematic. In this chapter we focus on these issues.

*Understandings of Ego Identity Problems in Mass Society*

In this section we examine primarily the work of psychologists who have attempted to understand identity from a developmental point of view—in other words, how identity formation might take place in an orderly, predictable sequence of increasingly complex stages over the life course.

### Culture and the Identity Crisis: Erik Erikson

Virtually all contemporary formulations of identity have been influenced by Erik Erikson. An obituary in Toronto's *Globe and Mail* of May 14, 1994, described Erikson as a "psychoanalyst who profoundly reshaped views of human development," noting that his popular recognition peaked during the 1970s, when the public embraced the term *identity crisis*, which he coined. Through Erikson's influence both the psychological and the sociological communities took interest in the concept of identity, and voluminous literatures have emerged.

Erikson first noticed the trend toward more problematic identities in the 1940s, and he wrote extensively for the next three decades about the "identity crisis" that he saw as an epidemic in modern societies. He originally conceived of the notion of the identity crisis when treating identity loss among war-trauma victims during the Second World War. Later he drew a parallel between this type of disturbance and the experiences of "severely conflicted young people whose sense of confusion is due to a war within themselves" (Erikson 1968, 17). He also wrote about the identity problems of adulthood that he saw to be "normal" responses to the vicissitudes and alienation associated with modern, technological societies. His work in this regard has informed most of the recent psychological and sociological views of identity (see Weigert, Teitge, and Teitge 1986; Gecas and Burke 1995).

Erikson's overall theory of the life cycle postulates eight interrelated stages of psychosocial development. His identity stage has received the most attention, perhaps because it is currently the most difficult stage for people to resolve. Erikson's writings suggest that the psychosocial identity that emerges during the identity stage can be seen to comprise three interrelated components: the subjective/psychological component (ego identity), the personal component (behavioral styles and characterological repertoires that differentiate individuals), and the social component (recognized roles and statuses within a community or society). These components need to come together during the identity stage, and when they do not, or as they are doing so, an identity crisis is evident. The identity crisis is characterized by a subjective sense of identity confusion, behavioral and characterological disarray, and the absence of a recognized role or roles in a community. Resolution of the identity stage is facilitated when (1) a community role is acquired, (2) behavior and character become stabilized, and (3) a relatively firm sense of ego identity is developed (cf. Côté and Levine 1987).

With this formulation, Erikson was able to study a variety of cultures where he found great variation in how adolescence is structured and therefore variations in the tasks associated with identity formation. However, he tended to slant his formulations toward modern American culture (in which he lived as an adult), where, far more than in most other cultures—especially "traditional" cultures—resolution of the identity stage is predicated around choice and "individuality" during a protracted and loosely structured adolescence (see Erikson 1963 regarding the "American identity" for a landmark statement). Although there is much in Erikson's writings that we could review here (see Côté and Levine 1987, 1988, for complete reviews), I believe it is important to highlight one feature of identity that is often missed: the question whether there is a common thread that would link all of its dimensions.

My reading of Erikson suggests that for him the crux of identity stability lies in the interplay between the social and the psychic. That is, a person requires a *viable social identity,* and when the person develops a workable social identity within a particular culture, the psychological sense of temporal-spatial continuity—the sine qua non of ego identity— should be nurtured (Côté and Levine 1987). Once a sense of ego identity is established, people are buffered and protected from the vicissitudes of social conflicts and tensions. This position describes identity formation in all cultures, not just those that are individualistic and choice-oriented. According to Erikson, people of all cultures can develop a strong sense of ego identity based on role validation and community integration, especially when there is no ambiguity regarding beliefs.

Another way to express this is to speak of three forms of continuity: between the self and itself, between the self and other, and between other and other. The first type of continuity is what Erikson had in mind when he coined the term *ego identity* (i.e., a sense of self-sameness over time). The second type of continuity pertains to a person's relationships with others. A continuity here maintains the stability of personal and social identities, whereas a discontinuity threatens the stability of those identities. However, a strong sense of ego identity will help people through periods of instability in their relations with others. The third type of continuity represents the stability of relations in a particular community or group. When community relations are stable and continuous, people's personal and social identities within the community are safeguarded. When those relations are unstable, people's personal and social identities come under pressure and may undergo revision. What is particularly important to note is that unstable community relations (problems in "other–other" continuity) make it difficult for those attempting the transition to adulthood to do so in a nonproblematic fashion. The transition is especially hard for those younger members of society who do not have a sense of "self-self" continuity (ego identity) and who have unstable "self-other" relations.

These three forms of identity problems are now commonplace among both adolescents and adults in contemporary mass society. We can see in this formulation just how important a stable and structured society is in the formation of identities, as well as in their maintenance. We can also see why unstable and poorly structured societies, commonplace in the West, make identity in its various forms problematic for the individual. In my view, herein lies one of the greatest challenges to late modern societies.

Over my much shorter career, I have undertaken a number of studies based on Erikson's ideas (e.g., Côté 1984, 1986, 1993, 1996a, 1996b, 1997). That research has produced a framework that integrates Mead's and Riesman's work with ideas originating in Erikson's work. The correspondences among societal stages (and implicitly Mead's cultural configuration of socializing institutions and Riesman's modal character types) presented in figure 3.1 are matched with ideas stemming from Erikson's work on identity in figure 4.1. In matching these concepts, the three-stage theory of cultural change can be coupled with (1) the ways in which adult social identities (people's roles and statuses in their society) differ in each type of culture, (2) the "abnormal patterns" of identity formation (in the sense that the society would actively discourage such behavior), and (3) the "cultural metaphor" that provides the guiding image of identity formation in each society.[1]

Based on Erikson's psychohistorical writings on identity, as well as on the sociological literature, it appears that in premodern societies social identities tend to be *ascribed*. In other words, ready-made identities are assigned mainly on the basis of inherited statuses. In the premodern society the anomic identity crisis (refusing to fit into this prescribed niche) would be negatively sanctioned because of the need for conformity and productive contribution among members of the society. Positive sanctions would encourage people to define themselves in terms of the roles ascribed to them (hence the "identity = role" metaphor).

As a result of the early modern transformations associated with industrial capitalism and the rise of the nuclear family, adult social identities can increasingly be accomplished based (ostensibly) on a person's efforts, skills, and achievements, independent of inherited status (cf. Bauman 1997). In early modern societies, the perennial or unresolved crisis would be negatively sanctioned because of the need for motivated and productive workers throughout adulthood, and the cultural

| | Type of Society | | |
|---|---|---|---|
| | Premodern | Early Modern | Late Modern |
| Adult Social Identity: | Ascribed | Accomplished | Managed |
| Abnormal Patterns (Negatively Sanctioned): | Anomic Crisis | Perennial Crisis | No Crisis |
| Cultural Metaphor (Positively Sanctioned): | Identity = Role | Identity = Choice | Identity = Image |
| Ego Identity Structure (Marcia): | Foreclosed | Achieved | Diffused/Moratorium |

*Fig. 4.1.* The Culture-Identity Link: Identity Concepts

metaphor would encourage people to shape their identities in terms of their "choices."[2]

In late modern societies it appears that adult social identities are increasingly in need of being *managed*. That is, people's inherited characteristics and prior accomplishments fail to give them legitimacy in a wide variety of social settings (although the obstacles associated with class, gender, and race still obtain in significant ways). Instead, people increasingly need to strategically guide and control their own actions in order to continually fit themselves into a community of "strangers" by gaining their approval through the creation of the right impressions. The wrong impression management can lead to an immediate loss of legitimacy and even censure in the minds of late modern citizens who judge character only by the concrete behaviors they witness.

There seems to be no clear abnormal pattern in late modern societies, perhaps because it is too early to identify it, or perhaps because this is an era of constantly shifting standards; basically "anything goes" when it comes to statements of identity. It is also possible that with social control mechanisms becoming "looser," or less effective as we move through the three types of societies, identity formation is affected in unforeseen ways (cf. Côté 1994). Thus it would seem that *not* having an identity crisis around certain issues will be increasingly negatively sanctioned, given the need for a flexible, change-oriented population. If this is the case, in terms of Erikson's original formulation of the identity crisis, the "abnormal" may have become the "normal." Finally, the cultural metaphor in late modern societies encourages people to equate themselves and their identities with "images," both managed and projected.

To summarize the differences among the three types of societies based on this neo-Eriksonian framework, in premodern, postfigurative society adult social identity is largely determined by one's characteristics or attributes (race, sex, parents' social status); in early modern, cofigurative society it rests more on personal effort and ability (which are ostensibly based on appraisals of merit); in late modern, prefigurative society it becomes a matter of impression management; one attempts to gain—and maintain—acceptance from others who often have little knowledge of one's social background or accomplishments.

The framework developed thus far, and represented in figure 4.1, has several advantages over any of the individual analyses examined in chapter 3. For example, one parsimonious structure incorporates the major elements of the strongest frameworks (Mead's and Riesman's) as well as the best of others, such as some of the observations made by Lasch and Gergen. In addition it is a logically consistent, historically based, and empirically verifiable framework with which to proceed in our analysis of the contemporary nature of adulthood. I refer to this framework as the "culture-identity link" (Côté 1996a, 1996b).

Using this framework, we can gain a better understanding of why things are the way they are and what effect they have on how people define themselves. For example, it is postulated that the identity crisis has been growing in prevalence and severity as we have moved through early modern society and into late modern society. Although we are historically rooted in a (premodern) culture in which the identity crisis was likely rare (and probably avoided through rituals), we now find ourselves in a culture in which identity crises of various forms are the norm. In other words, it seems that the abnormal has become the norm. It is likely that the now more normal, prolonged, and severe identity crisis is associated with the cultural destructuring that we have been examining in this book and that the prolongation of youth we have witnessed is based in part on these two interrelated phenomena.

A danger in accepting this situation as normal is that we also accept it as healthy. Erikson originally conceived of the identity crisis when treating war-trauma, shell-shock victims, we recall, and he drew a parallel with its pathological forms in "severely conflicted young people whose sense of confusion is due to a war within themselves" (1968, 17). Moreover, if we view the identity crisis against the backdrop of the entirety of human history and culture, where it always involved fitting into an adult role, we should be alert to the possibility that in late modern societies not only are forms of the identity crisis widespread, but many are also pathological and epidemic, when compared to the identity crisis in premodern societies. Accordingly, I am wary of attempts to create or "force" such crises as part of an attempt to stimulate development as recommended, for there may be unintended and disastrous consequences for those individuals unequipped to handle them (Côté and Levine 1987). An awareness of the difference between default and developmental forms of individualization should be more helpful as social scientists make recommendations regarding how to channel identity formation.

Erikson warned at the midpoint of the twentieth century that those factors represented by the right-hand column of the culture-identity link (see fig. 4.1) contribute to a weakening of the ego and hence adversely affect the ego development associated with mastering the eight psychosocial stages of the life cycle.[3] Not only might people be derailed in developing their psychosocial potentials, but ego weakness also makes them vulnerable to the types of manipulation about which mass-society theorists warned us. This appears to be exactly what has happened as mass culture (now referred to as pop culture, especially when applied to the youth segment of society) has increasingly filled the void that we call "adolescence" and now "youth." To the extent that the adult community segregated and isolated young people, depriving them of institutional supports and ritualized passages into adulthood, the industries of mass culture have moved in, selling young people common sources of ersatz identity and ritual. The pop culture that passes as youth culture now serves to exploit the young and maintain their separation from adult society, membership in which would give them a stable, validated adult identity and, likely, the best chance of resuming their progression through the psychosocial stages of the life cycle.

Another reason for being wary of the temptation to see disruptions of identity as normal and natural (as do postmodernists like Gergen) is the importance of the intergenerational link and the possibility that identities are the intergenerational glue that holds cultures together. The question that arises from the culture-identity link is whether cultural continuity is threatened; are we losing that continuity? That certainly appears to be the case in many developing countries, where the young have been culturally disfranchised by Western influences (Côté 1994). As adults lose their conceptions of what the future holds (they seem to have done so as each generation lives its life further and further into prefigurative society), so do the young, but it becomes particularly difficult for the young to develop a firm sense of identity when their own futures are uncertain. If we follow Mead's typology, we need to ask what follows the prefigurative culture. Does unified culture become untenable, and does the cycle begin over again after a breakdown of the identity-culture link? A total breakdown in authority is especially troublesome inasmuch as it sets the stage for arbitrary authority to assert itself by offering certainty to replace uncertainty (as mass-society theorists warned). Again, certain aspects of late modern society bear a striking resemblance to Aldous Huxley's Brave New World, where identities are predicated upon a conditioning into consumption, pleasing others, impression management, and sensory gratification. Based on the neo-Eriksonian framework, which argues that human identity is not infinitely pliable and that a sense of ego identity is necessary for effective psychosocial functioning, I believe that we should also be on guard against views that reify or uncritically glorify all conditions associated with late modern society, as if they are inevitable and natural unfoldings of social evolution.

Considering the framework as a whole, then, this integrated understanding of the relationship between culture and identity suggests that the young person attempting to find her or his way into adulthood today faces a formidable task. It would appear that most young people in prefigurative societies today have parents who can provide little in the way of guidance about what their future holds. This is in stark contrast to the past, especially in postfigurative societies. Many parents who make the effort to guide their children into that indefinite future often find their efforts shunned by their children; in turn, their children find support for their obstinateness in youth-oriented pop culture that often vilifies parental authority—indeed, all adult authority. Many of these young people also reject their ancestral past as evil in certain ways (e.g., racist, sexist, homophobic, etc.), also in stark contrast to the past. They often turn to their peers for direction and find themselves in a "blind-leading-the-blind" predicament.

But the root of this dilemma is quite understandable since their society also offers them little stability, in part because it is changing so quickly. Moreover, a "once-and-for-all" identity formation seems to be a thing of the past; the attempt to form and maintain an adult identity can constitute a continual struggle for acceptance in an ambivalent world. Not only is the future indefinite for the society itself in the sense that there is no single vision of leadership, but in addition most people face continual changes in their work and personal lives. Hence, for many people, whether in their teens or twenties or older, a key question is now "If I'm not my parents' child, who am I and where am I going?"

### Exploration and Commitment: James Marcia

As we have seen, late modern societies have been characterized as being governed by the process of individualization, namely, "the tendency towards increasingly flexible self-awareness as the individual must make decisions and choose identities from among an increasingly complex range of options" (Wallace 1995, 13). In other words, a normal course of development now involves developing one's self as an "individual," rather than as simply a cog-in-the-wheel member of a collective community. There can be tremendous benefits to this opportunity, but we know that there can also be serious pitfalls and liabilities. The problem is that this "freedom" requires a great deal from people because it places pressures on them to continually reflect on their relations with others; to be conscious of the necessity to think ahead; to make choices, the results of which they will have to live with; to be solely responsible for their failings and limitations; and to overcome structural obstacles such as social class, race, gender, and age barriers. In other words, fully benefiting from the freedom requires, among other things, an intelligent self-discipline in dealing with one's self and one's society, often in the absence of collective supports.

Many people seem unable to rise to the demands of this freedom, even well into adulthood. Others master these conditions only after a long period of trial and error during their adolescence and youth. Indeed, many act in the opposite manner, exhibiting rather foolish and irrational behavior patterns that reflect little control over their basic impulses or the increasing number of temptations offered them by those who have something to gain by influencing their behavior (which is a dominant force in consumer-corporate, late modern society). A major goal of this book is to try to understand why people have so much trouble being self-determining agents, especially since Western societies have such advanced educational systems that supposedly enhance people's understandings of themselves and the world.

A group of developmental psychologists have operationalized elements of Erikson's work on identity formation and conducted a large number of empirical studies. Their studies have mapped out several dimensions representing the extent to which a person, in effect, (1) attempts to individualize and (2) is consciously instrumental in that process. The majority of the studies are based on James Marcia's "identity status paradigm" (for recent reviews see Adams, Gullotta and Montemayor 1992; Archer 1994; Bosma 1985; Côté 1996b; Kroger 1989; La Voie 1994; and Marcia et al. 1993). In its most basic form, the research uses four categories, or identity statuses, into which most people can be placed, based on (1) whether or not they have consciously thought about their occupational options, political and religious beliefs, and various interpersonal matters such as friendship and sexuality, and (2) whether or not they are committed to certain courses of action or beliefs based on this conscious choice-making. The four statuses represent psychological, or intrapsychic, positions with respect to identity formation (what Erikson called "ego identity"). Note that *social* identity formation is a separate, but related, process (as in the previous section).

The four basic identity statuses are termed identity diffusion, identity foreclosure, identity moratorium, and identity achievement.[4] They are operationally defined as follows: diffusions exhibit low levels of choice and commitment formation; foreclosures demonstrate low levels of choice but high levels of commitment; moratoriums are involved in ongoing choice-making but have incompletely formed commitments; and achievements maintain high levels of commitment based on an extended period of conscious choice-making.

We can correlate this terminology from the identity status paradigm with the culture-identity link as represented in figure 4.1 (bottom row) in order to develop further a framework with which to understand how people in different societies psychologically adjust to the transition to adulthood in terms of identity issues. Accordingly, in premodern, postfigurative societies, where adult social identities are ascribed, identity foreclosure is likely to predominate as a developmental stance toward forming an adult identity; in early modern, configurative societies, where adult social identity is ostensibly accomplished through individual effort, identity achievement would be the developmental strategy that appears most beneficial for the individual; and in late modern, prefigurative societies, where adult social identities in adulthood need to be continually managed, identity diffusion and identity moratorium appear to be increasingly the predominant responses because long-term commitments seem to be more difficult to sustain. However, unlike the predominant patterns in the previous two types of societies, the diffusion stance may be "socially adaptive" as a conformity strategy in the same way that default individualization is but not ultimately beneficial for the individual or the society (although it may be for the market economy). In other words, I do not recommend the diffusion stance as an adaptive strategy; rather I am simply trying to describe what seems to be happening (i.e., I am describing rather than prescribing). The moratorium status has more positive features to recommend than does the diffusion status, by merit of its inherently active nature. However, remaining perpetually in "moratorium"— a state of delay—has obvious pitfalls, including being locked into a transitional stance endlessly looking for exits. Nevertheless, it appears that an increasing number of people are chronic "searchers," as Josselson describes in the next section.

With these four sets of concepts correlated, we can gain a richer understanding of the past and the present, as well as what the future might hold. For example, although a significant but declining proportion of people still seem to follow the foreclosure and achievement patterns, an increasing number seem to be following the diffusion pattern (Marcia 1989). This apparent increase in the diffusion pattern, whereby a person does not actively explore identity issues or maintain a committed adult identity, is revealing in light of the apparent increase in default individualization processes associated with late modern societies (see chapters 1 and 2). It is also understandable in terms of the notion that the individualization process has liabilities (default forms) as well as benefits (developmental forms).

The paradox of the overall "weakening" of identity can be understood in the sense that late modern institutional supports for making developmental transitions have been destructured and are often deficient (i.e., they have broken down or are functioning poorly—such as the linkages between the mass-educational and occupational systems in many countries). Consequently, many individuals are left largely on their own to make the transition to adulthood and manage their subsequent life courses, especially in setting and achieving goals. In addition, the other-directed character structure of late modern societies means that individuals are often more intent on pleasing and impressing others than on maintaining their own internal standards.

As we have seen, it is believed that sustaining stable, internal points of reference can be problematic for all individuals in late modern societies, but "preadults" seem to be particularly prone to other-directedness. That helps to explain why people have become increasingly susceptible to a compulsive "image consumption." It appears that forms of consumerism were introduced to successive cohorts throughout the twentieth century (especially after midcentury) by various profit-oriented industries via youth cultures and peer cultures. Indeed, the heightened need to conform during the adolescent period has likely made it relatively easy for a pattern of image consumption to be introduced that involves an immediate-gratification orientation to enhancing one's physical and experiential self as deemed appropriate by others. Hence, it is now commonplace to adorn the body with various fashions, jewelry, and cosmetics in order to project a particular image that pleases others while gratifying narcissistic desires; and it is customary to spend great amounts of time in experiences that similarly project an image while gaining validation from others, through the consumption of music, mass media, computers and assorted games, and drugs. These all involve image consumption in the sense that illusions are used as a basis for key interactions with others.

The diffusion pattern of identity formation helps us understand the mass of consumers that has been created who have little concern about what the future holds and who are receptive to shifting trends and values. Under such conditions, if there is to be any resistance to this economic manipulation and any reasonable degree of self-directedness, the resources at individuals' disposal become important, particularly those psychological resources that can contribute to an internal point of reference, like ego strength. In previous research I have suggested that the response to these increasingly anomic social conditions ranges from passive acceptance to active mastery (Côté 1996a). The passive response appears to be widespread and involves simply acquiescing to the identity manipulation that characterizes contemporary society--hence, the apparent increase in identity diffusion. In contrast, the active response represents people involving themselves in their own personal growth and self-exploration to compensate for the social-organizational problems of late modern societies already identified. This active response is more comprehensive than the identity "achievement" studied by the identity status researchers because it involves a longer-term strategic response to the world and one's place in it over one's entire life course. I describe this position, called the identity capital model, in chapter 6.

Before moving on, it is appropriate to comment on the relationship between the identity status paradigm and Erikson's original theory. As I have argued elsewhere (Côté and Levine 1988; Côté 1996b), the way in which the identity crisis specifically, and identity formation in general, have been operationalized by identity status researchers appears to be rather narrow and focuses on the conditions more closely associated with early modern American society. For example, it appears that the choice/commitment form of identity formation is not the only type of identity crisis that can be experienced. Other forms of the identity crisis may be more prevalent and more significant developmentally, but they have not been as extensively studied. For example, crises involving conscious and unconscious conflict resolution may be more common than the choice/commitment form, but those crises have not yet been thoroughly investigated (see Côté 1986 for an operationalization of more conflict-based identity crises). The conflict-based crisis may involve no grand plan and may be more emotional than cognitive (e.g., involving ambivalence and resentment) but may still result in a realignment of identifications (cf. Erikson 1968, 1979).

Yet another type of crisis may be associated with the "reflexive project of self" discussed by Giddens (1991) and others. This "project" can be seen as a crisis, especially in contrast to identity formation in premodern societies, and appears to be widespread in late modern societies in response to a deficit of meaningful social relations and a surfeit of commodified images. Given that these conditions can encourage a "dissipation" rather than an "accruing" of self in late modern society, the "reflexive project," without an active, agentic disposition, can be a poor path to follow in the attempt to find a viable resolution in an adult identity recognized by a stable community.

Yet another form of "crisis" may be so well institutionalized that it goes unnoticed, as in premodern societies where individuals are guided through an identity transformation with community-sanctioned rituals (see Côté and Levine 1987 for a discussion of various types of crises and stage resolutions). A seldom-cited quotation from Erikson helps highlight different forms of identity crisis and their import:

The identity development of an individual is always anchored in the identity of his group; although through his identity he will seal his individual style. Of individual differences we may often not have the fullest perception. Especially in an alien culture we may see somebody going slowly through an identity crisis, in which conformity seems more emphasized than individuality. This very conformity may keep some aspects of the crisis from verbalization or awareness; only closer study could reveal it. Or the individual's experience may seem entirely submerged in rituals and procedures which seem to exaggerate the horror of individual decision and to offer, as a way out, the narrowest choice of models. We will not know the nature of this process until we have learned to study its variations. (1959, 105–106)

We return to these ideas about identity formation in chapter 6, where I make recommendations about how people can more successfully adapt to late modern society. The remainder of this chapter deals with the identity problems many people are currently experiencing.

## Identity Pathways: Ruthellen Josselson

Ruthellen Josselson, a psychologist and psychotherapist, traced the identity development of a group of thirty women over a twenty-two-year period from the end of their college years in the early seventies to their middle years in 1993. Her findings are presented in *Revising Herself: The Story of Women's Identity from College to Midlife* (1996). The insights and analyses from this longitudinal study provide us with a rare glimpse into the problems associated with "normal" forms of identity development for women in a late modern society. We can see in these women the pressures toward other-directedness to which Riesman refers; we can also see how their adult social identity has been problematic and in need of continual management; and we can see how these problems are traceable to characteristics of late modern, prefigurative society. No comparable study of identity has been done for men, but a number of parallels can be drawn, especially for those aspects of life that men and women increasingly share.

Josselson used the identity status paradigm to initially categorize the women in terms of the "gateways" they took into adulthood during their college years and the "pathways" they subsequently followed up to middle age. We see in her analysis how the identity statuses largely reflect character structures that dramatically affect how the transition to adulthood is undertaken. In this sense the statuses seem to encapsulate the personality resources these women had upon entering adulthood. Their resources affected how they processed experiences and attempted to act upon the world as agents. Notably, Josselson found that this was not an easy process for any of them, regardless of which pathway they followed, primarily because there were very few models for them to emulate when functioning in the public sphere.

The terminology of the identity status paradigm was modified by Josselson to better suit the experiences of her subjects. In her more intuitively meaningful terms, achievements were called pathfinders, moratoriums searchers, foreclosures guardians, and diffusions drifters.

Regardless of their identity pathway, Josselson reports, adult life has been a struggle for all of these women. In fact, eighteen of the thirty had sought some mental health assistance by the end of her study: "All but one of the Drifters, two-thirds of the Searchers, and half the Guardians availed themselves of psychotherapy in one form or another" (1996, 252). Only one pathfinder had sought help, supporting the notion that this identity stance is the most psychologically healthy. For those who needed it, "psychotherapy was useful and productive, assisting them along the road toward insight and planning and helping them design their own paths" (252).

Josselson describes the women's struggles as "identity revisions," in which a process of self-discovery and growth is undertaken. The pace and timing of this process differs for each stance. She also submits that identity revisions follow a path marked by attempts to maintain "connections" while developing "competence."[5] Here is how she describes the process:

> All women want a sense of competence and a sense of connection—that is one generalization I can make with some confidence. . . . How to go about achieving them is often the enigma. Choice is a slippery process, as is self-knowledge. To "know what one wants for oneself" is not an easy matter and is often a lifelong quest. Freedom is liberating, but it can also be terrifying. (1996, 241)

In interpreting the behavior of the women in her study, Josselson emphasizes the psychological side of identity revisions, attempting to counter certain media depictions and feminist theory that simply portray women as knowing what they want but being held back by an oppressive society. She sees the identity revision process as one in which the social world may or may not play a part, depending on the issue at hand. The struggles she describes involve "very inchoate longings—to 'be someone,' to 'do something'—into realizable goals" (1996, 241). And these struggles are undertaken through individual effort, often with little support from others. She summarizes the courses of these revisions as follows:

> Guardians begin with certainty, adopting in large part the dreams and values transmitted by their families or carrying unchallenged childhood fantasies into adult ideals. They choose the weight of tradition propelling and buttressing them. Pathfinders and many Searchers, by contrast, wrestle through options and then make their choice, and they decide with less conviction than the Guardians. Searchers (most of them) chose only after an extended period of self-examination and experimentation, and remain most aware of internal conflict and struggle, of desire never fully satisfied. Drifters are at pains to know their own desire among the shifting impulses and dreams of the moment. They struggle to find themselves within their own volatility, but are vulnerable to being appropriated by someone else's design. (241)

Because there is reason to believe that identity is increasingly less rooted socially and less fixed psychologically in the late modern age, it is instructive to review what Josselson writes about people with the least stable identities: those patterns may be the norm in the future. Sigmund Freud once asked, while in a naive and perplexed mood, "What do women want?" Josselson responds, with regard to the "wanting" patterns of drifters and searchers:

> For them, desire is often self-generated but short-lived. What feels like conviction often shows itself in a short time to be passing infatuation. Many experience an intoxicating hopeful excitement that may conceal a poorly conceived purpose. At a given moment, they may appear to "know what they want," but the certainty is transitory and soon transposes itself into yet another impulsive plan. (242)

In the sample of thirty that she interviewed in 1993, over half fell into one of these two identity categories: 33% had been searchers since college and 23% had been drifters. In my view, these are strikingly high percentages that need to be interpreted more historically and sociologically, as we have been doing in this book—against the background of a society in which choice-making is both possible and problematic, in accordance with the models provided by Mead and Riesman (see chapter 3). Moreover, Josselson's observation that all of these women struggled through individual effort, often with little support from others, is understandable in terms of the individualization and cultural destructuring processes.

The difficulty with the purely psychological approach is that it tends to be acontextual and ahistorical, thereby missing a sense of contrast with other possible societies and other eras.[6] As Josselson notes, these women (and, I am sure, the men in their lives) have been on a frontier of cultural change that makes it very difficult for them to form, and then maintain, a stable sense of self. But that is the issue at hand—the one to which this book is devoted—and the one Margaret Mead and David Riesman warned the world about several decades ago. We see embedded in Josselson's descriptions of these women's lives how an other-directedness has deeply affected at least half them in a "normal" fashion. Indeed, it is likely that if we extended her study to a wider, less privileged population, the percentage of those affected by other-directedness would be much higher.

Josselson's research is further limited because she deliberately set out without any methodological safeguards to prove that women have a greater sense of "connection" than do men. Her notion of "connection" follows closely from the recent feminist claim, reviewed in chapter 3, that women are more "relational" than men. Although the women in her sample may have been more relational than most men, she did not take steps to scientifically test this by setting out null hypotheses (i.e., starting with the assumption that gender does not affect relationality) or by making direct comparisons with the experiences of men. Hence, in spite of the contributions her study makes, it has the same shortcomings as other work done using the "relational model." Nonetheless, she did attempt to describe how the women in her sample struggled with a sense of competence (agency) along with their sense of connection. For example, this is how she links these two attributes and the sense of identity: "Identity resides at the intersection of competence and connection: this is where people feel most fully themselves—and are most recognized by others as being who they are. Adult crises in identity among these women have most often involved the struggle to keep experience of competence and connection in balance" (1996, 178). We revisit the notion of balancing these two attributes in chapter 6.

## Clinical Identity Problems in Late Modern Society

The consensus is growing among social scientists that identity problems are the major "symptoms" of the times, in the same way that neuroses were the major "symptoms" of Victorian society. Neuroses seem to emerge under conditions of emotional repression, whereas identity problems seem to emerge when there are insufficient restraints put on behavior and experience. Without adequate structure and guidance, people tend to be confused or lose their sense of place in society. They tend to take longer to become "mature" members of the human species (it can become a matter of will *or* ability, depending on the circumstances). In late modern society we seem to have a population that tends to be confused about "who they are." Lacking a secure psychological foundation, people have a difficult time making the transition to "adulthood." In turn, an increasing number of people seem to become "adults" (in terms of age) who are "immature" in comparison to adults of earlier periods. This all seems "normal" now.

In the face of these changes, can we still make a distinction between normality and pathology when speaking of identity problems? It does appear that we can, although the line has become blurry. One starting point is with the personality disorders that took on epidemic proportions in the latter half of the twentieth century. The *DSM*-IV lists ten distinct personality disorders and an eleventh that is nonspecific. They constitute enduring, pervasive, and inflexible patterns of behavior and experience that cause significant distress and impairment for the individual inflicted. In part because much psychiatric theory was developed earlier in the twentieth century when different social conditions prevailed, and in part because many individuals with these disorders do not consider them a problem, the disorders have posed a significant challenge to the psychiatric community as they have grown in prevalence. Afflicted individuals think they are "normal," perhaps because they see similar traits in many people around them. However, afflicted individuals experience significant distress as a result of their underlying ego identity instability. The *DSM*-IV explicitly recognizes the slippery slope between the normal and the pathological, giving the following directions to clinicians: "Personality Disorders must be distinguished from *personality traits that do not reach the threshold for a Personality Disorder*. Personality traits are diagnosed as a Personality Disorder only when they are inflexible, maladaptive, and persisting and cause significant functional impairment or subjective distress" (*DSM*-IV 1994, 633).

The most prevalent of the eleven disorders is the borderline personality disorder (BPD), afflicting about 10% of patients in outpatient clinics, 20% of psychiatric inpatients, and between 30% and 60% of all those with personality disorders (*DSM*-IV, 652). This disorder is also distinguished from "Identity Problem" in the *DSM*-IV; the latter does not qualify as a mental disorder, although it did in an earlier version of the manual (the *DSM*-III).

### The Borderline Personality Disorder

In their book *I Hate You—Don't Leave Me: Understanding the Borderline Personality* (1989), Jerold Kreisman and Hal Straus provide a layperson's treatment of what has become one of the most common psychiatric impairments. They cite studies suggesting that the borderline personality disorder (BPD) afflicts some ten million people in the United States alone.[7] Yet they note that few people among the general public are aware of it as a psychiatric condition. One reason is that "borderline personality disorder" is a relatively new diagnostic label, gaining acceptance in the psychiatric profession only over the last two decades. Its recency suggests that it is in part "sociogenic," or rooted in sociocultural conditions, as certain neuroses were thought to be earlier in the twentieth century. According to Kreisman and Straus, "many in the mental health profession believe that we are living in a 'borderline era.' Just as the hysterical neurotic of Freud's time represented the repressive European culture of the early twentieth century, the borderline's fragmented sense of identity and difficulty in maintaining stable relationships may reflect the fragmentation of stable units in contemporary society" (xiii).

They observe that many of the symptoms of BPD are experienced by most people in this society, but the symptoms take on pathological proportions among those who have certain predisposing factors. Because of our atomized and alienating society, people are expected to experience loneliness, impulsivity, fear of abandonment, problems with intimacy, and stormy relationships from time to time. "Do we all display, to one degree or another, some symptoms of borderline personality?" Kreisman and Straus ask. "Yes," they answer, "but not all of us are controlled by the degree that it disrupts—or rules—our lives" (1989,

16). However, some people, without a stable sense of ego identity rooted in a trust of others, experience these symptoms continually and in the extreme, making their lives a hell, along with the lives of those they are close to. Some of the health consequences of BPD include anorexia, bulimia, substance abuse, and suicide. In other words, we live in a society in which both a sense of identity and stable relationships with others are problematic, but most people cope in some way, as we saw in Josselson's study.

Apparently, however, increasing numbers of people cannot cope. Borderlines attempt to respond to this confusing society by putting on an act for others, by being entirely other-directed. Kreisman and Straus explain these symptoms as follows:

> Central to the borderline syndrome is the lack of a core sense of identity. When describing themselves, borderlines typically paint a confused or contradictory self-portrait. . . . To overcome their indistinct and mostly negative self-image, borderlines, like actors, are constantly searching for "good roles," complete "characters" they can use to fill the identity void. So they often adapt like chameleons to the environment, situation, or companions of the moment, much like the title character in Woody Allen's film, *Zelig,* who literally assumes the personality, identity, and appearance of anyone around him. (1989, 9)

Recall that many postmodernists, including Gergen (discussed in chapter 3), celebrate these conditions.

There may be developmental (e.g., poor parental relations) and constitutional (e.g., genetic) roots of BPD, both of which are still under study, but it is possible that this disorder would not emerge in such proportions in a different type of society. For example, in premodern, postfigurative, tradition-directed societies, where adult social identities are ascribed and ego identity is foreclosed (as in figures 3.1 and 4.1), the symptoms characterizing this disorder would be less likely to emerge, in part because there would less tolerance for them. The *DSM-IV* lists the key symptoms of BPD:

> A pervasive pattern of instability of interpersonal relationships, self-image, and affects, and marked impulsivity beginning in early adulthood and present in a variety of contexts, as indicated by five (or more) of the following:
>
> (1) frantic efforts to avoid real or imagined abandonment

(2) a pattern of unstable and intense interpersonal relationships characterized by alternating between extremes of idealization and devaluation

(3) identity disturbance: markedly and persistently unstable self-image or
sense of self

(4) impulsivity in at least two areas that are potentially self-damaging (e.g.,
spending, sex,substance abuse, reckless driving, binge eating)

(5) recurrent suicidal behavior, gestures, or threats, or self-mutilating
behavior

(6) affective instability due to marked reactivity of mood (e.g., intense
episodic dysphoria, irritability, or anxiety usually lasting a few hours
and rarely more than a few days)

(7) chronic feelings of emptiness

(8) inappropriate intense anger or difficulty controlling anger (e.g., frequent
displays of temper, constant anger, recurrent physical fights)

(9) transient, stress-related paranoid ideation or severe dissociative symptoms (1994, 654)

In their chapter entitled "The Borderline Society," Kreisman and
Straus cite a number of possible social conditions specific to contemporary society that might be feeding the epidemic of personality disorders. Echoing the distinction between early modern and late modern
society, they note that the fixed nature of social roles and the prohibi-
tions against impulse expression have changed. Consequently, children
are raised in less structured environments, and more of them are probably experiencing poor, abusive, or neglectful parenting, as parents
themselves are under stress from changed social and economic circumstances (and are increasingly beset with personality disorders themselves). It is believed that the seeds of BPD are planted in childhood
with difficult parent-child relations. As children with that background
attempt to develop into adulthood, they encounter a loosely structured
society with changing (ambiguous and contradictory) gender roles
(some researchers have found that BPD is more prevalent among
women). In addition, the society in which they are expected to function
is geared toward immediate gratification, self-absorption, and a poor
sense of the past and future.

Citing Lasch approvingly, Kreisman and Straus agree that these social conditions are conducive to unstable personality traits that for
some become the person's entire character. And echoing Margaret
Mead, they argue that more and more people are "trapped" in a present in which past traditions and future directions are absent (cf. Bly

1996). They refer to a "loss of historical continuity [which] works both ways in terms of time. Devaluation of the past breaks the perceptual link to the future, which becomes a vast unknown, a source of dread as much as hope. Time is perceived as isolated points instead of as a logical, continuous string of events influenced by past achievement and present action" (1989, 68).

### Ego Identity Disorders and Problems

The diagnostic manual of the American Psychiatric Association currently is in its fourth major revision (the *DSM*-IV). The previous version, the *DSM*-III, listed "Identity Disorder" as one of several psychopathologies found among the adolescent population. Perhaps in response to the criticism that there was an unnecessary proliferation of psychiatric illness categories, identity disorder was "downgraded" to "Identity Problem," to be distinguished from BPD. According to the *DSM*-IV, "Identity Problem" "is reserved for identity concerns related to a developmental phase (e.g., adolescence) and does not qualify as a mental disorder" (1994, 654). Whatever their official psychiatric status, identity difficulties appear to be widespread enough not only to gain the attention of the psychiatric community but also to now be considered within the realm of normalcy. Moreover, the designation of identity problem does not include the "identity crisis" that Erik Erikson identified as a normative developmental passage. According to Sherman Feinstein: "The DSM-III defined identity disorders as subjective distress over an inability to reconcile aspects of the self into a relatively coherent and acceptable sense of self. The disturbance is manifested by uncertainty about a variety of issues related to identity, including long-term goals, career choice, friendship patterns, values, and loyalties" (1985, 1763).

As with BPD, most people seem to cope with these pathogenic social conditions without becoming seriously afflicted. However, a proportion of the adolescent population apparently does experience a severe reaction to these social conditions (perhaps with contributing constitutional and developmental factors). Feinstein describes the abreaction to the widespread identity question (Who am I?) in this way:

> The resulting transitory regression is characterized by an inability to make decisions; a sense of isolation and inner emptiness; an inability to

achieve relationships and sexual intimacy; a distorted time perspective, resulting in a sense of great urgency and a loss of consideration for time as a dimension of living; an acute inability to work, and at times a choice of a negative identity, a hostile parody of the usual roles in one's family or community. (1985, 1763)

In its listing of symptoms, the *DSM*-III indicates that a diagnosis should be given if there is "severe subjective distress regarding uncertainty about a variety of issues related to identity" (such as those just cited; 1977, M64). However, if we backtrack to research conducted by identity status researchers, we find that most young people have difficulties with these issues. There may not be severe distress concerning issues of long-term goals and career choice in the "normal" samples studied, but the bulk of the research suggests that most young people do not resolve the issues in a highly self-directed or committed fashion. In fact, it appears that most tend to be passive and other-directed, even the substantial population that goes on to college and university. In my view, the reason lies not so much in the failings of the individual but in the nature of a society that diverts the attention of children and adolescents elsewhere—mainly to short-term, impulse-oriented activities, from which pop culture enterprises generate profits for a few self-interested people.

## Social Identity Problems: Individualization and the Decline of the Collective

We saw how psychologists and psychiatrists view identity problems in late modern society. Although those views are helpful, in order to round out our analysis, it is appropriate to consider how sociologists look at the same problems.

A growing number of sociologists are voicing dissatisfaction with the "postmodernism paradigm," in reaction to the exaggerated claims of some postmodernists. There is general agreement that significant changes took place in most Western societies in the latter part of the twentieth century, but there are disagreements over how much change has taken place and why the changes have occurred. Andy Furlong and Fred Cartmel characterize this dispute in their book *Young People and Social Change: Individualization and Risk in Late Modernity*:

On a theoretical level, these changes have been expressed in a number of ways with sociologists holding different opinions about whether they signify the beginning of a new era, just as significant as the transition from medieval to modern society, or whether they represent developments within modernity. At one end of the spectrum, postmodernists . . . argue that we have entered a new . . . epoch in which structural analysis has lost its validity. . . . Patterns of behavior and individual life chances have lost their predictability and post-modernism involves a new and much more diverse set of lifestyles. The validity of a science of the social is rejected, along with the usefulness of key explanatory variables such as class and gender. . . . Other theorists have been more cautious in their interpretation of changes and have used terms like "high modernity," "late modernity" . . . or "reflexive modernization" . . . to draw attention to the far reaching implications of recent socioeconomic change, at the same time as expressing the view that, as yet, these changes do not represent an epochal shift. (1997, 1–2)

Furlong and Cartmel concur with the "late modernism paradigm," arguing that "radical social changes have occurred," but they "are extremely skeptical of the validity of post-modern theories." In particular, they do not believe that as much institutional destructuring took place in the latter half of the twentieth century as postmodernists contend. They acknowledge that "structures have fragmented, changed their form and become increasingly obscure" (2), but those structures associated with social class and gender have remained more intact than postmodernists will admit, at least in Britain.

Anthony Giddens, a chief proponent of the late modernism paradigm, has laid out the social psychological implications of his social theory in the book *Modernity and Self-Identity: Self and Society in the Late Modern Age* (1991). Giddens follows the sociological tradition (like Marx, Durkheim, Weber, and Parsons) of formulating comprehensive macro social theories about the changing structure of society. He has gone even further, however, in developing an elaborate framework for understanding identity from a macro perspective and in making important micro-macro links. Like other sociologists, Giddens believes that sustaining social identities have become more problematic throughout the life course, not just during the transition to adulthood. For Giddens, social identities are undermined by conditions associated with late modernity, an era in which the conditions of industrial capitalism have become heightened or exaggerated. These conditions have "undercut traditional habits and customs," radically altering "the nature of day-to-day social life" and affecting "the most personal aspects of our experience (1991, 1). Giddens carries on the earlier macrosociological view that selfhood or identity became problematic because the destructuring of social contexts by industrial capitalism created deficits in the "interior life" of individuals. However, he also ascribes intentional qualities to individuals to resist and adapt to this destructuring, and he describes various ways in which late modern societies have been restructured.

Notably, the late modern societal restructuring is at a higher level of abstraction than restructurings that occurred in previous societies, introducing a variety of risks that individuals must deal with in certain ways. This complexity places demands on individuals' intentional qualities that cannot always be met. Consequently, those with less "wherewithal" do not cope as well in late modern contexts. Yet Giddens rejects the notion that current conditions have obliterated the interior lives of individuals, as some postmodernists claim (1991, 100). Instead, he believes that impression management is a natural and inevitable response to the requirements of late modernity, in which people must be able to manage the impressions demanded by a variety of settings (by modifying their demeanors and appearances). He does not believe that this necessarily fragments the self or creates multiple selves, but rather that most people are well-adjusted enough to cope with these circumstances (Giddens deals in detail with issues of basic trust and ontological security that form the basis of this adjustment). But identity is existentially challenged on a more continual basis in late modern societies than in premodern ones, and some people handle these challenges better than others.

Thus, Giddens believes that under conditions of late modernity, it is important for individuals to develop their "agentic" potentials with which to construct reality and act in the world, not to surrender these, as Gergen suggests (cf. Côté 1996a, 1997). A person needs to be an "intelligent strategist" (Giddens 1994, 7) in dealing with the abstract dimensions of "place" and "space" in the late modern world. At the same time, the self requires the "external" in order to obtain the reflexive grounding (reference points to mirror the self) that is key to the senses of personal and social identity. Giddens (1991, 32–33) also argues that in late modern societies "the self becomes a reflexive project" extending over the entire life span. It does so in part because of the degree of institutional destructuring (in habits and customs) and in part because of continual institutional restructuring. A key difference between Giddens's work and the views of most postmodernists is his argument that late modern institutions are "reflexive" (just as individuals are): they make continual adjustments to new risks and constant social change (i.e., major institutions have mechanisms with which to monitor their environments, thereby continually anticipating risks and adjusting to change). In premodern cultures, in contrast, life was more highly structured and stable, and

> things stayed more or less the same from generation to generation on the level of the collectivity, [and] the changed identity was clearly staked out—as when the individual moved from adolescence into adulthood. In the settings of modernity, by contrast, the altered self has to be explored and constructed as part of a reflexive process of connecting personal and social change. (1991, 33)

In Giddens's judgment, self-identity "is not a distinctive trait, or even a collection of traits, possessed by the individual. It is the self as reflexively understood by the person in terms of his or her biography" (1991, 53). In other words, a person forms a self-identity by negotiating passages through life and reflecting on his or her actions during those passages. Self-identity is thus a product of meaning-making as a mode of adaptation to the vicissitudes of late modern society—vicissitudes created by the alienating and disjunctive experiences associated with the decline of local authority structures and the rise of interconnected global influences. Giddens believes that most people, so long as they have a foundation to support a stable sense of self-identity, are able to deal with those vicissitudes:

> A person with a reasonably stable sense of self-identity has a feeling of biographical continuity which she is able to grasp reflexively and, to a greater or lesser degree, communicate with other people. That person also, through early trust relations, has established a protective cocoon which "filters out," in the practical conduct of day-to-day life, many of the dangers which in principle threaten the integrity of the self. . . . the individual is able to accept that integrity as worthwhile . . . [and has] sufficient self-regard to sustain a sense of the self as "alive." (54)

But "feelings of self-identity are both robust and fragile" (55). The fragility comes from the fact that the individual's construction of his or her biography can be challenged in many ways; they are robust to the extent that the personality strengths bolster them.

Giddens's view, and that of other late modernists, is supported by the historical record we examined earlier, inasmuch as the life course in late modernity follows a large number of trajectories determined in part by individual preference (there is now compulsory individualization, unheard of in premodern societies) and in part by the uncertainty and risks of the global community in which late modern societies themselves attempt to cope (there is now less concrete, daily structure than in premodern societies). Although this sociological contribution to the study of adulthood is largely indirect (i.e., it is focused on the most common life situations of a population, not on the life course per se), it is worth looking at the dual impact of individualization and destructuring on social identity. To do this, we need to appreciate the relationship between individualization and destructuring.

In his book *Risk Society: Towards a New Modernity*, Ulrich Beck presents his "model of individualization"; he views individualization as an inverse function of destructuring processes (1992, 127). Beck begins by noting that the process of individualization dates back centuries, to the early phases of modernization, including the Renaissance, the decline of feudalism, and the rise of industrial capitalism. During this period three phases in the social structuring of individualization took place. First, people were increasingly "disembedded," removed from their "historically prescribed social forms and commitments in the sense of traditional contexts of dominance and support." In other words, they were "liberated" from traditional statuses, but they also lost many collective supports. This change in societal structure was followed by a change in cultural structure: there was a "loss of traditional security with respect to practical knowledge, faith and guiding norms" (128). In the third phase new social commitments were formed that "re-embedded" people, reintegrating and controlling them. By now, individualization has been institutionalized in place of the collectivization that characterized premodern societies.

Beck offers three theses regarding the "mode of reintegration and control" that now prevails. The first is his contention that neither status, nor class, nor family is the basic unit of society. Instead, the basic "reproduction unit" is the individual: "Individuals inside and outside the family become the agents of their livelihood mediated by the market, as well as of their biographical planning and organization." Beck's second thesis is that individualization has become paradoxically standardized. Because the market now prevails in place of traditional forms of noninstrumental culture, the market has standardized modern institutions such as education and the law. Because the individual is now thoroughly dependent on the market, he or she must adjust to these standardized requirements, must modify his or her biography and life-planning accordingly. Life courses therefore become idiosyncratic and "preference-based," but within the changing and chaotic requirements of market forces. His third thesis is that the separation of private and public spheres has been destructured and restructured with the public sphere penetrating the private one. Now private situations also have a public, institutional character. These spheres have "the contradictory double face of institutionally dependent individual situations." This means that those who are most involved in the individualization of their biographies are most dependent on the labor market and are therefore "dependent on education, consumption, welfare state regulations and support, traffic planning, consumer supplies, and on possibilities and fashions in medical, psychological and pedagogical counseling and care" (1992, 130–131).

As a result of the restructuring of Western societies by modern forms of capitalism, there are "inherent contradictions in the individualization process." People have been cut loose from traditional ties and obligations, only to be subject to control "by secondary agencies and institutions, which stamp the biography of the individual and make that person dependent on fashions, social policy, economic cycles and markets, contrary to the image of individual control which establishes itself in consciousness." Thus, the individual biography is increasingly "reflexive" in the sense that the individual can monitor and modify it, but this also means that people are held ultimately responsible for the outcome of their reflexivity, in spite of their dependence on the market. That situation, of course, suits capitalism quite well because its inherent inequality becomes obscured by people's belief that they have full control over their individual biographies. Different people within and between "social classes" share various aspects of modern life through their preference-based lifestyles, but underlying inequalities can remain. If players in the late modern identity markets of individualized biographies find that they can no longer sustain their lifestyle for economic reasons, it must be their fault, according to the logic of late modern individualization, because they made the choices (1992, 131–132).

The fact that countless others may be experiencing the same difficulties is not considered a legitimate reason for one's personal problems. Hence, no link is made with systemic problems or exploitation. Beck is not claiming that (social class) inequalities have disappeared. To the contrary, they have simply become less visible or obscured because economic risks have been individualized; no longer are they seen as shared. Moreover, there is less and less for people to fall back on in comparison with traditional, collectivist supports. Even the social welfare reforms put in place to compensate for the loss of traditional forms of culture and economics are being dismantled; the result is growing poverty and homelessness. People therefore find themselves in increasingly isolated and precarious situations. Since there is no benign restructuring in sight, what is called for is the type of developmental individualization I referred to in chapter 1 and the type of active agency I discuss in chapter 6.

Beck's model thus takes us back to a number of the points raised independently by others, including Buchmann in chapter 1. For example, Beck's model is entirely compatible with the ideas of mass-society theorists, as the following passage shows:

> Individualization means market dependency in all dimensions of living. The forms of existence that arise are the isolated *mass market,* not conscious of itself, and *mass consumption* of generically designed housing, furnishings, articles of daily use, as well as opinions, habits, attitudes and lifestyles launched and adopted through the mass media. In other words, individualization delivers people over to an *external control* and *standardization* that was unknown in the enclaves of familial and feudal subcultures. (1992, 132)

His analysis is also entirely compatible with much of the empirical evidence we examined in chapter 2 regarding the role of television in the decline of civil society:

> Television isolates and standardizes. On the one hand, it removes people from traditionally shaped and bounded contexts of conversations, experience and life. At the same time, however, everyone is in a similar position: they all consume institutionally produced television programs, from Honolulu to Moscow and Singapore. The individualization—more precisely, the removal from traditional life contexts—is accompanied by a

uniformity and standardization of forms of living. Everyone sits isolated even in the family and gapes at the set. (1992, 132)

With Beck's model we can gain a better sense of what individualization is and is not. He is clear as to what it is not: "It does not mean atomization, isolation, loneliness, the end of all kinds of society, or unconnectedness" (1994, 13). It does not mean a revival of bourgeois individualism. It is not a psychological state but a social form. Individualization can be understood in terms of social and economic changes that disembedded the traditional, collective institutional patterns governing life-course trajectories and replaced them with patterns that suit industrial-capitalist society, "in which the individuals must produce, stage and cobble together their biographies themselves" (13). In an "individualized society," individuals must learn "on pain of permanent disadvantage, to conceive of [themselves] as the center of action, as the planning office with respect to [their] own biography, abilities, orientations, relationships and so on" (1992, 135). Under these conditions, Beck argues, "a vigorous model of action and everyday life" needs to be developed by the individual—a model that "puts the ego at its center, allots and opens up opportunities for action to it, and permits it in this manner to work through the emerging possibilities of decisions and arrangement with respect to one's own biography in a meaningful way" (136).

We can also gain a greater appreciation of the different experiences of men and women in late modern societies with the use of Beck's model. Specifically, individualization is more taken for granted by men, but it can be more problematic for women because women may encounter informal resistance to their participation in the public sphere. This means that some of the difficulties that women in search of economic self-determination experience—in reality systemic failures—are blamed on them as individuals. Moreover, because of the institutional penetration of the private sphere, their lives are now more governed by anonymous, bureaucratized, and standardized forces than in the past. To the extent that institutional regulation of their lives presupposes that they have "partnered" themselves with an individualized male, it sometimes denies them recognition as an individualizing person in their own right.

Consequently, many women find themselves in emotional no-win situations. If they do not develop their market potential sufficiently, they may be blamed for neglecting their new "duties" of career planning. If they do not pay sufficient attention to residual private-sphere obligations, they may be blamed for neglecting their old "duties" of "family planning." "Men's situations," according to Beck,

> are quite different. While women have to loosen their old ascribed roles of an "existence of others" and have to search for a new social identity, for reasons of economic security among others, for men, making a living independently and the old role identity coincide. In the stereotypical male gender role as "career man," economic individualization and masculine role behavior are joined together. Support by a spouse (the wife) is unknown to men historically, and the "freedom to" work for a living is taken for granted. (1992, 112)

To the extent that this double standard is changing, women have fewer public-private sphere conflicts, but as we saw in our examination of Josselson's work, those conflicts have played a central role in many of their identity formation processes well into adulthood.

The work of these sociologists rounds out the work of others we have examined thus far. Giddens used Erikson's studies in formulating his views; the neo-Eriksonian framework is compatible with the late modern model; and Marcia's paradigm is easily integrated with the individualization thesis. For example, the exploration of commitments to which that paradigm refers seems to correspond to more active forms of individualization, or what I have referred to as developmental individualization. In contrast, the lack of exploration of commitments reflects more passive, or default, forms of individualization. Indeed, the identity status literature supports the notion that those who would be classified as achievement or moratorium have undergone more extensive cognitive, moral, and other forms of psychosocial development than have those who would be classified as foreclosure or diffusion. Thus, the work of sociologists provides explanations of the various social contexts in which identity formation can take place.

We should pause here in order to more clearly differentiate psychological and sociological conceptions of some processes in which the individual is central. For example, psychologists have used the term *individuation* for some time for the "separation-individuation process" that begins in early infancy when the boundary is established "between the 'me' and the 'not-me'" (Levinson 1996, 32). That is the process by which offspring develop an emotional distance from their parents and become persons in their own right; it does not require a rejection of those parents, nor does it require parents to withdraw support from their children. In contrast, *individualization* refers to the social processes by which people compensate for a lack of *collective* support from their community or culture. It designates the extent to which people are left to their own devices to meet their own survival needs, determine the directions their lives will take, and make myriad choices along the way.

It appears that most of the work on individualization processes comes from European scholars, whereas that on individuation processes comes from American scholars. It is possible that "individualism" (a political-economic process) has a longer history in the United States than we think and that American scholars have simply taken it for granted. Collective supports may have declined more recently in Europe, calling individualization processes to the attention of European scholars. Whatever the case, recent global changes have made it apparent that individualism is increasingly being thrust upon people around the world, and as this happens, collectivism seems to be in decline. Consequently, individualization processes need to be thoroughly understood and not confused with individuation processes.

If we restrict ourselves to the United States, we can propose that individuation processes existed in premodern society but that individuation was carried out under conditions in which identities were ascribed and parent-child relations were well structured. With collective supports intact, little individualization would have taken place, although it might have been a model for those who struck out to settle in the frontiers or to undertake voyages of discovery. In the early modern phase, both individuation and individualization processes would have been common, but again individualization would have taken place in more structured and collectively supported ways. If Riesman is right, parents would have expected a certain amount of individualization from their children (made possible by their internal "gyroscope" that gave them a sense of direction) but certainly not the extreme forms that we see in late modern societies. Now in late modern societies, both individuation and individualization processes seem to have taken extreme forms. If Mead and Bly are right, children are increasingly individuating from their parents by rejecting them wholesale rather than simply developing a healthy distance from them. And everything we have looked at thus far supports the notion that people are undertaking an individualization process under conditions of little preset direction and few collective supports.

In addition to these clarifications, it is worth pointing out gender differences in these various "individual" processes. In individualization, as we have seen, women have fewer role models for choice-making in the public sphere, and there are still guilt-producing pressures associated with the private sphere. Furthermore, it may be that women have more difficulties than men individuating from their mothers, given the greater role of mothers in child-rearing and given the processes of same-sex identification. When we look at the more general concept of individualism, it appears that women still experience more structural barriers than men to full independence as self-determining agents. In this sense their active agency is more restricted by structure. Gender differences are also discernible around issues of "individuality" (in which personal identity is displayed during interactions with others). Women seem to be under more "display pressures"; for example, they are encouraged to compete with one another over issues of attractiveness. All of those pressures are now manipulated and exploited by multibillion-dollar industries (Côté and Allahar 1996, chap. 3). I reiterate, however, that these gender differences are of degree, not kind, and that men and women are increasingly converging in terms of these issues, especially among the younger and more educated segments of the population (cf. Allahar and Côté 1998; Furlong and Cartmel 1997).

## Learning to Live with Psychological Uncertainty and Risk

In chapters 3 and 4 we have taken a conceptual journey though a variety of social scientific theories concerning the changing nature of intergenerational relations and character formation and the impact of those changes on identity formation. Informed by Mead's and Riesman's insightful typologies, Erikson's foundational identity theory, and the work of "late modernists," we have come to see key reasons why identity formation became increasingly problematic over the twentieth century. Now that we are well into late modern society, it is "normal" for a sizable proportion of the population to have a poorly formulated sense of themselves as agents in the world and to have a vague sense of their past and their future. This "diffused" or "default" identity appears to be increasingly "normal" because of social and economic conditions that encourage an other-directed, image-oriented personality, bent on immediate gratification through the consumption of goods and services sold by corporate-capitalist enterprises.

Not everyone falls prey to those influences, but an increasing number of people seem to. In fact, it is easily argued that for some time now people have been targeted from childhood on by corporate-capitalist enterprises with encouragement to be passive in their identity formation. Consequently, with each successive cohort, more people have passed through their adolescence and into their adulthood without actively engaging themselves in their own identity development, in spite of opportunities to do so.

Although an increasing proportion of the population seems to go through life in a state of passive confusion about themselves, their goals, and their values, many or most people seem to be able to hold themselves together in one way or another, as Giddens claims. There seems to be a lot of trial-and-error experimentation, along with considerable pain and joy, as Josselson argues. There also seems to be a lot of help-seeking through the various media (which profit from this confusion), including self-help books and "bare-all" talk-show television programming. However, many people cannot hold themselves together, and the mental health professions have their hands full as more and more people with various adjustment problems and mental disorders seek help for their emotional distress. We seem to be experiencing an epidemic of identity-related disorders that are not temporary adjustments made during late adolescence and early adulthood but permanent maladies that continue through adulthood.

But what has changed to create such problems? Primarily, it seems that the pendulum has swung away from the Victorian era, when impulses were repressed but roles were clearly defined and when people felt socially constrained but there was little question regarding how to behave. Now there appear to be few limits on many forms of impulse expression; roles are increasingly vague, contradictory, or rejected as too confining; social constraints have given way to shock behaviors, bizarre forms of dress, and eccentric, self-styled behaviors, especially among the young; and many people have only fuzzy concepts of what constitutes appropriate behavior in a variety of social contexts, partly because there is often little consensus about such matters.

That swing of the pendulum spans the transition from early to late modern society. Undoubtedly there were also swings during the transitions between premodern and early modern societies, and between early and late modern societies with similar laments about the passing of order and good taste (Putnam [1996] argues that the period between 1865 and 1895 was similarly disruptive). But the possibility is not eliminated that the changes we have been examining run deep and are far-reaching. Furthermore, they can be seen as a heightening of the changes that took place during the early modern era, when industrial capitalism rose as the dominant socioeconomic force in society. Though the *industrial capitalism* of the 1800s caused many social and personal disruptions that persist today, we may simply have become used to them and now take them as "normal." Accordingly, we may now be getting used to the more recent changes wrought by *corporate capitalism,* so that they seem "normal."

In these days, however, aided by media technologies, economic forces seem to be digging deeper into people's existential core—into the depths of their character. The person with borderline personality disorder complains of no "inner core," but that complaint is echoed by many others in society. The difference seems to be that others have coping mechanisms that are absent in the borderline. It is not uncommon for people to say that they "don't have an identity." Or they may say it of someone else. What do they mean? In late modern society they seem to mean that they are not a "somebody," or at least do not have a valued social identity as can be found in a career or a position of importance. This form of reasoning attests to the extensiveness of other-directedness, for many people seem able to define themselves only in relation to others' approval. In the past, people might look to their inner selves and to a rich emotional interior for an answer to the question of whether they "had an identity." Others interpreted a person's "identity" by the person's character, that is, by the person's acts and deeds that culminated in his or her reputation (Wheelis 1958). Now, with few restraints and rules, reputation often does not count for much, especially in those contexts where people know nothing about each other's pasts. Reputation is often limited to the present or the recent past.

The type of society that we have has been called an "identity society," not because identity is prominent but because it is problematic (Glasser 1972). *Identity voids* now characterize much of the social landscape and the psychological interior of numerous individuals. Accordingly, it is normal for people to do without a stable sense of identity or to continually search for one. Among the young, who would otherwise be moving into an adulthood characterized by contributions to their family and community, a glorified identity crisis is common, wherein great pride is taken in how much experimentation is undertaken or how many commitments are avoided or rejected as archaic or associated with one of many "isms" (especially sexism or racism). Although there is evidence that such a period of identity formation can be developmentally useful (as a moratorium), when it takes an exaggerated form or goes on indefinitely, it is more likely that there will be casualties—both emotional and physical—associated with it. The casualties affect no only the person seeking "an identity" or experiencing an identity void, but also the person's friends, family, and community—just ask a person with borderline personality disorder or his or her associates.

# 5

# The Brave New Society
## Forever Young in a High-Tech World

### A Kinder, Gentler World Order?

The belief in progress is widespread, supported by the vast majority of the population. Capitalism, in its various forms, has been the major engine of progress for the past five centuries. Surely the average citizen of the Western nations is better off materially and is healthier as a result of the technological progress made possible by capitalism. Yet, what can we say about capitalism's social advancements? Is the average citizen of the Western nations better off in terms of life-satisfaction, a sense of meaning, or spirituality? And just how much have the advances been distributed across the entire populations of the Western nations, or among those non-Western countries that have served as sources of cheap labor and raw materials?

Perhaps most importantly, to what extent has the social fabric of Western nations been sacrificed in the name of "progress"? To what extent is "progress" a euphemism for the manipulation of society by a few individuals who have profited by introducing technologies that have altered social relations and displaced people from their productive community roles? In this chapter we consider these questions, first by looking at a society that has been completely manipulated in the name of technological progress and profit, and second by examining the history of the transition to adulthood and how it has been manipulated in the name of progress and profit.

### Huxley's Brave New World: *How Close Are We to the Ultimate Mass Society?*

In my opinion Aldous Huxley's *Brave New World* (1932) was one of the most important books of the twentieth century. The book's message about the direction that Western civilization is taking has been grossly underrated and has not been as influential as it might have been in warning us about some of the political and economic choices "we" have made. Many people have read that book in their high school literature classes, but they probably encountered simplistic interpretations of its theme, its characters, and its portrayal of a dystopia. Moreover, the impact of a book is affected by the way it is presented and the age at which a person reads it: when *Brave New World* is read from the point of view of literary criticism, one can focus on deficits of style and miss the sociological insights; a teenager who reads it might focus on the sexual freedoms Huxley portrays and miss the emotional prisons in which his characters live. I suggest that a reading or rereading of *Brave New World* is now in order in light of what I say about it here. You can then better judge the validity of the comparisons I make.

What are the psychological, sociological, historical, and futurological implications of Huxley's book? Huxley used *Brave New World* as a vehicle for extrapolating from events in the first part of the twentieth century—when the social and biological sciences were reaching an alarming level of sophistication—into the future. In setting the heyday of his Brave New World six centuries into the future, he seems to have erred on the conservative side, because within one century we are in many ways well into the type of world he portrayed (he recognized this fast pace of social change in the foreword of the 1946 printing, noting that "it seems quite possible that the horror may be on us within a single century" [1932, 14]). We can also use his book to speculate about our future from the vantage point of seventy years of subsequent social change. And, given our poor collective sense of the future, I think we need all the help we can get in that regard.

Huxley wrote *Brave New World* in the context of the "nature-nurture debate," which raged during the first decades of the twentieth century among scientists who were attempting to promote opposing views of human nature. We are not so much interested in the debate itself here as in the scientific work that stimulated it. (See Côté 1994 for a discussion of this debate, its implications, and a current controversy stemming from it.) On one side of the nature-nurture debate were those who believed in the overriding importance of genetics (nature) in determining human behavior; on the other side were those who believed that what happens in the social environment (nurture) was of ultimate importance. In the context in which Huxley wrote his book, it does not matter who was "right" or who had the better argument. Huxley wrote to warn us what would happen if those working to perfect our "nature" and our "nurture" reconciled their differences and combined their techniques, that is, of what a world could look like if the principles of genetics and the principles of conditioning were perfected in concert. He portrayed a world in which the social and the biological sciences are combined to produce the ultimate means of political control.

Political control in the Brave New World is in the hands of corporate-capital interests that have learned how to maximize mass production and mass consumption. Huxley symbolized that accomplishment by the deification of Henry Ford, the setting of the calendar to Ford's date of birth, and the proscription against taking Ford's name in vain. This control ranges from small genetic structures (the ex-utero fertilization of human eggs) to the largest political structure (the "World State," a government-corporation that has supplanted all nation-states around the world). Genetic engineering, the chemical manipulation of embryos, and early childhood conditioning (especially using hypnopaedia, or sleep-teaching) all use (Ford's) assembly line techniques to predetermine in batches the abilities of people. The society then sorts people into castes, named Alphas, Betas, Gammas, Deltas, and Epsilons. "Innate" abilities are thus matched to social destination: development is incrementally arrested to make the lower castes more suited to perform the more menial labor—and like it. The D.H.C. (Director of Hatcheries and Conditioning) explains: "That is the secret of happiness and virtue—liking what you've *got* to do. All conditioning aims at that: making people like their unescapable social destiny" (1932, 24). The match of inborn ability with social function is designed to promote happiness: people perform jobs associated with their ability level (e.g., Epsilons, the caste with the most arrested development, are happy as sewage workers).

Conditioning techniques (developed by early behavioral psychologists) are employed to literally shape human consciousness—what thoughts occupy people's minds. Potential thoughts that are "antisocial" (i.e., not approved by the corporate government) are counterconditioned during infancy with negative stimuli repeated hundreds of times. Once people become functioning members of society, they are motivated by positive reinforcements (physical pleasures), which appear to work because they produce what people believe is "happiness."

However, these short-lived rewards are psychologically and spiritually shallow forms of fulfilment. In short, a system has been developed for the mass production and standardization of human beings—in the name of "social stability." The problem of social stability, according to the D.H.C., was solved "by standard Gammas, unvarying Deltas, uniform Epsilons. Millions of identical twins. The principle of mass production at last applied to biology" (Huxley 1932, 18). The D.H.C. explains further that the conditioning techniques continue until "at last the child's mind *is* the suggestions, and the sum of the suggestions *is* the child mind. And not the child's mind only. The adult's mind too—all his long life. The mind that judges and desires and decides—made up of the suggestions. But all the suggestions are our suggestions! . . . Suggestions from the State" (34). (The current situation, in which young children spend numerous hours passively watching television and absorbing its repeated messages, is but a benign analog of those conditioning techniques of repeating messages over and over hundreds of times.)

The society of the Brave New World is organized totally around the needs of commodity capitalism; in fact, the State has engineered social structures over the centuries so that all behavior involves some form of commodity production or consumption. Anything new, such as a new sport, must be approved to ensure that it involves a sufficient level of consumption. Behavior that does not directly contribute to commodity capitalism is targeted with early negative conditioning techniques:

> One of the students held up his hand; and though he could see quite well why you couldn't have lower-caste people wasting the Community's time over books, and that there was always the risk of their reading something which might undesirably decondition one of their reflexes, yet . . . well, he couldn't understand about flowers. Why go to the trouble of making it psychologically impossible for Deltas to like flowers?
>
> Patiently the D.H.C. explained. If the children were made to scream at the sight of a rose, that was on grounds of high economic policy. Not so very long ago (a century or thereabouts), Gammas, Deltas, even Epsilons, had been conditioned to like flowers—flowers in particular and wild nature in general. The idea was to make them want to be going out into the country at every available opportunity, and so compel them to consume transport.
>
> "And didn't they consume transport?" asked the student. "Quite a lot," the D.H.C. replied. "But nothing else." Primroses and landscapes, he pointed out have one grave defect: they are gratuitous. A love of na-

ture keeps no factories busy. It was decided to abolish the love of nature, at any rate among the lower classes; to abolish the love of nature, but *not* the tendency to consume transport. For of course it was essential that they should keep on going to the country, even though they hated it. The problem was to find an economically sounder reason for consuming transport than a mere affection for primroses and landscapes. It was duly found.

"We condition the masses to hate the country," concluded the Director. "But simultaneously we conditioned them to love all country sports. At the same time, we see to it that all country sports shall entail the use of elaborate apparatus. So that they consume manufactured articles as well as transport." (Huxley 1932, 29–30)

When conditioning techniques are ineffective in eliminating "antisocial" behaviors later in life, "soma" is prescribed. Soma takes the person on a mental "holiday"—a precursor to tranquillizers like Valium, antidepressants like Prozac, and designer drugs like Ecstasy, all now used by tens of millions of people worldwide. Force and exile are used only as a last resort. Huxley does provide one character, Bernard Marx, of the Alpha caste, who shows signs of "antisocial" behavior. He tries to decondition himself and to convince another character, Lenina Crowne, to look at things differently. When Bernard tries to convince Lenina that spending some time alone might be pleasant, she is shocked and accuses him of "not wanting to be a part of the social body." In their conversation, during which Bernard tries to reason with her, Lenina blocks out what she can, in part by childishly repeating mantras she was taught during her infant hypnopaedia conditioning, such as "Never put off till tomorrow the fun you can have today." She asks Bernard whether he is free and happy, to which he replies: "Yes, 'Everybody's happy nowadays.' We begin giving the children that at five. But wouldn't you like to be free to be happy in some other way, Lenina? In your own way, for example; not in everybody else's way." Bernard goes on to reflect about their condition and says: "I want to know what passion is . . . I want to feel something strongly. . . . It suddenly struck me the other day . . . that it might be possible to be an adult all the time." To this Lenina says, "I don't understand." Bernard replies: "I know you don't. And that's why we went to bed together yesterday—like infants—instead of being adults and waiting" (79–82).

The World State, which oversees all of this carefully conditioned "happiness" is actually a huge corporation run by ten World Controllers. Since "happiness" is the goal of all human activity in the Brave New World, there is no need for political vision or guidance, so political structures in which debate and discussion take place are not present. The population has been deconditioned from engaging in intellectual inquiry or expressing historical curiosity. Indeed, any books that might encourage those mental activities are long gone, although the State continues to condition people to hate books by associating them with loud noises during childhood conditioning. Instead, not only is capitalism glorified—it is deified; organized religion is replaced by a form of reverence and worship of the World State, and Henry Ford is the new Christ. Among the worst crimes defined by the World State are the possession of literature and artifacts that are not part of the State-endorsed after-Ford world. The questioning of pleasure and commodity production are also crimes because they could give the citizenry a sense of history and tradition (and hence a critical consciousness) that the World State fears would upset the "Community, Identity, Stability" that it has spent centuries establishing.

The State has long since produced mass conformity through various forms of information control. People dare not think too deeply about things, for if their anxiety level does not become unbearable because of their past conditioning, their fear level paralyzes them because of the sanctions they know the World State will evoke. Thus, all citizens of the Brave New World, even the high-functioning Alphas, live a mindless existence with no interior life. They find an other-directed happiness through mandated consumption, required promiscuity, and a variety of group hedonistic activities (such as the "feelies"—movies during which people experience the tactile sensations of the actors—an anticipation of virtual reality technologies).

The characters in Huxley's dystopia are extremely shallow. People are highly narcissistic, other-directed, and obsessed with managing their impressions on others (e.g., Lenina is obsessed with making sure that people think that she has a perfect body and that she is sexually "pneumatic," but she refuses to empathize with those from the lower castes or to recognize that emotional attachment should precede sexual relations). There are no parents to guide and direct offspring, so this is a truly prefigurative society. Along with the impoverished interior life, there is little sense of an inner core or personal continuity independent of external stimulation. Instead, people are reliant on continual validation from others, and others' companionship, for their sense of identity, meaning, and direction. To the extent that people are fully relational in

Gergen's sense (see chapter 3 of this volume), we can see a possible homology between Gergen's postmodern world and Huxley's Brave New World, but it is not one that reflects well on the postmodern vision. Novel situations that do not match early conditioning and consciousness control are met with panic (reflecting a poor sense of ego identity), during which there is a regression to the infant state at which early conditioning occurred. People's sense of identity is precariously tied to "place"—the environment into which they have been conditioned. Venturing out into other "space" is too anxiety-provoking for most (cf. Giddens 1991).

Relationships within castes are entirely peer-oriented, and the State has long before done away with parenthood and marriage. Children are manufactured in huge factories and then receive a regime of conditioning that prepares them for their place in life (thus, identity ascription has returned). For "adults," no children need to be planned, raised, or guided. In fact, no one really "grows up"; infantilism is an acceptable behavior pattern. The vast majority of the population stays in a state of half-adulthood or half-childhood, with the few people who run the State making all decisions and giving all directions. Disputes are settled either with banishment or by increasing the rewards to the injured parties. Thus, "maturity" and "identity" in Huxley's Brave New World are reducible to the pursuit of "happiness" through infantilizing forms of hedonism that have been structured by a World State (corporation) to maximize production and consumption.

In effect, Huxley describes the ultimate mass society in which a hierarchical series of internally undifferentiated, but externally differentiated, segments of the population coexist. Within each of his castes, people are virtually identical, and their differences from people in other castes constitute functional divisions of production and consumption. In essence, there is no traditional society; instead there is the equivalent of a popular culture that provides people with diversions from the reality of the situation; the diversions establish patterns of mass consumption that support the system of mass production. Aside from Huxley's use of irony, his tendency toward farce, and a few technological advancements that he did not foresee, the world he envisioned remarkably resembles the corporate-capitalist mass society of late modernity with its popular culture increasingly penetrating every aspect of people's lives. No, there is not yet a World State ruling people, but the trend is certainly in that direction as corporations grow in size and wealth, dictating policy over sovereign nation-states. For example, in some cases transnational corporations purchase the debt of a country for a percentage of the dollar value of the debt, a practice called debt swapping, so that they can dictate policies to suit their interests (cf. Beauregard 1993; Eisenstein 1998; Koth de Paredes 1993; Teeple 1995).

## How Did Things Get So Confusing?

It appears that we have moved considerably closer to Huxley's Brave New World much faster than he originally imagined. How did this happen? In my view, through its various phases capitalism has fundamentally changed Western civilization, both directly and indirectly. To the point at hand, changes wrought by capitalism can be seen in the institutions providing the *normative structure* for the transition to, and hence through, adulthood (i.e., what to do, when to do it, why, where and with whom). As I have argued elsewhere (Côté 1994), the most effective way to change a culture is to alter "coming-of-age processes" incrementally on a cohort basis, so that the intended changes are introduced to the most impressionable and vulnerable members of society. As each cohort attains adulthood, it accepts the changes as normal and inevitable, but the next cohort is open to further changes in the same way. The adult segment of the society would have been more resistant to these changes if they had been directed at them.

We can discover the changes in the passage to adulthood that have emerged at the institutional level, beginning roughly two hundred years ago, by looking at the changing relative importance of the social institutions involved. In this type of analysis, it is necessary to use approximations about the relative influence of each institution because, obviously, it is difficult to be precise in such matters. Nonetheless, plausible scenarios can be offered. My analysis is intended to apply to all Western countries. Although these institutional changes occurred at different rates in different countries, their direction and outcome appear to have been much the same in all. For the sake of simplicity, then, I present one model; it can subsequently be empirically tested within each nation to determine its accuracy. From the literature I have examined, however, it appears that Western nations are generally converging in the ways described here (see Langlois et al. 1994 for detailed analyses of this).

## The Discovery and Conquest of Youth

The primary institutions governing the transition to adulthood that have been affected since 1800 are the family, religion, education, the state, and the market economy (first in its industrial phase, and more recently in its corporate phase). Figure 5.1 represents my estimations of the approximate relative influence of each institution in providing normative structure for the transition to adulthood from 1800 to 2000.

Around 1800 the family and religion were the institutions providing most of the normative structure for the transition to adulthood for the vast majority of the population. It is most likely that the family exerted the greatest influence for most people, especially in the frontier communities. Since then, the family has been in steady decline as a direct overriding influence. Two centuries later, as individualization processes have intensified and broadened, the family provides something of a "safety net," protecting the young from an unwelcoming economy, but for most young people it is no longer a strong influence in determining their major life choices as an adult (e.g., what to do for a living, whom to marry, and so forth; cf. Modell, Furstenberg, and Hershberg 1976).

By the mid-1900s, as we saw in chapter 2, religion began a precipitous decline. In Canada, which is generally and reliably in line with other Western nations in this trend, now only 12% of young people attend services regularly (Clark 1998; cf. Bibby 1993; Bibby and Posterski 1992), down precipitously from earlier twentieth-century figures. Looking at the adult population as a whole, among whom young people's parents are found, in the 1940s two-thirds of Canadians attended services regularly, but by 1996 the percentage was only 20. Clearly affected by the individualization process, people are now more likely to "pick and choose" their religious beliefs cafeteria style, as evidenced by the fact that most people still believe in a god, but they have developed their own ways of showing it.[1]

Returning our focus to the early 1800s, the other three institutions of interest here all had a negligible influence on the transition to adulthood. By 1850, however, education began to emerge as an influence for the children of affluent parents who sent their daughters to college to find suitable mates and their sons to make appropriate professional contacts (Collins 1979). Since then, the influence of education has grown, rippling through the social classes, so that now it is one of the most important institutions providing structure to the transition to

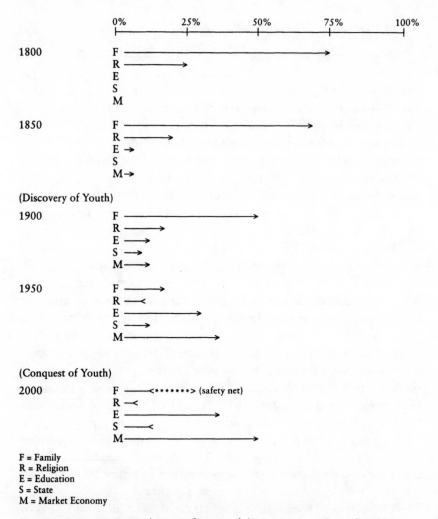

F = Family
R = Religion
E = Education
S = State
M = Market Economy

*Fig. 5.1.* Approximate Relative Influence of the Institutions Providing Normative Structure for the Transition to Adulthood

adulthood. Currently, in most Western countries the majority of teens are in school, and in some countries between one-third and one-half of those in their early twenties attend colleges or universities. The increased influence of educational institutions was partly due to their own initiatives, for example through educational lobbies, and partly due to the efforts of the state, as compulsory education and labor laws were passed (Collins 1979; Côté and Allahar 1996). By the second half of the twentieth century, mass and private education systems had become enterprises in their own right, occupying up to one-third of the population and holding a monopoly in providing the labor supply for corporate capitalism. Indeed, education and the market economy now fit together like a hand in a glove, in many respects. The mass education system in particular produces a compliant labor force with just enough knowledge to perform the necessary tasks but not enough universalizing ethical awareness (Erikson) to seriously challenge the inequities and injustices inherent in the capitalist system.

By 1900 the state began to emerge as an influence, largely through its mediation of other interests. For a time the state worked somewhat against the interests of the market economy on behalf of the youth segment by passing labor laws (mainly when key reformers pushed to stop the blatant exploitation of the young). By the early 1900s the state worked on behalf of the educational lobby with compulsory attendance laws. After the mid-1900s, the state continued this support, bolstering higher education with publicly financed expansions and tuition subsidies. Note, however, that this support of the educational sector has also had the effect of subsidizing the market economy, and therefore corporate capitalism, by financing the training of specialized labor and the production of literate consumers. Corporate capitalists in Western countries now have access to a highly educated labor pool with little or no cost to themselves. Ironically, labor now foots most of the bill for labor reproduction with taxes imposed on it by the state.

It was not until the 1970s that the state began to more deliberately work against, or ignore, the youth segment, siding largely with corporate capitalists in matters of wage rates and working conditions (e.g., with low minimum wages and age-graded wages). In the late 1900s the state in many countries abdicated its mediating role between corporate capitalism and labor. With respect to youth labor, the state withdrew from many of its social safety-net obligations and higher education subsidies, leaving youth in a laissez-faire situation confronted by powerful market-economy interests.

The increasing role that the market economy has come to play in the transition to adulthood has not been adjudicated by any democratic process. This period of transition has been penetrated more and more deeply by profit-driven pop culture, an amoral, anonymous market force with little regard for the well-being of its consumers. There is no "adult authority" overseeing these developments—just an elite group of adults profiting from them. To fully understand how a culture gave over control of its recruitment of new adult members to a group of exploitative capitalists requires an appreciation of the changing meaning of being "young" and the political-economic implications of the changing meaning.

At the beginning of the twentieth century in North America, the mid- to late-teen years were quite different than when the century came to an end. For example, around 1900 only a small number of male teens attended secondary schools; almost half were involved in agricultural labor, and the rest were employed in one of the three major labor force sectors (i.e., in the resource, manufacturing, and service sectors)—often making a living wage or close to it. Many lived with their families, but there was paid work available for them (without the age prejudices we now witness), and those who lived in their parents' home made considerable financial contributions to the family (Modell, Furstenberg, and Hershberg 1976). For working-class families, their most prosperous years were often when their female and male children worked and lived with them (Allahar and Côté 1998).

As of the year 2000, in most Western nations the vast majority of teens attend secondary schools. In Canada and the United States, over one-half of secondary school graduates go directly to postsecondary institutions (Nobert and McDowell 1994). However, only a minority (less than one-third) in this age group (eighteen to twenty-four) are engaged in employment that is sufficiently well paid to afford them independence from their parents. Those who stay with their parents rarely contribute much financially, and they make only minor contributions to household labor (although young females do more housework than young males); thus, they are free to pursue various leisure activities (White 1994; Modell, Furstenberg, and Hershberg 1976). In effect, their parents often subsidize them with free or cheap room and board and or allowances, and their mothers often provide "domestic" services for them. Referring to Canadian youth, Lindsay, Devereaux, and Bergob found that those "aged 15–19 devote less time than the overall population aged 15 and over to productive activities, while they have more free time and spend more time sleeping" (1994, 5). And referring to American youth, Arnett argues that "adolescents in many American households are treated not like equal adults but like indulged guests. This is not a healthy arrangement, either for adolescents or their families" (1996, 162). Moreover, if a person in the late teens or early twenties can get a decent job and does not have to pay room and board, his or her discretionary income can exceed that of his or her parents (Mogelonsky 1996).

What happened over the twentieth century to transform young people from productive citizens to dependents of their families, the educational systems, and/or the state? And on what basis were they denied their right to contribute to the society and the economy to their full productive capacities?

Perhaps the most significant development was that as a consequence of industrialization and advances in mass production, the labor of the young was no longer needed in the same way and to the same extent as in the preindustrial and early industrial eras, when the young were integral to the economy and were typically granted partial or full autonomy during their teen years (Steinberg 1990). As the young were "technologically displaced" from the economy (Rifkin 1995), and as child labor laws were passed to justify their exclusion, an increasingly idle youth population was viewed as a problem in need of social control. Misbehavior among some of the idle and economically displaced young soon drew the attention of social scientists and mental health experts, who were looking for objects of study and clients for their fledgling professions.

On this issue, those on the nature side of the nature-nurture debate originally prevailed and defined signs of misbehavior among the youth segment as biological in origin—adolescent storm and stress resulting from a supposedly hormonal turbulence associated with puberty (for discussions see Côté 1994; Mead 1928). Consequently, the period of adolescence itself was "discovered" as a distinct period of the life cycle with its own properties and problems (see fig. 5.1). The social contexts (i.e., nurture influences) producing adolescent behavior were downplayed by many, especially in psychiatry and psychology (cf. Proefrock 1981).

As it turns out, the storm-and-stress model of adolescence has been exposed by recent research to be one of many myths of modern social science. I will not dwell on that model—and its popular equivalent of the "raging hormones" stereotype—except to say that it prevailed during the twentieth century in several of the social sciences, and it has indelibly stamped public consciousness regarding the adolescent. The psychopathology attributed to adolescence came to be used as a legitimation for the juvenile justice system in North America and that system's suspension of the rights of adolescents (Proefrock 1981). Current laws justify the custody and treatment of the youngest segment of young people (usually under age sixteen) for what are called "status offenses," namely, offenses by virtue of their age-based status as a "preadult." These de jure conditions have been accompanied by de facto conditions whereby widespread discrimination exists toward the young, not only in the workplace but also in their day-to-day lives, as when they are denied access to restaurants and public places.

Over this period the needs of social scientists and mental health practitioners cross-fertilized with those of educators, who were also trying to legitimate and expand their fledgling profession. A consequence of these combined efforts has been to prolong childhood and adolescence. In fact, the term *teenager* was coined only recently, in the late 1930s (Danesi 1994; Palladino 1996). During the 1950s teenagers were the first major target group of mass marketers (Owram 1996; Frank 1997a, 1997b). Now the concept of teenagers has a self-evident reality; moreover, this age-segregated group constitutes a multibillion-dollar market.

As a result of these developments, a significant proportion of the population has been denied full participation (citizen rights) in mainstream society because of ageist assumptions, based on the faulty belief that youthfulness is a form of incapacity caused by raging hormones. This pathologization of "the adolescent" contributed to events during the twentieth century that marginalized the young from adult society and made them more vulnerable to the manipulations of market-economy interests. Viewed as biologically inferior and in need of control and segregation (in schools), successive cohorts were increasingly kept in holding patterns before being allowed entry into adulthood and a full productive participation in the community. Thus, the young have become increasingly more important as consumers in the market economy than as producers. This situation has not only further contributed to the downward spiral of their social status; it has also kept them at the mercy of market forces. In these ways we can say that the "conquest of youth" has been accomplished.

The association of youth with a "biological condition" helped disfranchise this age group as well as homogenize its range of acceptable behaviors, particularly among the teen segment. Further, more and more we see people in their twenties being treated as teenagers used to be treated, such that there are really two segments of youth today, those in their teens and those in their twenties (Keniston 1975; Klein 1990). One now may speak unchallenged of the young (though not of women or racial minorities) as somehow biologically inferior, with inherent mental problems (ostensibly caused by raging hormones), and use that stereotype to justify their unequal treatment in society, thus perpetuating their lower social status. Indeed, the stereotype is so pervasive that it is held by many young people themselves. To the extent that this happens, a spiral of causal reactions occurs, setting up a series of self-fulfilling prophecies whereby the stereotype creates realities.

## The Rise of Youth Culture and the Fall of Adulthood

Young people have reacted in various ways to the "imperialistic" institutional activities that have structured the current political economy of youth. Some of their reactions have been attempts to fill the voids in meaning created by gaps in the institutional configurations and to resist indoctrination into, and subjugation by, these institutions. Clearly, not all of the youth segment, especially in the fifties and sixties, has passively accepted these changing conditions. Rather, a proportion of the young have exhibited a considerable degree of agency and resistance, largely in reaction to the imposition of the market economy on their present and future lives.

However, market forces have "learned" how to feed off this agency and resistance, appropriating and coopting them at each turn by marketing products as "hip" or "cool" in the various youth industries that emerged in the latter half of the twentieth century. Now many symbols of youth resistance to market forces are commodified and sold to younger cohorts so that they too can feel "hip" or "cool." Thomas Frank documents these marketing tricks in his recent book *The Conquest of Cool: Business Culture, Counterculture, and the Rise of Hip Consumerism* (1997a). Frank makes explicit reference to theories of mass society, noting how marketers have used the concepts of "cool" and "hip" to trick the mass consumer into believing that he or she could be set apart from the masses and meaningfully react against a standardizing and exploitative establishment. In a similar analysis, Lacayo (1994) argues that these marketing efforts have created the "hipness paradox," namely, that being "truly hip" is a status to which almost everyone aspires but cannot achieve by definition (because it is an awareness associated only with extreme social marginality), yet through shrewd marketing almost everyone is made to believe that they have achieved "it."

Marketers have developed a variety of strategies to make people think that consuming their product is hip, liberating, or growth-enhancing. The chief marketing strategy documented by Frank (1997b) is "liberation marketing," which presents ads critical of mindless middle-class consumers, who are depicted as dumb suburbanites, trapped workers with sadistic bosses, or executive automatons in gray uniforms. Liberation ads tacitly admit that business now rules the world but claim that its own products or services can liberate consumers from this oppression, if only momentarily (e.g., the advertising of shampoos that give women orgasms in public or soft drinks that enable impossible risk-taking adventures). Marketers have also nurtured new brand loyalties that provide models of existential rebellion, in which a product is used as an expression of resistance against, or escape from, the drudgeries of work and urban life. They have also worked to create brand identities, which help consumers assimilate a product into their own sense of identity (e.g., Apple computers are associated with a humanistic vision of the future, and Benetton with a libertarian vision, achievable by overthrowing communication conventions).

Frank argues that business culture is replacing civil society and that corporations are the dominant institutions of our time, replacing the nation-state. He refers to the United States as the "Republic of Business" run by a "corporocracy" that does not "demand order, conformity, gray clothes, and Muzak; it presents itself as an opponent to those very things." Moreover, he argues that the "defining fact of American life in the 1990s is its complete reorganization around the needs of corporations. The world of business, it seems, is becoming the world, period. The market is politics, the office is society, the brand is equivalent to human identity" (1997b, 44). He goes on to argue that "advertizing is taking over the cultural functions that used to be filled by the left. Dreaming of a better world is now the work of marketers. We used to have movements for change; now we have products" (47).

The marketing techniques of the early part of the twentieth century (fine-tuned in the 1920s) appealed to the mass consumer's desire to emulate the upper classes and the elites. With the entrenchment of mass society—and the public desire to escape this condition, however symbolically—marketers changed their strategy to appeal to a rejection of elitism and an embracing of antiestablishment, life-on-the-edge images. That strategy, of course, works best among the youth segment, and this segment has become a formidable consumer force. Ads now commonly portray the crudest, most bizarre and outlandish behaviors to appeal to the restless and rebellious spirit in young people and those adults who still feel that way.

More generally, mass culture has been delivered to the widest audiences through a "dumbing down": the lowest common denominator is targeted, namely, passive and uncritical consumers who prefer not to expend any mental energy during their leisure time. Marketing strategies now include multimedia penetrations of consumers' lives (products presented not only in explicit ads but also in movies, music videos, television programs, and magazine articles) and merchandising spinoffs that often have the consumer voluntarily advertising products (via names brands stamped on T-shirts or other products such as knapsacks and "Walkmans," now called "personal CD players"—perhaps the ultimate symbol of atomized mass society, in which separated beings are linked to a series of common sources, all a great profit).

Frank contends that the attempts to appropriate youth culture have been highly successful, stating that contemporary "youth culture is liberation marketing's native tongue" (1997b, 45). He makes note of the academic controversy in cultural studies regarding how much youth culture constitutes a resistance to these efforts at appropriation and expresses skepticism that "mass produced culture" is a site of rebellion (1997a, 17). In reference to such academic glorifications of mass culture, Frank argues that "glibly passing over . . . the culture of capitalism . . . seriously miscontextualizes American daily life" (19). The issues are not "hip versus square" or "conformity versus individualism" but the extent to which consumer culture has penetrated people's lives: "Consumer capitalism did not demand conformity or homogeneity; rather, it thrived on the doctrine of liberation and continual transgression" of norms of restraint and thrift, especially in terms of spending in search of pleasure (18).

In spite of such attempts to appropriate youth culture and co-opt the young into the capitalist cycle of consumption-production (i.e., the endeavor to make as much money as possible so that one can buy as much as possible), we can still speak of distinctive youth cultures that emerged in the latter part of the twentieth century, in which there are signs and degrees of resistance.[2] Two such general cultures can be identified: a "mainstream" youth culture (MYC) and a youth counterculture (YCC).

The MYC has emerged as a by-product of the activities of the institutions that have affected the transition to adulthood, especially secondary education and the identity industries of the market economy now dominated by corporate culture as described by Frank. The MYC is thus inextricably linked with "popular culture" to the extent that a segment of youth *conforms to* these institutional pressures and/or attempts to utilize these cultural resources in creative and personally agentic ways in formulating their identities. Owram (1996) speaks of the teenage culture that began in the 1950s but is now shared by people well into their twenties.

The YCC can be seen as a product of *resistance against* institutional forces experienced as oppressive; it represents an actively agentic alternative to them (hence, it is depicted on the right side in fig. 5.2, opposite MYC). YCCs in North America are often focused around a heavy or extreme involvement with drugs and music (Owram 1996), sometimes in a cultlike fashion with some unfortunate consequences (Arnett 1996). These forms of counterculture tend to be apolitical and hence not a threat to mainstream society or corporate interests. Nonetheless, the state periodically attempts to exert its authority over these countercultures, and corporate interests continually attempt to appropriate their symbols of rebellion (as discussed earlier). There is nothing currently organized in any youth countercultures that approximates the type of political resistance that emerged in the 1960s, but that could change.

The growth of the MYC in the early 1800s was mainly among the segment sent off to school by their parents, many of whom were benefiting from the affluence of early industrialization. It began with upper-middle- and upper-class males, then spread to females and has trickled down through the classes since (see, e.g., Mørch 1995). By the 1950s the MYC included middle-class males and females, stimulated by the segregation of the "teenager" in schools and the targeting of them by the early identity industries. During this same period we saw the emergence of distinct countercultures (germinating in the 1950s but especially prominent in the 1960s). By the late 1900s, both forms of youth culture had become options for youth of all social classes. Because of the co-optative nature of capital enterprises, however, it should be

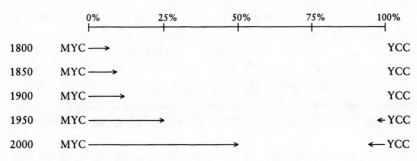

MYC = Mainstream Youth Culture
YCC = Youth Counterculture

*Fig. 5.2.* The History of Youthhood

noted that it is now sometimes difficult to distinguish the two—new forms of resistance are quickly commodified and sold to conformist youth.

## Mass Culture and Arrested Development

The institutionalized delay of adulthood undoubtedly has many positive features, such as giving people time to experiment with possible future identities, but those who would rather not, or cannot, take advantage of it find themselves having to "wait" anyway, and the wait often has negative consequences (cf. Petersen 1993). In fact, a pattern of enforced idleness or of reduced contribution to the community now characterizes youth, forcing many young people to live as dependents of their parents well into their twenties. This custom is increasingly taken as a normal and natural sequence of events in North America (Lerner 1995; Schultze et al. 1990) and in many European nations (Cavalli and Galland 1995).

Having a large proportion of the population kept in a state of partial or full dependency may seem like an entirely unintended consequence of social change. Indeed, it was not "planned," but it has proven to be quite advantageous to the businesses associated with the production of mass culture. The chief advantage lies in the fact that these businesses are given mass markets of identity-hungry consumers. Thus, on the one hand, the identity moratorium allows people to experiment with various identities and future selves, but on the other hand it leaves them open to various forms of identity manipulation, the very thing mass marketers are looking for.

Moreover, the identity moratorium has helped create a virtually powerless political group, with no one to speak positively and forcefully for it. The "time out" from adulthood also means a time out from political and economic participation in mainstream society. Together, these factors have contributed to the economic disfranchisement of youth.

When such effects are spelled out, we gain insight into how the concept of the identity moratorium taken from developmental psychology can be reframed in terms of the political economy of youth. It is not that the developmental perspective is wrong, but rather that it can overlook the "big picture" provided by the political-economic perspective.

The economic disfranchisement of youth can be seen in the fact that over the past thirty years there has been a steady and significant redistribution of wealth in North America (and most Western countries) based on age. For example, in the United States in the late 1960s, males aged sixteen to twenty-four made about 90% of what those over twenty-four years of age made. By the 1990s that percentage had steadily dropped to below 70. Moreover, whereas the overall drop in the earning power of young males has been about 25%, for African American youth it has been almost 50% and for Hispanic youth, about 30%. It should be noted here that the gender convergence of wages mentioned in chapter 1 has been a result not only of the rising wages of young female workers but also of the declining wages of young male workers (Allahar and Côté 1998). In a sense, then, had young males not been disfranchised to this extent, young females might have been empowered to a much greater extent.

While the youth segment has become economically marginalized, it has paradoxically become a major source of consumers, often at the expense of parents. Youth constitute a large market, estimated at almost three hundred billion dollars per year in the United States, one-third of which is their discretionary income and two-thirds of which comes from their parents (Palladino 1996). But that consumption is almost entirely geared to mass culture, or rather popular culture that has been disseminated via the various mass media. In the past, popular culture was shared by all in a community regardless of age, but popular culture is now fueled by leisure industries such as music, fashion, and cosmetics and targets those consumers who await the next craze or fad to follow. Young people undergoing the identity moratorium are particularly vulnerable to these influences because fads can give consumers a sense of identity, however illusory, fleeting, or partial (cf. Lunt and Livingstone 1992). Ewen and Ewen (1982) document a number of these techniques directed at the general population (not just the youth segment) in their book *Channels of Desire: Mass Images and the Shaping of American Consciousness*.

As figure 5.1 suggests, in accord with the ideology of youth as "vulnerable dependents," major institutions fell into line over the twentieth century to maintain these new boundaries: schools became part of normal development, endorsed by the state as guardians of the youth; market enterprises sprang up to give structure to the void in meaning that emerged and, at the same time, to take advantage of youth's vulnerabilities of identity; families increasingly had to provide their young with a period of relative leisure extending into what had hitherto been the transition to productive adulthood, subsidizing capital enterprises with room, board, and allowances for its cheapest labor and at the same time giving up real control of the transition to adulthood (becoming instead a safety net as the welfare state diminished); and from these influences youth cultures emerged, as young people themselves struggled to define this new phase of the life course. It is ironic that many young people who live for free with their parents, but who have reasonable jobs, have more discretionary income than do their parents (Mogelonsky 1996), who themselves are saddled with heavy debt loads from mortgages and credit cards. Most of this discretionary income, not surprisingly, is spent on the consumer items of popular culture.

As we enter the twenty-first century, these institutional patterns are well entrenched; they feed on one another, and they exhibit a variety of tensions that make the transition to adulthood precarious for a significant proportion of the population—it is a precariousness that ironically validates the storm-and-stress myth. Thus, stereotypes about the biological inferiority of the young are confirmed in many people's minds, but it is social circumstance that generates this self-fulfilling prophecy.

Although it may seem rather curious, one way to gauge how social change has affected the youth segment of society is to consult the marketing literature. When we do so, we find that not only is there tremendous attention directed at understanding this change, but also there is great interest in affecting that change. This stands to reason, given the vested interests of marketers: they need to be able to chart current consumption patterns because they make their wages by predicting and affecting future consumption patterns. The most accessible marketing journal is called *American Demographics: Consumer Trends for Business Leaders*; it is published monthly in magazine format with short, informative articles in which observations are firmly based on the most recent statistical analyses. A cursory review of the content of this journal reveals scores of articles about youth consumption patterns and a number about what the changing life course means to marketers. Within the past few years, articles with the following titles have appeared in *American Demographics*: "Marketing to Generation X" (Ritchie 1995), "Talking to Teens"[3] (Zollo 1995), "Getting inside Kids' Heads" (McGee 1997); "Marketing Street Culture: Bringing Hip-Hop Style to the Mainstream"[4] (Spiegler 1996); and "College Come-Ons"[5] (Speer 1998).

Two recent articles illustrate the depth of the analysis mass-marketing consultants employ in their attempts to stay on top of ways to penetrate the minds and the culture of the young. The first is titled "The Boomerang Age" and has the telling subtitle "Don't Assume 18-to-24-Year-Olds Are Adults." Its headnote proclaims, "The pre-adult life-stage is here to stay" (Farnsworth Riche 1990, 25). The author argues that "the path toward independent living is more twisted than ever, intertwined with increasing choices about education, work, and marriage. Because people are delaying marriage, they are living with their parents longer. They are delaying marriage because they're going to school. They're going to school because most well-paying job now require a college degree." In Farnsworth Riche's view, it does not "make sense to call someone an adult if they don't live independently." She goes on to observe that in the United States over "two-thirds of young people age 18 to 24 live with their parents or other relatives. Only 25 percent of young men live independently, and only 38 percent of young women do" (26). She also notes that there are many "false starts" in the attempt to live independently, with about 40 percent returning to live with their parents at least once. The "failure rate" of those attempting to forge on into adulthood by getting married is increasing among those in their early twenties—their divorce rate has risen to that of early-marrying teens.

This "marriage boomerang" seems to be accompanied by an "educational boomerang," with more young people taking longer to complete their education. Not only are more people postponing adulthood by enrolling in postsecondary programs, but they are also taking substantially longer to complete those programs; less than 10% complete a B.A. in the standard four-year period after high school. More and more are "stopping out" of their educational paths, either after high school or during college. Farnsworth Riche also identifies a "job boomerang," noting that it takes more time for young people to settle into the labor force, and when they do, they no longer find it easy to work their way up the ladder. Moreover, college graduates are increasingly likely to take "stopgap jobs" rather than career entry ones, thereby competing with their less-educated peers and further "lengthening their transition to full adulthood" (1990, 52). And once into one "career stream," young people are more likely than ever to have to change occupations.

Farnsworth Riche concludes from her analysis that these "trends suggest that the new pre-adult stage in the life cycle is here to stay. Businesses are already taking advantage of it" (1990, 52). But perhaps what is most telling is the way in which these trends are interpreted by analysts like Farnsworth Riche, a national editor of *American Demographics*. That is, she ends her article with a double-sided claim, on the one hand admonishing critics for raising the issue of this situation, and on the other hand apologizing for the system that has created the disarray (minimized by her as "boomeranging") in so many people's lives:

> Pop culture critics love to complain about the prolonged adolescence of today's young adults. They blame television, apathetic parents, and "consumerism, narcissism, and the instant gratification of desire," as *Newsweek* put it. These critics ask when young adults will learn to make commitments. They will learn later. When facing so many choices, the best decision may be no decision—at least for a while. Boomeranging is a rational response to changes in our society and economy. It's here to stay. (52–53)

In essence, Farnsworth Riche is recommending passive, default, and diffused forms of identity formation (discussed in chapter 4) as an adaptive response to the transition to adulthood. As we saw, although this may be an increasingly common response, we are hard pressed to see how it is one to be recommended; in fact, it seems irresponsible for adults, who are ostensibly the guardians of youth, to recommend it. Indeed, this type of position simply feeds into the worst of what we have been examining by recommending that young people make more decisions associated with default individualization than with developmental individualization. But of course, the more people there are who take paths of least effort and least resistance, the better things are for those marketers and businesses who make their living by manipulating people's lives and the decisions they make.

The second article from *American Demographics*, titled "The Rocky Road to Adulthood" (Mogelonsky 1996), also takes up the matter of young people living with their parents and effectively delaying adulthood. What is of great interest, again, is how that trend is analyzed (this author is a contributing editor). Noting the later age of first marriage in the United States (24.5 for women and 26.7 for men, up three to four years from 1970) and of having first children (four years later than in 1970), Mogelonsky believes that "a new phase of life between dependent childhood and independent adulthood" is being created (32), and she speculates that many people in recent cohorts may never "grow up" according to conventional standards. Citing experts in the field, Mogelonsky discusses "planners" versus "strugglers," among those attempting to find their way along the "winding path" to adulthood. So far, so good. This author's analysis corresponds to everything we have examined thus far. Unfortunately, once again we are left with a Pollyannaish conclusion:

> As more and more young adults return to the nest as a deliberate step on the path toward their future, the phenomenon is losing its stigma as a last resort of the insecure and irresponsible. What looks on the surface like a denial of adulthood is taking shape as a bridge to true maturity. Maybe the kids are more grown up than we thought. (56)

I wish I could share Marcia Mogelonsky's optimism, but in light of what I have seen, I cannot; at least I cannot apply such a generalization to all of those struggling to find their way through the currently disjunctive period of youth.

## Using the Past to Predict the Future: The Rise of Youthhood and New Trajectories

### Youthhood as a Destination

From the preceding analysis it is clear that institutions other than family and religion have come to direct the development of the young.

Both the family and religion are "losing" to other institutions in the amount that they can guide and structure youth. Of the other institutions, the biggest winner seems to be the capitalist marketplace, which has penetrated the lives of the youth segment mainly through the guise of popular culture. Increasingly, the market economy provides young people with ersatz forms of identity through fashion, music, electronics, and leisure services. The educational system has also benefited, by selling identities based on credentials. At the same time the state (and local community adult leaders) is abdicating its responsibilities toward the young, leaving the task of welcoming the young into adulthood up to education; educational systems in turn seem at best rudderless and self-interested and at worst (as in some high schools) the equivalent of violence- and hate-breeding prisons.

We can also witness how the new life stage that can be called "youthhood" (Mørch 1995) is emerging, involving half of the American youth population, and soon to do so in Canada and European countries (a common government target is to get 50% of the youth into colleges and universities). Thus, the institutionalized identity moratorium—an imposed delay of adulthood—appears to be emerging as a permanent feature of the life course, segregating more and more of the young, including those well into their twenties, from adult society and putting them "on hold" (Côté and Allahar 1996). At the same time, the corporate interests that have created a popular culture around the concepts of cool or hip may play a large role in locking many people into this new stage of youthhood. Most vulnerable is that segment of youth that heavily invests its identity in these false notions of resistance as part of a rejection of mainstream identities, thereby remaining on the periphery of society throughout their formative years. Delaying the acquisition of life- and human-capital skills until the twenties can prove to be a liability because habits become rigidly set, and the critical period for the acquisition of certain skills (e.g., music, language) may have passed. Those who delay the transition for too long may find the final stage of the passage to adulthood more difficult in that they will have to relinquish their youth culture identity ties. At best, such individuals may enter a form of quasi-adulthood.

Based on these trends, what does the future hold? To some extent that depends on how the distribution of wealth shifts over the next few decades, but all indications point toward continuing polarization.

There are distinct signs that the middle class is in decline (see, e.g., Myles, Picot, and Wannell 1988; Rifkin 1995), and the state fiscal panics of the 1990s resulted in a withdrawal of the state from the institutions built at midcentury that created much of the professional middle class (e.g., health care, education). That signals a decline in the economic prospects of successive cohorts; it has already begun with the past few cohorts, as they fail to reach the standard of living of their parents' cohort. Thus, we may see a growing underclass based on generational replacement, whereby the economic prospects of upcoming cohorts continue to decline, leading to an increasingly age-based poverty structure—already under way. In both the United States and Canada, the poverty rate among the youth segment has doubled in the last couple of decades (Côté and Allahar 1996).

Thus, if we make projections into the twenty-first century based on the trends over the last two centuries, several dramatic changes are suggested, as illustrated in figure 5.3. First, youth as a mainstream institution (MYC) will likely become as institutionalized as childhood and adulthood, constituting the new life stage of youthhood. Its moratorium characteristics will become more entrenched and prolonged with each successive cohort, to the point where a sizable proportion of the population may never enter adulthood as we have known it. For many, remaining in youthhood will not be a "choice" so much as an exclusion based on their lack of "identity capital," a resource that is becoming increasingly important in order for a young person to be accepted by adult communities (see chapter 6). Hence, we may see the end of adulthood as we know it, at least for much of the population, especially regarding qualities like independence, responsibility, and commitment (cf. Arnett and Taber 1994).

This state of affairs will be viewed as normal and inevitable, and few will question why such a large portion of the population enters a terminal stage of youthhood and is locked out of adulthood. Moreover, many of those who remain locked into youthhood will find it a relatively pleasant experience because they will be encouraged to consume to their capacity, but little will be required of them in terms of mental effort expended on their productive capacities. This group will constitute a sort of "working class" (equivalent to Huxley's Gammas or Deltas) that performs services and does contract work for the "techno-class," the highly educated and competent 20% of the workforce that steers or controls the society via high technology (Rifkin 1995).

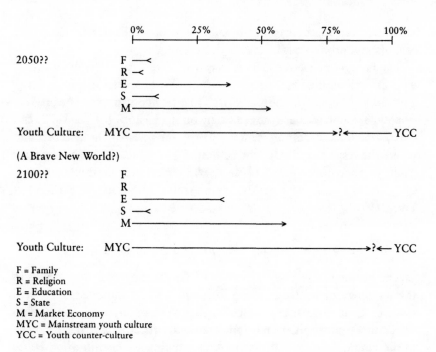

F = Family
R = Religion
E = Education
S = State
M = Market Economy
MYC = Mainstream youth culture
YCC = Youth counter-culture

*Fig. 5.3.* The Future of Youthhood

Second, because this is a capitalist society, a stratified system will be prominent. A significant segment of "youth" will function as marginal workers—perhaps an underclass, or at best a "servo-class" (equivalent to Huxley's Deltas or Epsilons). We may well see a return to the class system of the nineteenth century, with its extreme wealth polarization. If so, this polarized class system will be reintroduced through the youth segment and will become more extreme with each cohort. Perhaps eventually class placement will be fully determined early in life, as Huxley predicted.

Third, struggles will ensue in which a YCC attempts to resist, but it will likely diminish in influence relative to MYCs as more and more people are enticed to follow the pleasurable enticements provided by capitalist enterprises in the feel-good society that they produce. Rather than any organized attempt to rebel, and rather than constituting any real threat to the capitalist system, much of this resistance will be at the interpersonal level, as in youth-on-youth conflict, tension, and violence. The beginnings of such conflict in the late twentieth century were obvious, even to the casual observer of youth behavior in secondary schools and urban gangs.

The most negative scenario is that by 2100, if these trends continue, we may well witness Huxley's Brave New World several centuries early: a world in which all activity is geared to either consumption or production; where activities are judged solely on the basis of the pleasure principle, which is so complementary to the interests of the market; and where the responsibility for the community and subsequent generations is left to controllers—who I believe will most likely be the "captains" of "global capital" now making nation-states into nominal entities (cf. Ewen 1976).

## Cultural Variation in the Transition to Adulthood

The prolongation of youth is one of the most agreed-upon trends in the sociology of youth. Not too long ago, some sociologists contested this trend, claiming that their colleagues were simply displaying "typical adult" (uninformed and nonempathetic) reactions to the behavior of the young. In originally attempting to publish *Generation on Hold: Coming of Age in the Late Twentieth Century*, Anton Allahar and I met with considerable resistance of this sort from our colleagues. Those days appear to be over, both among social scientists and among the general public. The contested area now is subgroup variations among youth, especially between males and females and among various countries (see Davis 1990 and Tanner 1996 for the stances that can be taken toward youth behaviors).

A degree of consensus has been reached among life-course experts concerning how to view changes in the life cycle affecting both youth and adults. For example, there is little resistance to the ideas central to this book that the life course has undergone destructuring and individualization. Indeed, many of the researchers have gone on to look at different degrees of these processes across nations, between genders and social classes, and among races and ethnic groups (see, e.g., Ashton and Lowe 1991). It is not that I think these differences of degree are unimportant and do not affect life chances in significant ways. But for the task at hand—understanding the changing nature of adulthood at its most general levels—these *differences of degree* should not be confused with *differences of kind*. In other words, both youth and adults in all Western nations, whether male or female, white or nonwhite, seem to have been affected to some degree by the dual processes of cultural destructuring and individualization. Summing up the results of numerous recent studies carried out in western and southern Europe, Lynne Chisholm (1995) writes:

> On the basis of wide-ranging empirical evidence it can be argued that the contemporary youth phase extends further into the social life course than in the past, and that the social boundaries between life course phases are more fluid than they used to be. Quite simply, the trends summarized by the terms extensions, destandardization, fragmentation and individualization of the life course are not in dispute, although their intensity varies between societies and social groups. (127)

I leave it to others to hash out the details of these differences of degree regarding the impact of destructuring and individualization. Those differences affect mostly the timing of different life transitions or the sequencing in the transitions associated with leaving school, entering the labor force, establishing an independent residence, marrying, and becoming a parent. For example, Galland (1995) has observed three models of the prolongation of youth in Europe:

> a Mediterranean model, whereby family life is extended; a "Northern" and French model, which may be characterized as an extension of living away from home, since leaving home is not immediately followed by starting a new family; and a British model denoted by early entry into the job market and an extended phase of living with a partner but without children. (6)

In another study comparing the United States with Great Britain, the primary difference reported was that in Great Britain young people leave school and the parental home and enter the labor force earlier than in the United States, yet they marry later. Moreover, the timing of the major transition events are more spread out, but they follow a more common sequence in the United Kingdom than in the United States (Kerckhoff 1990). In yet another study of social class and gender differences in Great Britain, Gill Jones and Claire Wallace (1992) report that "the working-class leave full-time education, start work, marry or cohabit and have children before the middle-class. Women marry or cohabit and have children before men, and in consequence heterosexual partnerships tend to contain male partners who are on average two years older than females. . . . men have longer in the labour force than women, before forming partnerships" (100–101).

I could go on citing the results of numerous studies of such differences in timing and sequence, but I believe the point has been made that the need is to attend to the higher-order changes affecting the life course if we are to understand the bigger picture of what is happening to young people in each country around the world.

## Youthhood, Adulthood, and Happiness

When we examine Huxley's dystopia in light of recent social, economic, and political changes, we can identify alarming similarities with contemporary Western societies. It appears that a sizable portion of the adult population has already been affected by these trends and that these trends have escalated with each successive cohort over the course of the twentieth century. We are now at the point where popular culture, a contemporary analog of Huxley's Brave New World, is able to penetrate the lives of many young people and at earlier and earlier ages.

When viewed from a very general perspective, the adult segment of the population can be identified as having shirked its responsibility to the youth segment: adults have not looked after the well-being of the youth and ensured that they receive benign guidance into adulthood. However, "adulthood" is experiencing its own set of pressures, leaving a void in the life course that is being taken up by what can be called "youthhood." With adulthood in relative disarray and youthhood targeted for exploitation, we can expect numerous trends and events that shock people's sensibilities. The least of these will be the rise of unconventional adulthoods, or perhaps more properly, youthhoods. We are clearly in an era in which the following trends are either entrenched or escalating: declining marriage and fertility rates; open promiscuity with increasing sexualization among younger and younger people; widespread problems with impulse control, along with a sense of entitlement regarding impulse gratification; an increasing number of people for whom infantilization is normal and who take little or no responsibility for their actions. In effect, the overall adult community has abdicated responsibility for the control of culture and cultural reproduction and has relinquished that oversight to a small group of highly self-interested half-adults who rule more and more segments of society in the name of "progress."

Given these circumstances, there should be little wonder why violence among the youth segment has increased. Between the mid-1980s and the mid-1990s, the rate of violence doubled for males and quadrupled for females (Artz 1998). The manufacture of dissent (Côté and Allahar 1996) intensified in high schools where various competing cliques emerged as local manifestations or variants of the mainstream youth cultures most affected by popular culture (e.g., sports and music cults). With these developments, the ingredients were supplied for the types of revenge mass murders that became more common in the late 1990s.

Behind this form of dissent is, first, the segregation and exclusion of young people from adult society, which effectively marginalizes them and severely reduces their participation in adult activities. Second in importance is the placement of youth in mass educational systems. The large and anonymous nature of these schools encourages the formation of a variety of distinct and competing peer cultures and subcultures (they could be called peer cults), each with its own forms of segregation and exclusion (often carried out through teasing and various forms of harassment of individuals and cliques). Third is the saturation of this segment of the population with various forms of mediated violence. The violence on television, in movies, and in video games not only desensitizes viewers but places the consequences of such behavior in an unreal "cartoon" context. The media provide role models and actual training (in the case of point-and-shoot video games), but they do so in a context where no real persons are actually hurt. It comes as a shock to these young people when they see that the real-world consequences are permanent and irreversible. Indeed, so saturated are many young people with various media cultures that in some recent high school mass-murder rampages, the first phone calls from besieged students to outside "authorities" were to news media like CNN, not the local police. Traditional authorities apparently are exercising little in the way of guidance in these respects. Patricia Chisholm makes a similar argument in reference to the spate of mass murders in high schools:

> Parents, teachers and other counsellors may . . . share some of the blame. Too often . . . children have virtually no adult guidance when it comes to confronting the underside of mass culture. Adults frequently shy away from investigating teenage subgroups, hoping that a fascination with death or anarchy or Hitler . . . is merely a "phase." At the same time, the traditional buffers of extended family, religion and community have atrophied, forcing many kids to rely on each other for support. Add

firearms to this unsavory brew and the explosive results start to look almost predictable. (1999, 22)

Of course, not all young people are adversely or similarly affected by these influences. But for the proportion of the youth population with a weak sense of ego identity (with its distortion in time perspective) and an active fantasy life, this set of ingredients provides what is needed for them to seek—and know how to take—revenge for perceived injustices. For those who have spent their short lives immersed in "mediated" cultures, outrageous acts can bring them the promise of momentary fame, however perverse that short-lived identity might be.

# PART III

# Coming to Grips with
# Late Modernity
*New Forms of Maturity and Identity*

# 6

## Learning to Love an Indefinite Future?

### What Societies of the Future Have to Offer

Five hundred years of capitalism have irrevocably altered the course of human history. Not only have Western cultures been transformed, but also the influence of capitalism is now global in proportion. As I have tried to emphasize—anticipating critics who will try to dismiss some of my arguments regarding capitalism—there have most certainly been tremendous benefits associated with the history of capitalism. But the world is complex, and one cannot take it all in with a one-sided view that looks only at those benefits and is afraid to consider the possibility that capitalism has some deleterious effects. Even if we set aside issues of the morality of capitalism (such as the inevitability of inequality in capitalist societies), we still confront the double-edged nature of both the impressive technological progress made possible by capitalism and the initiative it rewards.

For example, by making life so easy for so many people, technology can remove the challenges that stimulate people's intellectual and emotional growth. Although much of high technology is challenging in these ways, only a small percentage of the population actually interacts with technology in a way that requires high levels of mastery. Those who do are usually the *producers* and maintainers of high-tech systems, such as computer hardware and software systems. For most people, technologies are *consumed* in ways that eliminate the need to think at complex levels or to master anything more than a rudimentary or repetitive set of nongeneralizable skills. Technologies are consumed for pleasure, or at least to make performing essential labor more pleasant, and one way they have been marketed is by claiming that the technology will reduce the effort people have to put into their day-to-day lives. Hence, certain high technologies have contributed to an increased passivity among the population, as we saw in chapter 2. Moreover, they have made life *too easy* in some respects. When things get too easy, or when too many rewards are associated with an activity, there can be a loss of meaning and value.

At the same time that the need for active mastery has been reduced in many spheres of activity, these technologies have made possible new forms of control of people's consciousness. It is now possible to penetrate people's lives—and minds—in ways unprecedented in human history. Those who wish to control the population for political or economic reasons have a variety of means available to them, from the television that occupies center stage in people's homes to the computers that sit on their office desks or monitor (and broker) their spending habits from far-away corporate headquarters. Curiously, these pervasive and intrusive influences receive little attention compared to other matters, such as the sex lives of politicians. And when reservations about them are expressed, experts come out of the woodwork to deny that they have a demonstrably negative effect (but these experts are often from think tanks paid by vested interests). Common sense is often eschewed as part of the widespread fear, in the United States at least, of criticizing the fundamentals of the economic system that is clearly the most influential factor in Western societies today (cf. Caldicott 1992). Critics of capitalism experience tremendous rebuke in many circles; they can be marginalized, ostracized, and persecuted. The lack of leadership, or even dialogue, on the liabilities of capitalism is obvious in many countries. In particular, one need only monitor the news and political-analysis programming on television to see how shallow and evasive the discussion is of issues related to this matter. There is simply too much power at stake related to corporate capitalism for most analysts to feel that they can speak up; they fear losing their jobs.

What does all this mean for adulthood? Most adults face a paradoxical situation in which the most obvious and most pervasive force affecting them—the capitalist economy and its myriad industries—cannot be discussed in an "adult" manner. Like children afraid of being scolded for being impertinent, adults in the United States (and other similar countries) face reprisal for identifying and criticizing the reality they face. Capitalism is in this way much like a religious orthodoxy; those who appear heretical can face inquisitional reactions, as in the McCarthy era. Consequently, the vast majority of American adults do not speak up on such matters; instead, they go along with the shallow and scapegoating explanations that tend to blame the victims of inequality for their own plight (as occurs in the debates over welfare, education, and health care). This paradox adds to the complexity of contemporary adulthood. When it is coupled with the positive rewards for not speaking out and the ease with which people can passively go along for the "technological ride," the outcome is that the citizens of many countries appear unprepared to move into the future in a thoughtful and morally responsible manner.

So what do societies of the future have to offer? More of the same, as far as I can tell, except that corporations will use their growing economic and political power to continue to refine the ways they manipulate people's (mass) behavior and consciousness, and more and more of the population will be enticed into passive stances that reflect forms of default individualization. In my estimation, the path we are taking is directly toward the type of world Huxley warned us about.

## The Normality of Narcissism

The normalization of narcissism is perhaps one of the most telling signs that dramatic changes have occurred in Western societies. It is also potentially one of the most ominous signs regarding the future of Western societies. As we saw in chapter 3, Lasch brought the notion of cultural narcissism to public attention, but since then others have followed up on his ideas. Writing in 1981, Maxine Schnall referred to narcissism as a "generational virus." In her book entitled *Limits: A Search for New Values,* she argues that many people have discovered "hedonism without happiness" when they were really looking for, but unwilling to give, "unconditional love." She sees the problem of narcissistic entitlement as a problem that has especially infected the post–World War II cohorts, but it can be found among people of all ages. She describes her counseling experience with people thus afflicted as follows:

> We can call any behavior normal if enough people do it, but if it fails to bring them happiness over the long run, they will begin casting about for a new answer. And that is precisely what great numbers of people, from their twenties to their sixties, are doing today. The hundreds of people who come through the doors of my counseling agency year after year are beginning to say, in one way or another, the same thing. They are disillusioned with narcissistic pleasure-seeking, fragmented relationships. They

have found this extreme to be no less frustrating in its own way than the opposite extreme of dutifully fulfilling socially established role requirements in the all-consuming, locked-in relationships that the nuclear family represented thirty years ago. (1981, 19)

Schnall goes on to connect these problems with the rise of Riesman's other-directed person. She notes that in contrast to the inner-directed person, the other-directed person is easily made unhappy, because constantly comparing oneself with others will inevitably lead to disappointment, especially if one's only internal reference point is a narcissistic personality organization rooted in infancy. Schnall has found in her counseling practice that the narcissistically driven, other-directed person looks to external sources of validation, primarily in "experiences." But the obsessive nature of this search for validating experiences turns potentially pleasurable experiences into *work*. Hence, the other-directed person *works* for validation through experiences that often do not bring the fulfillment one would expect. Schnall concludes that

> other-directed people have so little sense of self that they need experience to prove they exist. The Cartesian syllogism "I think, therefore I am" becomes "I *feel* therefore I am." But in today's era of superconsumerism, when the concept of "fun morality" has been applied to sex and has turned into work, the cultural narcissist withdraws from even that proof of . . . existence. So what is left? (1981, 21)

Schnall's solution to the problem the contemporary adult faces is to adopt a position that incorporates elements of both inner-directedness and other-directedness. She argues that "positive freedom is possible only for the person who is neither exclusively inner-directed nor exclusively other-directed but a combination of the two—the self-steerer, if you will, whose compass is a set of *freely chosen* internal personal standards shaped by both parents and peers. The magnetic north is the individual's own particular sense of *purpose*" (1981, 23). Schnall goes on to claim that "we can begin to transform ourselves from a *selfish* culture, characterized by avaricious distrust of the self and others, into a *self-directed* culture, one in which, by virtue of depending on our own resources and finding satisfaction in them, we can find even greater fulfilment by sharing our resources with others and concerning ourselves with the common good" (305).

I believe there is merit in Schnall's recommendation for people to be more self-directed in a "sea of temptations," but I think there is more to this, as I indicate in a subsequent section, where I discuss "identity capital." Before moving on, however, let us examine the notion that narcissism is not only a normal malady of late modern society but can actually be "adaptive."

Wink and Donahue (1995) recently reported findings in the *Journal of Adult Development* that support Lasch's contention that narcissism is an asset for success in contemporary society. They traced a sample of about one hundred women from 1958, when they were seniors in college. The women were given questionnaires measuring their levels of narcissism at ages twenty-one, forty-three, and fifty-two. Two forms of narcissism were studied: covert narcissism (narcissism coupled with an introverted personality) and overt narcissism (narcissism coupled with an extroverted personality).[1] They found considerable stability in the degree of narcissistic elements in the personalities of these women over their life courses and concluded the following about the impact of narcissism on these women's lives:

> In the case of covert narcissism, insight and a differentiated view of the inner self were accompanied by negative affect directed at self and others. In the case of overt narcissism, assertiveness and the capacity for creative achievement at work were accompanied by interpersonal conflict and problems in accepting limits. In its juxtaposition of diverse, conflicted, and often unintegrated selves, narcissism may be truly a construct for our times. (84)

What they found, in other words, was that introverted narcissists deteriorated with age in their personal lives and did not experience successes or achievements as a result of their narcissism. It was the extroverted narcissists who were better adjusted and more successful in their work environments, but they paid a price in their personal lives. Wink and Donahue summarize their findings regarding the lives of the overt narcissists as follows:

> We anticipated that . . . overt narcissism should lead to an involvement in high-status occupational careers and found evidence for this at both ages 43 and 52. By their early 40s, high scorers on overt narcissism tended to have launched, and continued to adhere to, upwardly mobile careers and, in the early 50s, their jobs tended to be rated as high in status and occupational creativity. . . . [However, high] scorers on overt narcissism proved to be less successful in their family relations than in their careers. (83)

Wink and Donahue speculate that overt narcissism might have been particularly useful for women of that generation, given their minority status in high-prestige occupations. We do not know from their sample whether overt narcissism was as functional for men of that generation. However, their quantitative analysis is supported by anecdotal evidence provided in a recent book written by the career management expert Barbara Moses. In *Career Intelligence: Mastering the New Work and Personal Realities* (1997), Moses bases her advice on years of experience as a human resources consultant. In reading the real-life stories she relates, it seems that the conditions Lasch and Schnall described in the 1970s became more severe in the 1990s. These stories also support the possibility that success in the corporate world is associated with a high degree of overt narcissism.

Moses lists four conditions associated with the challenges of the new lean and mean workplace of the 1990s: loss of predictability, loss of security/enforced self-reliance, the "commodification" of self, and a loss of connection (1997, 29–35). Of most interest here is the commodification of self. She finds that this is key to getting and retaining jobs, as it has been for some time. In times of contract work, downsizing, and poor job security, however, it can be a continuous activity, including "endlessly gathering testimonials, documenting . . . achievements, and making proposals for new pieces of work." Only freelancers and independent contractors did this in the past. In fact, Moses argues that some people spend as much time "selling themselves" as they do on their current work assignments: "In today's workplace, workers have to constantly resell/market themselves—to constantly manage other people's impressions of how well they are performing" (33). The following story that Moses relates illustrates how important it is to sell oneself *and* be extroverted about it:

> As one senior manager told us: "There were two high-level professionals on my project team. The assignment was coming to an end, and both faced an uncertain future. One of them, Terry, started to actively market his services through proposals and offers to provide support to other senior managers. The other, John, did nothing to let people know what he was capable of offering. He thought that it was 'unseemly' for a professional of his standing to have to do that, sell himself so aggressively. He told me, 'people know I'm good at what I do.' And he was very good—better than Terry, actually. But not enough people knew it. And where Terry was able to hook up with another project team, John was let go." (33–34)

In this example we catch a glimpse of the survival-of-the-fittest business world of late modernity, where the "fittest" is not necessarily the most competent (as Lasch argued). Instead, the one who survives is the one who does the best job of impression management and self-commodification. Increasingly, it appears that overt narcissism is not merely an asset in the workplace—it actually appears to be a requirement in some settings. As we have seen, though, other conditions have changed, placing new demands and constraints on contemporary adults.

The reason I revisit the issue of narcissism as a normal and/or adaptive aspect of late modern character is to help set the present in relief against the past. The narcissistic character trait was in the past actively opposed in Western Christian culture, as we see when we review the "seven deadly sins." And, as we saw in chapter 1, until quite recently adults were expected to be duty-bound, not self-absorbed. This change is perhaps one of the most significant for projecting where we are going in the future, for the loss of a sense of adult duty and responsibility (with nothing to replace it) threatens to upset the very generational continuity that will determine how well future generations are provided for. If the adult community is now dominated by narcissists, and its leaders' narcissism is their greatest asset, the prognosis for the well-being of future generations is indeed in question. We now focus for the last time on the issue of how to characterize contemporary adulthood.

## A Working Typology of Brave New Adults

Throughout this book we have reviewed a variety of attempts to understand the changing nature of adulthood in a changing world. Although observers have used different terminologies and have taken different approaches, and although they have targeted different periods, they have tended to identify many of the same characteristics and problems attendant on contemporary adulthood. This concurrence of analyses can be taken as one form of evidence for validity, namely, that a consensus exists about the "existence" of something. I will briefly review this consensus about what individuals increasingly experience as adults and what characterizes the culture in which they now function. We can then move to a more abstract level of analysis and develop a synthesis in the form of more general categories that help us make sense of the variations in the trends we have observed.

It appears that the most debilitating psychological problem that contemporary adults face involves difficulties in experiencing a sense of core (ego) identity. Developmental psychologists now consider this a "normative" or "normal" problem of adolescence (i.e., most people routinely experience it). As we have seen, some postmodernists believe that this is a "healthy" state that adults should embrace. Those who hold that view are silent about the possibility that they are celebrating chronic debilitating problems that psychiatrists refer to as personality disorders. James Glass (1993) is particularly upset with the glorification of these conditions by some postmodernists. After discussing the multiple personality disorder in general and a particular case of it, Glass concludes:

> Postmodernism's dalliance with disconnection and chaos may either be trivial, just plain false, or more likely, dangerously irresponsible. To suggest that persons live as if they had no connections, no histories, or core selves, is to literally throw the self into a psychologically contingent world. . . . The postmodern theory of multiplicity . . . is an extreme rejection of boundary, stability, historicity, and any concept of a cohesive self. To live the life (the facts) of multiple selfhood is to not know where one self begins and others end. It is to be lost, without any sense of historical continuity to one's being. I would submit this kind of "freedom" is not liberation, but enslavement to a contingent world, a frightening internal and external set of perceptions that have the power to impose serious, if not deadly, emotional fragmentation and psychological dislocation. (276)

With this quotation, I believe I have said enough in this book to make a case that the postmodern position regarding the nature of the changes affecting Western societies is seriously flawed, if not reckless.

In addition to narcissism and problems of identity, it also appears that people are increasingly other-directed, especially during the period of youth when their sense of self-definition is vulnerable. This means that they can be acutely sensitive to the opinions of others and are therefore more easily shaped and controlled through psychological threats and anxieties. Most humans no longer experience continual threats to their physical survival as they have throughout most of human history; instead, their psychological well-being is vulnerable to verbal slights and nonverbal community social sanction. Consequently, threats to their psychological well-being are often mistaken as threats to their survival, probably because their sense of identity is involved.

In these respects many adults are now precariously positioned in terms of day-to-day identity management with others and are deathly afraid of being singled out as "offensive," "different," or somehow out of step. For to attract such censure can bring the overt wrath of the empowered, especially the newly empowered half-adult who is as happy squabbling as being courteous and respectful. Even though most of the sanctions associated with other-directedness cannot "hurt" anyone physically, they can do psychological or even financial harm. These sanctions include social humiliation and isolation on the basis of rumor and gossip, as well as having one's career disrupted or terminated. Of course, there is little defense in the court of public opinion, so many people are horror-struck at the prospect of being targeted by a "rumor mill." Teenagers are especially sensitive in relation to their peer group, but the fear also increasingly affects workers in relation to their (half-adult) colleagues and parents in relation to their immediate community—and increasingly in relation to their "empowered" children. In the "sibling house," what once applied to children's peer groups now applies more and more to adult society.

As Bly argues, the sibling society gives people the permission to be narcissists, to remain as half-adults, and to engage in complex forms of sibling rivalry wherein they demand what they feel they are entitled to from an "authority" they have learned to hate (their actual father, some imagined patriarch who is long gone, the government, the "establishment," "men," or what have you).

When we combine these ingredients with the increasingly blurred line between youth and adulthood and the new requirements of a psychological adulthood, we can see why many people are confused about what they should do to help themselves mature or to chart their lives on a stable, satisfying course. As a consequence of these developments, we can also understand why an increasing number of people no longer base their identity management on an inner core they have learned to appreciate and develop (e.g., on an intellect derived from deep thought about knowledge, a repertoire of talents and skills, a rich interior life based on an appreciation of the arts and literature, and so forth). We can also see why an increasing number turn to hedonism as a default response (it takes little skill or discipline to be a pleasure-seeker). And it is understandable why more and more people are turning to others for leadership and direction so that they can "identity shop" (Schnall 1981, 107) among offerings of fashion, New Age spirituality, self-help courses, and the like.

In short, a case can be made that an increasing number of people are arriving at the antithesis of "traditional adulthood" as their "needs and wants" expand and their "obligations and attachments" contract. Underlying this situation is a decline in the number of people with a stable sense of inner identity and an increase in the number who are confused, angry, and selfish half-adults. But it is obviously more complex than this simple (but heuristic) dichotomy of responses. In fact, a more complex synthesis of these late modern tendencies can be offered in a typology that might help us understand in a parsimonious manner a variety of Brave New Adults. The typology that I offer should also help us to understand who the adults of tomorrow will be. My hope is that it will be useful in generating *adult* discussions about how we can all cope with the present and plan for the future.

This analysis places in context the types of adaptation people make in societies with varying degrees of structure and varying opportunities to individualize in ways that I have described. Thus, it is designed to help us understand the adaptations people seem to be making to decoupled life courses in a destructuring society driven by factors (especially consumer-corporate interests) that have heightened the process of individualization.

I propose that we think in terms of four categories of adults: traditional, inner-directed modern, other-directed modern, and unconventional.[2] The four categories are illustrated as a product of the cross-tabulation of the dimensions of community structure and individualization in table 6.1.[3] The result of this cross-tabulation is referred to here as the "structure-agency" template. Note that for the sake of simplicity there is not a distinction between default and developmental forms of individualization, as I have made earlier. Instead, the more generic notion of individualization is employed (see, e.g., Beck 1992; Furlong and Cartmel 1997).

The traditional adult appears to be the dying breed of late modern society. These individuals have been socialized during childhood into remnants of a traditional cultural group, especially one of the ethnic groups that has insulated itself from mainstream Western influences. In Mead's model, these adults maintain some sort of respect for intergen-

TABLE 6.1
*The Structure-Agency Template*

| Community Structure | Individualization | |
| | High | Low |
| --- | --- | --- |
| High | Inner-directed modern | Traditional |
| Low | Other-directed modern | Unconventional |

erational obligations (for the past and the future), preserving a three-generation familial link if they can. In Riesman's model, they tend to be largely tradition-directed. In terms of the structure-agency template, these individuals fall into the high community structure/low individualization sector. Thus, sociologically they favor more collectivist forms of life-course development within a more highly structured community. They attempt to follow the coupled life-course trajectory of their ancestral culture as modeled by their parents, except when externally disturbed (e.g., by a death). For Bly, these people are more than half-adults; for Lasch they would exhibit low levels of narcissism; for Gergen, they would be remnants of a previous "romantic" era in which there was a belief in an inner core identity.

Both types of modernist adults adhere to life courses dictated by higher levels of individualization. The key difference is the extent to which they anchor their individualization within normative structural arrangements. Because of the higher level of individualization, both types reject collectivist aspects of their cultural heritage or "parental group" for various reasons (emotional, ethical, etc.). For those who have no sense of an ethnic or cultural past, there is nothing to reject, so other elements may be the object of rejection: social-class lifestyle, religion, connections with the "establishment," and the like. People may do this wholly or in part, but they then need to seek out new models of adulthood to follow as well as new communities within which to find validation for their chosen lifestyles.

The inner-directed modern adult maintains a type of "gyroscope" adopted from his or her parents, as Riesman suggested, but lives without a close intergenerational linkage (in Mead's terms). The break in the intergenerational linkage is partly a result of this adult's career-making and the identity construction required by geographical mobility and partly because of the emotional detachment associated with rejection of elements of the culture represented by his or her parents.

Inner-directed modern adults follow a loosely coupled life-course trajectory as modeled by their parents, but they are willing to alter it in accord with the "realities" and exigencies confronting them, making sacrifices to suit their careers or constructed identities. Although these adults may exhibit some degree of overt narcissism, they take certain adult responsibilities seriously (therefore are less likely to be half-adults). And they have a relatively strong sense of an inner core identity, which gives them the strength to follow a self-chosen path and cope with the stresses of late modern society. This type of adult appears to be decreasing in number.

The other-directed modern adult is similar to the inner-directed except for the "radar" orientation Riesman discussed and the consequent erratic behavior patterns and life-course trajectories that might ensue from this adult's attempt to stay in tune with ongoing trends, fads, and the like associated with mass culture. Other-directed modern adults are also more likely to adopt many of the symbols of mass culture as their own, substituting its illusions for their reality. They are more likely to have a quasi-family comprising peers—to which their primary loyalty is devoted—than a sense of obligation to their family of origin or their ancestors. They are also less likely to have a stable family of orientation, because they experiment with different lifestyle options, and many of these experiments fail. Their life courses are considerably decoupled in relation to the traditional adult, and they would likely be considered half-adults by Bly. For them, the line between youth and adulthood may be either irrelevant or invisible, so they may remain in a period of youthhood throughout their lives, unless something jogs them out of it. Lasch would see a high degree of narcissism in their behavior, and Gergen would see them as exhibiting signs of some stage in the development of the postmodern self (especially the strategic manipulator or the pastiche personality). Psychiatrists would likely find evidence of the traits associated with personality disorders. This type of adult appears to increasing in numbers, and is "at home" in late modern society.

The unconventional adult rejects traditional patterns of adulthood and the life course but is not likely to construct a stable or significant model to replace them. Instead, he or she maintains preadult patterns with a loose (but strained) connection with parents and peers. This adult lives far into Mead's prefigurative society but is often not concerned about the risks or consequences of continuing as a narcissistic half-adult. His or her sense of self may be fragmented, and his or her sense of temporal-spatial continuity impaired. The consequences of the person's unconventional behavior may be disturbing to her or him and to others, but the pattern remains. In this category Gergen would see the strategic manipulator, who takes advantage of other people who also have poorly formed senses of identity. However, this person would have difficulty managing impressions well for any sustained period of time, because of an unstable inner core. Psychiatrists would likely see mixtures of narcissistic, borderline, and antisocial personality disorders among these adults. This type of adult appears to be increasing in number, as a by-product of destructured, hedonistic late modern society.

Although this typology is not strictly based on empirical evidence, it does appear to have a sound theoretical base that can provide directions for future empirical analysis. In the meanwhile, the utility of this sort of typology is found in its ability to help organize otherwise complex and disparate formulations. And its validity can be initially assessed according to its ability to explain and predict social patterns.

With this synthesis we have a working model of the forms that adulthood might be taking in late modern society. For the most part, given the trends I postulate, I do not see any reason to be overly optimistic about the future. Nonetheless, there is room for optimism if we can gain control over the various forces shaping human consciousness, especially economic ones. If we truly want to avoid creating a society like Huxley's Brave New World, we need to acquire the type of insight necessary to avoid moving blindly in that direction.

In the meantime it is clearly an onerous task to make the transition to adulthood in contemporary late modern societies and to maintain a stable adulthood once "there"—not necessarily because the job has become more complex, but rather because it has become trickier, partly as a result of the destructuring that has occurred and partly as a result of the consumer-corporate forces that have moved in to replace traditional forms of culture. Now the rules are less clear and more contextual, and there is less institutional guidance pointing to clear developmental pathways. Hence, there is a need for more individual maneuvering and for people to take more strategic approaches to their life courses. At the same time, many pressures push people toward the paths of least resistance and effort, and fewer influences encourage them to undertake the more difficult forms of self-development that improve their intellects, skills, and senses of identity. It would be easy to simply disparage those who are not doing well in spite of the opportunities ostensibly available in late modern society, but what is needed is a way of understanding them and the forces that move them in the direction of least effort.

## Structure and Agency: Is the Glass Half Empty or Half Full, and for Whom?

The individualization thesis has been criticized for underestimating the continuing impact of social structures on people's lives (Furlong and Cartmel 1997). Although there is widespread agreement that various elements of Western societies have been destructured, there is disagreement about the nature and extent of the destructuring. There is also disagreement regarding its potentially positive repercussions. Beck (1992), for example, argues that the decline in the extent to which social structure governs people's lives has increased the potential for personal agency among the citizens of Western societies. Certainly, more and more has been left to individual choice, but some of that choice is not welcomed or based on meaningful alternatives. As we have seen, many people find themselves in situations requiring that they make choices for which they are unprepared (e.g., they lack emotional maturity, economic resources, or intellectual ability).

Furlong and Cartmel (1997) agree that the conditions facing young people in the 1990s differ considerably from those of previous generations, but they disagree with others on the nature of the changes. In particular, they believe that social class and gender continue to structure people's life chances in a range of contexts. What has happened, they argue, is that the continuing impact of social class and gender has been obscured in important ways as a result of individualization processes. Many people now believe that their futures are entirely a matter of choice when in fact "economic and cultural resources are still central to an understanding of differential life chances and experiences" (109). Furlong and Cartmel identify a "paradox of late modernity" in which the structural foundations of social life have become "more obscure," yet they "continue to provide powerful frameworks which constrain" people's activities. Accordingly, the focus on individual preference has helped to further weaken "collectivist traditions" (109).

Although their analysis is specifically focused on Great Britain, it is consistent with much of what I have described regarding North America. Moreover, even though there is now a "greater diversity of experiences" available to people, Furlong and Cartmel argue that

> the timing of domestic and housing transitions and the chances of successful completion still reflect traditional class and gender divisions. Whereas the protraction of domestic and housing transitions has created the potential for young people to develop as individuals and experiment with different living arrangements, new forms of vulnerability have also been introduced due to the removal of State support and increasing unreliability of access to family resources. In this context, we have suggested that establishment of adult identities has become more problematic. (1997, 111)

Furlong and Cartmel also see evidence of a convergence of social classes and genders, especially in the areas of leisure and lifestyles:

> This convergence partly reflects the extension of youth as a stage in the life-cycle and with young people from all social classes being denied access to enhanced resources through employment. However, changing leisure patterns and lifestyles also highlight the extent to which preferences have been manufactured through mass marketing techniques. In other words, lifestyles are increasingly shaped by the market and therefore should not be viewed as an expression of individual choice. Moreover, those who lack the resources to participate in consumer markets face cultural as well as financial exclusion; in this respect, our evidence highlights a polarization of social life in which those occupying disadvantaged socioeconomic positions face the prospect of total exclusion. (1997, 111)

Furlong and Cartmel have several important things to say that are relevant to the sociological positions we have reviewed in this book. In reference to Giddens's and Beck's works, although they agree "that one of the central characteristics of late modernity is the weakening of collective social identities," they argue that individual reflexivity and personal agency have been overemphasized (Furlong and Cartmel 1997, 113). They claim that a considerable amount of manipulation has taken place, particularly through the media, which serves to "distort reality," not to give people a clearer sense of their choices or places in the world. The new technologically mediated experiences simply provide illusions, shape opinions, and make people feel that they are part of a wider community, when many people are actually constrained by the material conditions associated with social class and gender, which continue to define their *place* in the world.

I am in general agreement with Furlong and Cartmel's analysis. I would add, however, that race and ethnicity need to be added to the list of structural obstacles that continue to determine people's life chances, especially in countries like the United States, although there is evidence there of convergence with respect to certain forms of leisure and lifestyle. Thus, when we ask the question "Is the glass half empty or half full?" it is also appropriate to ask "For whom?" To the extent that race, class, gender, and age continue to structure people's experiences and life chances, these structural obstacles will determine perceptions of what the future has to offer. Those who are favored by these structures will be more optimistic about their future life chances, and rightly so. Those who are not favored by the structures, rightly, will be more pessimistic about their future life chances. To the extent that capitalism requires a certain amount of inequality among its workers, the glass will seem "fuller" for those who benefit from the inequality, and it will seem emptier to those who do not benefit. This does not mean that reality is merely a matter of perception, but that one's perceptions are influenced by how one is affected by that reality. Similarly, those who stand to benefit from the continuing inequalities of capitalism will tend to view it as an inevitable, even natural, economic system that stems from basic human nature. In contrast, those who stand to lose will tend to view it as the product of human activity and a social construction in which those with more power have found ways to maintain or increase that power out of their own individual greed (cf. Unger, Draper, and Pendergrass 1986).

What I believe we particularly need to attend to is the heightening disparity based on age. Trends clearly suggest that age is increasing in importance as a structural obstacle affecting people's life chances, with the most recent cohorts finding more and more obstacles in the way of their transition to independently functioning adulthood. As each cohort has done worse over the last several decades, the face of disadvantage has been changing. Possibly, this is a temporary problem, but if it is not, we face increasingly polarized societies in which being young is a serious financial liability. If this situation maintains itself over several generations, and if the scenario outlined by observers like Rifkin (1995) unfolds, social class and age may become more and more correlated, so that a new age-based proletariat emerges that comprises up to 80% of the population. The other 20% will be either those who managed to escape this proletariat because of their skills and intelligence in mastering the high technologies or those who have been sponsored by wealthy parents who gave them privileged, private educations (but, assuming they have productive roles, even most of the privileged will need to have the skills and intelligence to master high technologies).

If that occurs, gender will decrease as a structural obstacle dividing the population, because there will be a gender convergence based on widespread poor economic prospects (this has already occurred over the past two decades as the prospects of young males have plummeted, meeting those of young females, which have risen [Allahar and Côté 1998]). Similarly, race may become less of a structural obstacle because 80% of the population will face similar dismal prospects in the capitalist labor force. Hence, the "face" of the new bourgeoisie (the 20% class) may become "diverse" in race and gender (global capitalism is "faceless" in some respects) but more homogeneous in age, with entry occurring well into what we now consider adulthood (the 40s and 50s), with the exception of a few highly intelligent younger people who help the bourgeoisie make more money and the (intelligent) children of the existing bourgeoisie.

## Charting a Course: The Happiness of Pursuit

Based on what we have examined throughout this book, what can we say about how adults have charted a course through recent history, and what can we recommend about how people might cope with the outcomes of this history? First, I present some thoughts on the major transformations that have made possible the forms of adulthood that I have identified, and then I make recommendations about how adults in the late modern era can manage the situations in which they find themselves.

### The Seven Deadly Sins: Collectivism and Individualism Reconsidered

The seven deadly sins are pride, greed, lust, envy, anger, sloth, and gluttony. These are the base, human tendencies that the Catholic

Church of the Middle Ages identified as implicated in social decay and as impeding spiritual development. So long as these tendencies were avoided by people and actively censured by the Church, a certain collectively based social stability was maintained, and the impact of capital accumulation was mitigated. However, as history shows, the former "sins" have become "the seven cardinal virtues" (Mumford 1944, 162) that constitute the cornerstone of contemporary capitalism. Indeed, capitalism would not have grown so fast or so extensively if the seven deadly sins continued to be socially proscribed. Slowly, over time, increasing with each generation since the Middle Ages, these character traits have become so widespread that they are now considered normal and even essential for the individual who must function within a capitalist society.

Louis Mumford (1944, 162–163) encapsulated the impact of capitalism on Western civilization in the following way:

> The whole moral change that took place under capitalism can be summed up in the fact that human purposes, human needs, and human limits no longer exercised a directive and restraining influence upon industry: people worked, not to maintain life, but to increase money and power and to minister to the ego that found satisfaction in vast accumulation of money and power. . . . [Before] the emergence of capitalism, economic life had had a strong moral foundation. It was rooted in the notion that every act of life was under the Judgment of God: the trade of market stall no less than the judgments of the market court. Hence the conception of the just price: a price determined by the intrinsic value of the commodity and its actual cost of production, divorced from the accidents of individual preference or material scarcity. The guilds set themselves to establish standards of workmanship and to maintain price levels: an active war went on against those who debased commodities, who tried to corner them, or who sought to avoid selling them in the open market at the standard price, first come, first served. Against the Roman legal motto, Let the buyer beware, the medieval economist held rather, Let buyer and seller both fear God. Medieval production, down to the sixteenth century, centered on security, regularity, equity: social justice was more important than private advantage. (1994, 162–163)

Of course, we have changed the names of the seven deadly sins: pride has become self-esteem, individuality, and vanity; greed has been redefined as materialism: anger has been sublimated into competitiveness and drive; lust has become sexuality, sex appeal, love life, and fashion; envy is now channeled into initiative and incentive; sloth has become leisure; and gluttony is associated with the "good life," which many people seek (either through retirement or by trying to strike it rich). Whatever terms we use, the point is that the level of mass consumption that now characterizes Western societies would not have been possible if these traits had not been nurtured and openly encouraged. Moreover, their nurturance involved a long-term, strategic manipulation of people's values and of the culture into which people would come of age. As Rifkin (1995) outlines, the twentieth century saw a massive assault on the type of behavior patterns that had previously buffered people from the seven deadly sins. With the perfection of mass production techniques, industrialists needed populations of mass consumers, and it was no small task to transform Americans (for example) from a frugal people into "spendthrifts," and to lure them from seeing self-sacrifice as a virtue to expecting "immediate gratification." Indeed, according to Rifkin (and others), the "American business community set out to radically change the psychology that had built the nation—to turn American workers from investors in the future to spenders in the present" (19–20).

Marketing and advertising came of age themselves in the twentieth century, honing their techniques in the 1920s. People were made to feel ashamed for wearing or using homemade products (which were still the norm then), instead of store-bought or factory-made products. Young people were especially targeted, as advertisers preyed on their fears of feeling out of place. Products were advertised with the label "modern" (the equivalent of cool or hip) as opposed to old-fashioned (not cool).

In my view the radical transformation of the seven deadly sins tells us exactly where we have gone off course as a civilization. I am not saying that we should enforce a monastic existence, but these seven weaknesses, coupled with the decline in collective supports and the consequent rise in individualization, seem to be at the heart at most of what is wrong with capitalist-dominated Western societies. It is interesting to speculate about what a capitalism would look like with those seven qualities proscribed. For example, would capitalism be as vital as it now is in breaking down the barriers to human toil? That is difficult to say for sure, but a more "collectivist capitalism" is certainly not out of the question. In fact, there are models for such an entity in the social democracies of the Nordic countries and the communalism of some oriental cultures. Americans seem to assume that capitalism has to be deeply embedded in a high degree of individualism, but this need not be the case. The challenge for the future of highly individualistic, capitalist countries, as I see it, is to reintroduce forms of collectivism, whether it be in civil society through social capital investments (Putnam 1995a, 1995b; Rifkin 1995), education-work integration schemes, or active employment strategies. The theory and practice are there to be observed—the challenge is to adapt them to countries like the United States.

By suggesting that collective supports and networks be revitalized, I am not proposing a return to earlier models of adulthood in which self-development was eschewed in favor of self-sacrifice or where duty and responsibility overrode choice. To the contrary, I am proposing that we consider models of adulthood that combine the best of both worlds: wherein people balance their commitment to self with commitment to others and where people accept responsibility, especially for the choices they make. My recommendations are based on seeing the best, and the worst, of what adults did during the twentieth century, as described in the preceding chapters. For example, I am especially impressed by what Maxine Schnall has to say about character development and the combination of inner- and other-directedness to fight the tendency toward narcissism. I also take seriously Bly's warnings about a society in which half-adults prevail and in which decisions are made by what are in effect bickering siblings. Here are some specific recommendations I have made in my own academic writings.

### Identity Capital: Agency and Human Potential in Individualistic and Communal Societies

In a series of ongoing investigations, I have been studying two responses—passive acceptance and active adaptation—to the condition of late modern society described in this book (Côté 1996a, 1997). As I have noted, the passive response, which involves simply acquiescing in the identity manipulation that characterizes contemporary consumer-corporate society, appears to be widespread. Individuals who undertake more active responses are more involved in their own personal growth; they follow more difficult developmental paths and social/occupational attainment patterns. The social-organizational problems of late modern societies translate to deficient guiding structures, which are often "replaced" by the manipulative influences of consumer-corporate culture. Accordingly, the more auspicious responses to these contexts involve active, agentic dispositions and behaviors that lead individuals to resist the paths of least resistance and effort and instead to explore their potentials, build personal strengths, nurture a critical consciousness of the world around them, and sustain some sense of direction and meaning (i.e., to make choices involving forms of developmental individualization). Thus, agentic dispositions should lead people to explore their potentials and build personal strengths in spite of a nonnurturant environment (cf. Stein, Newcomb, and Bentler 1992; Vallacher and Wegner 1989; White 1979). With those strengths, people should be in a better position to act in the world on the basis of conscience, even though those around them do not.

This work is represented by the "identity capital model," a developmental–social psychological approach to identity formation that integrates psychological and sociological understandings of identity. Most generally, the term *identity capital* denotes what individuals "invest" in "who they are." Such investments potentially reap future dividends in the "identity markets" of late modern communities. To be a player in those markets, one must first establish a stable sense of self, which is bolstered by social and technical skills in a variety of areas, effective behavioral repertoires, psychosocial development to more advanced levels, and associations in key social and occupational networks. At the very least, given the apparent chaos of late modern society, key resources for bargaining and exchanging with others in late modern communities are apt to involve skills in negotiating life-passages with others, such as securing validation in communities of strangers and obtaining membership in the circles and groups to which one aspires. The most successful investors in the identity markets presumably have portfolios comprising two types of assets, one more sociological and the other more psychological.

These assets can be *tangible* in the sense that they are "socially visible." These more sociological features include educational credentials (educational capital), fraternity or sorority and club or association memberships (social capital), personal deportment (e.g., manner of dress, physical attractiveness, and speech patterns), and the like. Tangible resources should be effective as "passports" into other social and institutional spheres, inasmuch as they are needed to get past the "gatekeepers" of various groups in which one wants to be a member, as well as to be accepted by established members. Such groups vary in their concreteness (from those with specific memberships to abstract reference groups), making one's tangible resources important in the micropolitics involved in identity negotiations. As a person interacts daily with others over a period of time, these resources should also increase one's identity capital through the accruing of negotiable self-concepts and self-presentations.

Other identity capital resources are *intangible*. These more psychological factors probably include qualities like the holding of commitments, ego strength, self-efficacy, cognitive flexibility and complexity, critical thinking abilities, moral reasoning abilities, and other character attributes that can give individuals certain vitalities and capacities with which to understand and negotiate the various social, occupational, and personal obstacles and opportunities they are likely to encounter throughout late modern life. Hence, in addition to the more tangible social components, there seems to be an internal subjective/experiential component to identity capital that can be relevant to the external demands of micropolitics and impression management. In Eriksonian terms, these various attributes are tied to well-developed ego-synthetic and ego-executive abilities (cf. Côté 1993). Note, in this context, that I am not saying that making use of identity capital means fostering false impressions and engaging in trickery in dealing with others. To the contrary, the personality takes on a complexity and a flexibility so that it can adapt to the multidimensional contexts of late modern society. Identity capital is thus a set of strengths, not a bag of Machiavellian tricks or a tactic used by Gergen's strategic manipulator.[4]

I would like to emphasize that by speaking in terms of "active" responses and "agency," I am not endorsing what some might call a "male" model of behavior. The problem is that the concept "agentic" is often counterposed with the notion "communal" (e.g., Bakan 1966), and then a leap is made to the idea that females are more communal; agency, then, must be a "masculinist" concept. I believe the careful reader will know that that is not my intention and that, further, it is not an implication of the identity capital model. It does not take much thought to realize that the dimension "active-passive" is not parallel to either "male-female" or "agency-communion." Instead, active-passive is orthogonal to both; for example, females can be both active and passive. Active-passive *is* parallel to the developmental-default individualization dimension I introduced in chapter 1. Accordingly, agentic (choice oriented) patterns can be active (developmental) or passive (default), as can communal (collectively oriented) patterns.

To elaborate the agency-communion distinction, identity capital resources are context specific—what is effective in one context may not be in another. For example, my own academic identity capital is negotiable in university settings but of little value in other contexts (e.g., in dealing with bureaucracies in which I am but one of tens of millions of customers or in getting my car repaired). More to the point, identity capital resources probably differ considerably between individualistic and communal societies. In individualistic societies, attributes that reflect the types of intangible qualities identified here seem to function quite well, but they may not function so well in communal societies. The difference seems to be the amount of "space" the individualist self is given. In individualistic societies, people are expected to actively construct an elaborate interior or psychological space that they carry with them into situations that are often competitive (nonsupportive) and/or ambiguous, but they are expected to fill in what is missing in anomic contexts (or, in the long run, if they are to be successful in their society they need to actively capitalize on what is "missing" normatively in these contexts). For example, when I want my car to be repaired quickly and cheaply by a mechanic whom I do not know, it is helpful in that situation to present my identity to the mechanic as a "regular guy" with "car sense." To present an identity as an "academic egghead" or a "money bags" with only "book sense" or with "more dollars than sense" can result in poor service and a larger repair bill.

In contrast, in communal societies, there is a greater expectation that a "collective self" will be actively constructed that enters cooperative and well-defined situations. Attempts to "fill in" or "capitalize on" contexts can upset the traditions that form the basis of the collective interactions and are thus inappropriate. This does not mean, then, that collectivist behaviors are normatively passive, although they may be in certain contexts (Huxley's Brave New World is an example). Instead, a certain amount of active engagement is both appropriate and welcome in well-functioning collectivist societies. For example, appropriate behaviors in more cooperative societies would be those that contribute to the community's stock of social capital, as Putnam argues (see chapter 2), and these require active engagement. Part of the problem with contemporary Western societies is that people have disengaged from these collective enterprises and have either become passive or have invested their active initiatives outside their communities.

Elsewhere I examine communal forms of behavior that are not passive, and I trace the deleterious influences of capitalism in introducing individualistic, competitive behavior patterns (Côté 1994). But in reference to Western cultures, which have long histories of capitalism and individualism, it does appear that active, agentic responses constitute the most effective forms of identity capital, for both females and males (as opposed to passive, communal). Moreover, theoretical or moral positions that reject the types of active responses to the social conditions of late modern society recommended by the identity capital model risk encouraging people to adopt the very passive, agentic responses that feed into consumer-corporate interests' manipulations and do nothing to ameliorate the negative conditions that many people face. Most certainly, as should be clear to the reader by now, I would like to see far more active, communal-cooperative patterns adopted by people, but I recognize that these patterns may do little in certain Western (individualistic) contexts (e.g., some higher educational settings) to help discrete individuals cope with daily performance demands. It is also self-defeating for people to refuse to be actively agentic when there are obvious benefits to both themselves and others in their lives.

It would appear that our way out of this dilemma is to once again seek a balance that does not recommend one extreme over another. Hence, forms of intangible identity capital that enhance and link up with forms of social capital need to be examined if we hope to get Western civilization back on course, away from its current trajectory toward extreme atomization and alienation. In the next section we turn to a guiding principle that may help us change this course.

## A Model of Maturity: A Universalizing Consciousness with a Caring Particularism

The issue of gender differences in the structure and content of adulthood has been touched on in several chapters. The key issue to emerge in discussions of gender differences is whether women are more relational or caring in their orientations. Many observers who have evaluated the evidence argue that those differences that have been found are either contextual or the product of socialization, not biological dispositions.

The original impetus for the relational model was based on the assumption that existing models of moral development are male biased. However, empirical research has found this not to be the case. Still, there is something in the relational model that needs to be taken seriously. Specifically, we need to understand how a care paradigm (as in Gilligan 1982) can be integrated with a justice paradigm (as in Kohlberg 1979). I have suggestions about how to do so.

Gilligan's care paradigm is obviously most useful for understanding how people can meaningfully relate to others in their immediate environments—an understanding that seems to be lacking in Western societies. Whether it is five centuries of capitalism, many more centuries of patriarchy, or conditions inherent to gesellschaft societies that are behind this lack may not matter at this point. What matters now is what we do about it. But more than one academic has pointed out the limitations of a strictly care-based relational paradigm. The problem is with the inherent particularism of that orientation. Specifically, one can only care in a meaningful fashion for a limited number of people, usually one's immediate family, friends, or community. Those outside of these circles cannot possibly be the beneficiaries of the same type or amount of care. Most certainly, even the most relational person cannot extend genuine care to all the six billion people on planet Earth.

Joan Tronto raises these sorts of questions in her article "Beyond Gender Difference to a Theory of Care." Among other things, she argues that a purely care-centered orientation is limited by its own conservatism. This conservatism has three manifestations. First, as suggested above, "we do not care for everyone equally. We care more for those who are emotionally, and even culturally closer to us. Thus, an ethic of care would become a defense of caring only for one's own family, friends, group, nation" (1987, 659–660). Second, the care orientation focuses on a preservation of existing relationships. If the person's care orientation is unreflective, there is no basis for judging "whether those relationships are good, healthy, or worthy of preservation." As Tronto argues, an unreflective care orientation can breed a hatred of difference, because people will not reflect on whether they should care for those outside of their primary groups. Third, Tronto says that "an ethic of care might lead to the reinforcement of existing social patterns," raising "the question of relativism" because it would likely "embody different moral positions in different societies and at different times" (660). In this respect the relational model would not distinguish the morality of Nazi Germany from Mother Teresa's Missionaries of Charity.

What is lacking in all three instances is an awareness of the moral necessity of applying the same principles of care to all people regardless of whether or not one knows them personally. In other words, one needs a set of universal principles that applies to all persons, not a set of particularistic preferences. This is exactly what Kohlberg offered with his theory of moral development, which emphasizes a justice orientation with a concern for rights, rules, and principles. The error that Gilligan and others have made is to label the concern with abstract principles of justice as a "male" orientation, when in fact that is more likely the "counterbalance" of the care orientation. What seems to have happened is that these two complementary orientations have become divorced from each other, at least in some people's minds and in some societies. The challenge lies in developing an integrated care-justice perspective both for individuals and for societies. For example, sometimes we need to be able to concretize abstract principles to be fair in a caring, compassionate manner, and other times we need to universalize concrete principles to be caring in a just manner. In addition, we need to understand better the connections and overlap between the two moral orientations; we need to see how to make concrete realities more just or more ethical in terms of abstract principles (e.g., Conger and Galambos 1997; Dreyer 1994; Kohlberg, Levine, and Hewer 1983; Walker 1991).

A similar challenge presents itself with respect to the apparently contradictory notions of the autonomous self and the relational self. The more balanced view is that we should encourage people to develop both sides of the self—the autonomous and the relational. Such a balanced personality structure would develop a set of caring and sensitive attachments to others but would also have an interior life and inner strengths. A person who is both autonomous and relational would be able to reflect upon and evaluate her or his relationships in terms of their morality and utility and would be capable both of self-direction and of resisting blatant attempts at manipulation. The person who has a well-developed relational side but not a well-developed autonomous side is likely to be wide open to the types of manipulation we have examined throughout this book. The person with a well-developed autonomous side but without a relational side would be prone to the types of narcissistic excesses we have also examined throughout this book. Thus stated, there is little question as to what character structures we should attempt to foster. However, insisting that these are opposing "yin and yang" orientations inherently rooted in gender will do little to take us in that direction. To the contrary, it will likely increase the polarization between men and women (and inhibit their finding common causes) and potentially set up self-fulfilling prophecies that actually push men and women to differentially value and adopt these orientations.

With a synthesis of the care and justice orientations as a moral outlook, in conjunction with a synthesis of the autonomous and relational "self" as a character structure, I believe that we have the basis of a model of maturity that can both help put us back on course societally and correct some of the excesses now exhibited by certain of the Brave New Adults. If the bulk of the adult-aged population were capable of a universalizing consciousness with a caring particularism and had the active, agentic personality structure to actualize its ethical outlook, I believe that many of the problems created by late modern society could be rectified by the collective political will that would emerge. I also believe that a critical mass of adults equipped with these moral and character structures would be catalysts for action to rectify the problems associated with the transition to adulthood created by corporate-capitalist society. As a gesture toward rectifying these problems, the final section of this book considers the issue of intergenerational justice.

In the meantime, I think it is worth pointing out that the position I have just outlined is similar to the one Erik Erikson took several decades ago with his work on generativity and ethics. Erikson built upon his research on identity in adolescence with formulations of adult development. He argued that the development of a stable sense of ego identity was a necessary precursor to stable forms of adulthood. The development of the stable sense of ego identity—which means a sense of temporal-spatial continuity—is a logical necessity for establishing stable relational bonds to others. Without experiencing stability in one's self, one has a difficult time maintaining stable relations with others, at least in any active sense. Hence, he theorized that a stable sense of adult identity is necessary for stable senses of intimacy and generativity, the two stages constituting much of adulthood in his eight-stage psychosocial theory.

In Erikson's view, "ego strengths" are attributes that are slowly built over the life course. They are necessary for people to make sustaining adaptations to their societies. These strengths also make possible secure bonds with others. It is not until the adult years, however, that people can develop the maturity necessary for a truly relational consciousness, and even then that consciousness can be slow to develop. According to Erikson's theory, adults eventually reach a point at which they "need to be needed" in order to avoid "the mental deformation of self-absorption," as a result of which they become their "own infant and pet" (1964, 130). In view of this tendency, Erikson "postulated an instinctual and psychosocial stage of generativity," in which care "is a quality essential for psychosocial evolution." We can see in Erikson's definition of care a synthesis of particularism and universalism: "Care is the widening concern for what has been generated by love, necessity, or accident; it overcomes ambivalence adhering to the reversible obligation" (131). His concept of generativity, characterized in this way, appears to be the developmental trajectory that nonnarcissistic people take. Narcissistic people, in contrast, would be more likely to take the trajectory toward self-absorption in adulthood. As we have seen, narcissism in middle adulthood is implicated in a variety of dysfunctional behaviors. Indeed, Erikson went on to identify a typology in which those who do not move into an "adult adulthood" move into either an "adolescent adulthood" or a "childlike adulthood" (137). Those who are derailed from the path toward "adult adulthood" have, for one reason or another, not developed one or more of the ego strengths associated with the first five psychosocial stages.

Erikson's definition of adulthood is inherent in his psychosocial theory of the life cycle, particularly with reference to the identity stage: "The problem of adulthood is how to *take care* of those to whom one finds oneself committed as one emerges from the identity period, and to whom one now owes *their* identity." Without this definition of adulthood, "the question of identity is a self-indulgent luxury" (1968, 33). In my view, developments over the last several decades suggest that more and more of the adult populations of Western societies have taken the course toward self-indulgent luxuries and away from the central problem of adulthood. Moreover, I believe they have been increasingly enticed to do so by the economic influences that I have discussed throughout this book. Given that some cultures promote a generative responsibility for the next *seven* generations (Bly 1996), current Western cultures stand in stark contrast in their inability to demonstrate responsibility for the generation currently attempting to reach adulthood, let alone those yet to be born.

When framed in this way, the question of what constitutes adulthood becomes clearer from an Eriksonian perspective. For example, a sine qua non of adulthood is a sense of caring responsibility for others, within one's generation and in subsequent generations. Accordingly, various lifestyle criteria become less relevant. For example, the growing diversity of lifestyles characterizing late modern society is not necessarily a threat to generative adulthood. What is a threat are those lifestyles built exclusively upon narcissism, hedonism, and consumerism that we have examined.

To develop further the psychoanalytic perspective, there is widespread consensus that over the last few centuries there has been a general decline in the level of "superego strength" (the "conscience" internalized during early childhood as a result of disciplining techniques) in Western societies (Côté 1993; Erikson 1958; Wheelis 1958). This lessening of the superego control over behavior has made possible increases in the level of ego strength that people could develop. Erikson identifies the critical juncture for this transition with the Renaissance (1958, 193). After that period the ego had more freedom and autonomy in diverting its energies to the development of politics, science, and other secular activities that represent mastery rather than mindless conformity to an absolute authority. However, the decline in superego strength also seems to have permitted greater levels of id cathexis (immediate self-gratification) in Western societies. For example, numerous holidays have emerged that appear to be primarily in the service of the id but holidays have their origins in "holy days" that hark back to the time when Western societies were more superego-oriented (Christmas is a perfect example).

Along with the decline in superego-oriented activities and the rise in id-oriented activities, it appears that recently an increasing segment of the population has exhibited a less well developed ego orientation. This is suggested by the already examined fact that an increasingly large segment of the population is not developing in significant ways the two primary ego functions that build the types of ego strengths that Erikson says are essential for passage through all of his eight psychosocial stages. Perhaps in response to the conditions of mass society and the manipulations of consumer-corporate society, more and more people seem to be socialized to practice and develop lower levels of ego synthetic (reality testing) and ego executive (taking action) abilities. With each successive cohort in the twentieth century, people seem to have been increasingly lulled into the fantasy worlds of popular culture and positively rewarded for remaining passive. From a psychoanalytic perspective, then, we can expect to see that a growing segment of the population has a poorly developed sense of conscience and a poorly developed sense of ego mastery but a well-developed sense of pleasure and immediate gratification.

If the psychoanalytic perspective is valid, it is easy to see how those psychohistorical developments are complementary to the interests of consumer-corporate society. Indeed, it is easy see why a consumer-corporate society might encourage the development of a population that has well-developed id impulses but poorly developed ego and superego qualities. Not only is such a population easier to entice with positive reinforcements (as in Huxley's *Brave New World*), but it has less capacity to resist those enticements, either on the basis of unmodifiable principles held by a superego or by means of the cognitive activities of a strong ego that would closely scrutinize attempts to influence it.

As we have seen in this book, a substantial body of evidence supports this theoretical perspective. One final piece of evidence is worth mentioning, however, because it speaks directly to the issue of successive cohort change. A series of studies has been carried out since 1966 by Alexander Astin and his associates of the life goals of large samples of first-year college students in the United States (Astin et al. 1994). They found that in the mid-1960s only about 45% of college students rated "being very well off financially" as a very important objective for them. By the mid-1980s this figure reached about 75%. Conversely, "developing a meaningful philosophy of life" was endorsed by over 80% of incoming students in the mid-1960s but only a little more than 30% in the mid-1980s. In other words, money-seeking goals and meaning-seeking goals have traded places among those undertaking the transition to adulthood. Assuming that these orientations are stable into adulthood, the American college-educated population is far more interested in "making money" then "making meaning."

## Political Vision and Will: Toward Intergenerational Justice

Will the Brave New Adult develop the emotional maturity, ego capacity, and ethical wisdom to resist the detrimental directions that Western societies are taking? Will an adult population that tends to be self-absorbed, narcissistic, and other-directed be capable of the political vision and will to take Western civilization into the future in a manner that guarantees the health and well-being of generations to come—not just one or two generations but hundreds—as was done for them by the five hundred preceding generations of recorded history? From what we have seen in this book, there are many reasons not to be hopeful. Some predict that the excessive lifestyles that Western adults have adopted will create a global ecological crisis by the year 2070 that will make it impossible for capitalism to continue at its current pace (Jhally 1997). This ecologically based collapse of capitalism would make it impossible for people to continue their high levels of consumption and their hedonistic lifestyles. That may seem like an overly pessimistic outlook, but anyone who considers himself or herself to be an "adult" must at least consider it seriously.

One call that may stir Brave New Adults from their comfortable existence is the appeal for intergenerational justice, which may be expressed with the notion of a quid pro quo, or in this case an "intergenerational quid pro quo." Quid pro quo literally means "something for something." In an intergenerational sense it means that one generation does something for another and receives something from the other generation in return (cf. O'Neill 1994). This is a key feature of many well-functioning nonindustrial societies: they are able to sustain an age-based reward structure that receives widespread intergenerational endorsement and support. Some nonindustrial societies have been known to exist for millennia on the basis of an intergenerational quid pro quo that linked age cohorts across the division of labor (Côté 1994).

In my view the key problem in late modern, corporate-capitalist societies is that the youngest segments of the population have been increasingly excluded from the meaning-based reward structures of adult society and given instead ersatz materialistic reward structures from which a small segment of the adult population profits. This protracted period of childlike dependency has created a rather paradoxical situation in which there is an increasing sense of entitlement along with an increasing sense of being disfranchised. More and more people want things done for them, but those very people have a diminished right to be productive members of the community. Not only has the status of the young been lowered in general, but their sense of obligation to other members of society has also been reduced. In a cycle of decline, instead of being valued for their productive contributions to and membership in the community, the younger segments have increasingly been thrust into more-or-less enforced idleness or leisure in relation to older age groups. Although this enforced idleness is made to be "fun" for them—indeed, they feel entitled to a certain level of fun—it is a short-sighted deal. The stark fact is that we know of no societies throughout history that have enforced so much idleness on their hitherto most productive members (namely, young adults). Certainly one is hard pressed to find a society in which the youngest segment of the population feels entitled to such material benefits without giving much in return.

But the fact remains that when the intergenerational quid pro quo is lost in a society, the young see less reason to cooperate with their elders. That has happened in many parts of the world, particularly in developing countries, where its consequences can be quite severe for the welfare of the citizenry (Côté 1994). However, there is a pressing need to grant the young greater *meaningful* productive social and economic roles. When that happens, not only their social status will rise, but so too will their willingness to cooperate in improving their society. Moreover, anomic and nihilistic reactions should diminish (cf. Arnett 1996). The adults of late modern society must also do something to thwart those avaricious members of consumer-corporate society who have been carefully constructing the popular culture that increasingly dictates how the transition to adulthood plays out. The adults must be able to distinguish between "freedom to" and "freedom from" (cf. Fromm 1955). Their children need to be free *from* exploitation, and that freedom should go beyond the freedom of others *to* exploit them. When such a moral position is finally taken, we should see a decline in the senseless violence that spread through America's high schools in the 1990s.

As I have indicated, it is not that there are no models that we might study. For example, Sweden has for most of the twentieth century endeavored to create the type of society to which I have referred. A recent publication by the National Board for Youth Affairs in Sweden (*Young Sweden* 1998) provides statistics that show how the transition to adulthood might be more benignly structured by adult society. Currently in Sweden only about twenty persons per year under the age of twenty-four receive prison sentences; of twenty European nations studied, Swedish students feel themselves to be the least bullied; and less than 10% of those aged twenty to twenty-five live with their parents (compared to 30–40% in Canada and 60% in Spain). These are but a few of the statistics suggesting that the transition to adulthood in Sweden is far more benign than in many other Western countries. In *Generation on Hold* (Côté and Allahar 1996) we discussed the policies that were in effect until the late 1980s. Although Sweden suffered some economic setbacks in the early 1990s that increased unemployment among all age groups, Swedes have maintained their efforts to guide and nurture their young. For example, active employment policies have been maintained to help businesses recruit young people, all unemployed young people are eligible for training programs, and young Swedes work within the same job categories as other age groups. Moreover, local authorities and schools are responsible for providing forms of work experience. Teenagers over sixteen who remain in school receive a study allowance, and generous, low-interest student loans are available for those who want to undertake postsecondary education. Those who cannot find work and who are not in school are guaranteed unemployment benefits. In other words, everyone is guaranteed some form of income.

Adult Swedes have also seen to it that young Swedes have opportunities for growth-enhancing activities during their leisure time. Young Swedes have ample opportunities to develop skills through their local schools with respect to the arts and classical music, and fifteen hundred youth recreation centers provide places to meet for young people who are not involved in clubs or sports organizations. At these centers facilities are provided for rehearsing plays, for dancing, and for playing rock music. Two-thirds of the males and one-half of the females are members of some sort of sports association. Clearly, then, the adult community provides social capital for their young. I do not offer the Swedish system as a panacea but rather as an example of what can be done when the adult community makes an attempt to truly care for all of its young and establish a quid pro quo for those making their way to adulthood.

The world of the future will require new identities and roles if we are to steer the course back to one where social justice is seen as the responsibility of each citizen, including business and political leaders. Currently, as a consequence of the changes in the transition to adulthood that we examined in chapter 5, many young people do not feel they have a stake in the society in which they are ostensibly full citizens—instead they feel disfranchised. Without a sense of connection to a society, people—whether young or not—do not feel it is in their interest to care about, or work for, a common good, either in their own "group" or in the world at large. To make matters worse, many teenagers find themselves segregated into high schools in which they are subjected to a "prisonlike" adult-imposed society where their only access to a "culture" is an adult-produced popular culture that seems only to divide them from each other by means of manufactured identities (e.g., skateboarders) that can breed resentment and violence. To the extent that Western societies are becoming masses of disconnected people without a sense of obligation to and reward from others, we are all increasingly impoverished. No amount of corporate activity can fix that, nor will corporations try because it is not in their bottom-line interest. Certainly, intergenerational justice is not part of any corporate-capitalist strategy. Intergenerational justice has been, and remains, the province of the adult segment of the population, which is entrusted with the task of keeping its offspring (and their offspring, and their offspring, and so on) "free from" harm but "free to" live full and complete lives.

I give the last word to Maxine Schnall. She recommends that we "reset our inner compass." She argues that if we are to move "from a narcissistic culture into a socially responsible and caring one," we need to build a society that

> provides the self with empathic guidance from infancy throughout life—to ensure the unfolding of personal fulfilment not only for ourselves, but for future generations. In a self-directed society the individual's capacity to make moral choices will not be blunted by a compliance or overindulgence. It will evolve naturally from our having learned to set healthy inner limits and to organize these limits collectively into a cultural moral code that each of us may be guided by in his or her own way. In such a society the narcissistic use or neglect of children by their parents will cease—and so will our moral aloneness. (1981, 319–320)

# Notes

NOTES TO CHAPTER 1

1. This is a composite sketch of a fictional character based on F. D'Emilio, "Mamma MIA! Gen X clings to home in Italy," *Ottawa Citizen*, April 20, 1996, B1. See also Cavalli 1995 for a discussion of the nature of contemporary youth transitions in Italy.

2. These two stories appeared in the September 1977 issue of *Glamour* magazine in an article titled "Casual Sex: Why Confident Women Are Saying NO," pp. 14–17, by Lynn Harris, who argues that women are increasingly motivated by "enlightened self-interest" and "powerful pragmatism."

3. This is a fictional character based on a composite sketch of life in the United Kingdom for many young men of working-class origin. For an extensive treatment of youth transitions in Britain, including youth crime patterns such as those described here, see Coles 1995.

4. Jacobus Arminius (1560–1604) argued that Christ died for all, not just an elite, thereby opening the way for the "democratization" of Calvinism.

5. According to the *American Heritage Dictionary, Bookshelf 98*, to consume means, among other things, "To expend; use up: To waste; squander: To destroy totally; ravage." Its Latin root is cúmere, to take. See also Rifkin (1995, 19).

6. It has been very difficult to coax most men into the private sphere in all Western countries, including those that have tackled this problem head on. In Sweden, for example, where the "Swedish experiment" has been attempting for some thirty years to accomplish this, little success has been achieved. Only a minority of Swedish men have embraced the private sphere to the extent that the majority of women embrace the public sphere. For details, see Jacobsson and Alfredsson 1993; *Equality* 1997; *Men and Equality* 1999.

7. An indication of the extent of sphere crossover can be seen in the growth of dual-earner families. Crompton and Geran (1995, 26) argue that one of the most radical changes in Canadian society has been the growth of dual-earner husband-wife families. In the past thirty years, their proportion has almost doubled, from 33% to 60%. Thus, in less than a generation, the norm of the traditional family, with a breadwinning husband and a stay-at-home wife, has

been transformed into a new norm, according to which both spouses work outside the home. In addition, the percentage of married women earning more than their husbands has doubled, from 11% in 1967 to 25% in 1993, and the percentage of single-earner families in which the wife is the breadwinner rose from 2% in 1967 to 20% in 1993.

8. The media continue to report gender disparities in the amount of household labor performed. However, when *all* labor—paid and unpaid—is taken into account, Canadian men and women do the same amount, because men on average work more paid hours outside the home than women. The problem lies in sharing the labor in an equitable fashion, with women gaining more in paid labor and men doing more of the unpaid labor. In this sense, then, equal contributions *are being made* by men and women to the welfare of the community.

9. At the same time, as we see below, new structures have emerged to fill some of the voids created by cultural destructuring. However, this "restructuring" has been largely taken over by business interests that have encouraged mass consumer behavior patterns, and these have come to structure family activities, peer groups, leisure time, and the like. A significant outcome has been the transformation of the transition to adulthood into a period increasingly influenced by market-driven popular culture in the guise of an ostensibly rebellious "youth culture."

NOTE TO CHAPTER 2

1. The implications of Kegan's work are more far-reaching than those of Herrnstein and Murray's *The Bell Curve* (1994), which argues that persons of less-than-average intelligence will have increasing difficulties as the technological basis of Western societies becomes more complex. If Kegan is right, even many with above-average intelligence will have difficulties meeting the mental demands of future societies if they do not embark on the types of developmental trajectories to which I have been referring. And if Rifkin is right in his predictions in *The End of Work* (1995) about the effects of technology on the workplace, perhaps only about 20% of the population will be fully functioning members of future societies, with the remaining 80% functioning as service providers and consumers.

NOTES TO CHAPTER 3

1. Note that her prefixes tend to be counterintuitive—she meant "post-" to refer to the past (the cultural configuration has been set), and "pre-" to refer to the future (the cultural configuration remains to be set). See Muuss 1996 for a discussion of this formulation.

2. In Bly's sibling society we can find updated characterizations of Mead's

prefigurative society. For example, he identifies the same general problem as did Mead: "In a sibling society, it is hard to know how to approach one's children, what values to try to teach them, what to stand up for, what to go along with; it is especially hard to know where your children are" (1996, xiii). And in specific reference to university students:

> We can now see an entire generation of students living in an impoverished landscape. The elders are without power . . . The young, black or white, tend to be rationalists and skeptics, and have nothing to live up to; the mutual dependence of generations breaks down. . . . The students' diminished interior landscape, upon which only pop culture shacks have been erected, corresponds with the blasted cultural landscape of adults. Where the mental countryside of the adults once included well-built old houses and even gardens and those squares where people talked, now adults live in the ruins. The adults have had their ability to admire deeply damaged. (161–162)

3. Riesman's other-directed society is "updated" in Bly's sibling society in a number of respects. We see this in Bly's portrayal of a population that needs public acclaim (as evident in the numbers of people who will appear on television talk shows for validation in spite of the ridicule and shame) and is mesmerized by media-fabricated nonevents that stimulate collective fantasies for profit. In addition to being easily manipulated through fantasies, Bly believes, people use others as "mirrors": "In a sibling society we want other people to be like us; we pay attention to the ways we resemble other people. They tend to reflect back our own image [which is inexact]. . . . Seeing our inexact image over and over finally floods our receptors, and we don't know who we are" (1996, 233–234).

NOTES TO CHAPTER 4

1. This framework is largely based on observations of Western cultures and likely applies most readily to the public domain of the middle classes (especially in modern societies). In this sense it is "Eurocentric" and is most relevant to the experiences of middle-class males since they have dominated the public domain. Though this may be a liability, middle-class, public-domain Western cultural patterns have set the standards that many other cultural groupings aspire to or must follow. I prefer to leave this potential bias as an empirical question to be answered on the basis of research that assesses the validity and prevalence of these patterns.

2. On the issue of gender, it follows that because men and women have traditionally occupied different spheres (public versus private), and because women are aspiring to move into the public sphere more than men are aspiring to move into the private sphere, women are merging these spheres more than

are men. The case can still be made, however, that more choices became available for both men and women in the early modern period as ascribed statuses became less common. If we compare the "common" woman and the "common" man, it is not likely that their latitudes of choice differed significantly around matters like mate selection or occupation. The gender gap was likely greater in the middle classes, where men had more options than either middle-class women or working-class men.

3. Note that psychoanalysts like Erikson assign special meanings to the term *ego* (i.e., it represents psychological processes that attempt to test reality and direct behavior), quite distinct from its popular meaning of inflated self-esteem.

4. This terminology is somewhat awkward and has a rather Calvinist tone, which Erikson himself noted (1963). Nevertheless, it has been in use for several decades now, so changing it would lead to some confusion. In the next section of this chapter, we see Josselson's more intuitive terminology.

5. Josselson does not provide elaborate definitions of these terms, but she argues that they coincide with the concepts of agency and communion (Bakan 1966), except that "competence requires less individualism and separateness than Bakan's 'agency' and . . . connection includes disharmonious relational experiences as well as satisfying ones and requires less merging of self than does Bakan's view of 'communion'" (1996, 278). Her notion of competence seems to correspond with what Erikson called a "special competency," which I operationalized as "a purposive use of skills" (Côté 1997, 585–586). I operationalized a separate measure of agency based on a configuration of personality traits including self-esteem, ego strength, internal locus of control, purpose in life, self-actualization, and ideological commitment.

6. The psychological approach therefore tends to treat the experiences of people in the current era as exemplars for people in other eras. Thus, for example, Josselson makes bold statements about what identity "is" and claims that life-stage approaches are not useful, when in fact she may be observing a highly anomalous era in which identity is extremely problematic and life stages have been thrown into flux. It is quite possible that she would draw different conclusions about identity and life stages based on a study of other eras.

7. The *DSM*-IV puts the prevalence at only 2% of the U.S. population, which translates to about 5 million in a population of 250 million.

### NOTES TO CHAPTER 5

1. I do not wish to belabor this point, but assuming that surveys of American religious attendance are unreliable, with weekly attendance being overreported by a factor of two (as I reported in chapter 2), it still remains to be explained why religion holds such popularity in the United States, to the point where significant numbers of people misrepresent themselves on this issue

(whereas people in other Western countries seem not to). Certainly, the individualization thesis seems to hold in the United States, but the degree of religious entrepreneurship seems to be unprecedented compared with that of other Western nations. Bibby (1993, 113) explains it by the same attributes that have brought Americans success in economics, entertainment, and sports; namely, "organizational knowhow, investment, initiative, and imagination." Indeed, there appears to be a burgeoning "religious economy" in the United States; groups have competed "with each other for truth and market shares" (184) as the old mainstream religions have declined in popularity. As a result of shrewd "marketing models," the number of denominations doubled between 1965 and 1990 (from about 800 to 1,600). Some of them now provide entertainment, sports, and recreational centers at churches, catering to the one-stop-mall, consumer mentality that has worked so well commercially (cf. Brady 1991).

2. In North America youth culture is much less defined than in Europe—the term "peer culture" appears to be the more appropriate designation (Brake 1985). Peer cultures seem to have emerged more from mainstream institutions than from countercultural ones in the sense that they have been "sponsored" by mainstream institutions such as secondary schools and result from a socialization context in which there is a low ratio of socializers to socializees. This arrangement encourages socializees to develop resistance to their socializers and to develop their own ersatz culture or counterculture (cf. Gecas 1981, 169). But again, in North America peer-oriented youth culture does not seem to have the coherence and cohesiveness of European youth cultures.

3. The subtitle is "The Teenage Market is Free-Spending and Loaded with Untapped Potential." In this article, "a veteran of teen marketing explains what's cool, what's not, and how to tell the difference" (Zollo 1995, 22).

4. The headnote for the article is "Many of the hottest trends in teenage music, language, and fashion start in America's inner cities, then quickly spread to suburbs. Targeting urban teens has put some companies on the map with the larger mainstream market. But companies need an education in hip-hop culture to avoid costly mistakes" (Spiegler 1996, 29).

5. The headnote is "Today's college students have more money than their predecessors, and they don't mind parting with it. Product and service providers want a piece of the spending now, but the ultimate goal is to cultivate long-term customers" (Speer 1998, 41).

NOTES TO CHAPTER 6

1. Wink and Donahue describe narcissism as follows:
The self-concept of a narcissistic individual [is] . . . fragmented and consisting of both a grandiose and expansive self as well as a self characterized by feelings of inferiority, vulnerability, and sensitivity to slight. . . .

These two contradictory selves lack adequate integration and are the product of an early parental deprivation that prevents the child and then the adult from fully integrating good and bad representations of the self and others. . . . The narcissistic individual is driven in life by the need to keep separate two contradictory views of the self. In the case of overt narcissism, this is achieved by using the grandiose self to defend against inferiority. In the case of covert narcissism, the inferior self is used to protect a more vulnerable, grandiose self from an outside threat of disconfirmation and rejection. (1995, 73-74)

2. A word of warning about this typology is in order. Like all such categorical systems, it is a simplification of a complex reality designed to help us gain a grasp of that reality in order to discuss it. Many people may not find themselves fully represented by any one category. Accordingly, we can identify "mixed types," whereby people combine elements of, say, a traditional adulthood with an inner-directed early modern one, or an other-directed late modern adulthood with an unconventional one.

3. If current trends continue unabated, it is likely that we will see a dramatic reduction in the size of the middle class in the next century, along with a polarization of income. Rifkin argues that this polarization will reshape the class structure such that only about 20% of the population has any real access to affluence via the high-tech and information sectors of the economy. He believes that only this proportion of the population will be needed to maintain and renew the engines of our advanced technological society. The other 80% will function mainly as unskilled and semiskilled laborers who carry out the menial tasks that have not, or cannot, be accomplished with robotics or computers. If this happens, successive youth cohorts are going to face the fact that they will not do as well financially or career-wise as their parents.

4. Preliminary investigations of this model confirm that agentic attributes are indeed important, even more so than the tangible assets studied (such as social class and gender [Côté 1997]). For example, among a group of university students, agentic personality attributes (self-esteem, purpose in life, internal locus of control, ego strength, self-actualization, and ideological commitment) combine to predict identity capital acquisition over a two-year period—in this case formulating a stronger sense of adult identity.

# References

Adams, G. R., Gullotta, T. P., and Montemayor, R. E., eds. 1992. *Adolescent identity formation.* Newbury Park, Calif.: Sage.

Allahar, A. L., and Côté, J. E. 1998. *Richer and poorer: The structure of social inequality in Canada.* Toronto: Lorimer.

Anderson, D. 1991. *The unfinished revolution: The status of women in twelve countries.* Toronto: Doubleday Canada.

Archer, S. L. 1994. *Interventions for adolescent identity development.* Thousand Oaks, Calif.: Sage.

Armstrong, P., and Armstrong, H. 1994. *The double ghetto: Canadian women and their segregated work.* Toronto: McClelland and Stewart.

Arnett, J. J. 1994. Are college students adults? Their conceptions of the transition to adulthood. *Journal of Adult Development* 1:213–224.

———. 1996. *Metalheads: Heavy metal music and adolescent alienation.* Boulder, Colo.: Westview Press.

Arnett, J. J., and Taber, S. 1994. Adolescence terminable and interminable: When does adolescence end? *Journal of Youth and Adolescence* 23:517–537.

Artz, S. 1998. *Sex, power, and the violent school girl.* Toronto: Trifolium Books.

Ashton, D., and Lowe, G. 1991. *Making their way: Education, training, and the labour market in Canada and Britain.* Toronto: University of Toronto Press.

Astin, A. W., Korn, W. S., Sax, L. J., et al. 1994. *The American freshman: National norms for fall 1994.* Los Angeles: Higher Educational Research Institute, University of California.

Bakan, D. 1966. *The duality of human existence.* Chicago: Rand McNally.

Bauman, Z. 1997. *Postmodernity and its discontents.* Cambridge, U.K.: Polity Press.

Beauregard, M. 1993. "Analysis of debt-equity and debt-for-development swaps." In *Is there life after debt?* ed. A. Allahar and R. Cecil, 120–126 . Conference Proceedings. London, Ont.: Inter-American Organization for Higher Education.

Beck, U. 1992. *Risk society: Towards a new modernity.* London: Sage.

———. 1994. "The reinvention of politics: Toward a theory of reflexive modernization." In *Reflexive modernization: Politics, tradition, and aesthetics in the modern social order,* ed. U. Beck, A. Giddens, and S. Lash, 1-59. Stanford, Calif.: Stanford University Press.

Bee, H. L. 1996. *The journey of adulthood.* 3rd ed. Upper Saddle River, N.J.: Prentice-Hall.

Bell, D. 1961. *The end of ideology.* New York: Basic Books.

Bennett, W. J. 1994. *The index of leading cultural indicators: Facts and figures on the state of American society.* New York: Touchstone.

Best, P. 1995. Women, men, and work. *Canadian Social Trends* (Spring): 30–33.

Bibby, R. W. 1993. *Unknown Gods: The ongoing story of religion in Canada.* Toronto: Stoddart.

Bibby, R. W., and Posterski, D. C. 1992. *Teen trends: A nation in motion.* Toronto: Stoddart.

Björkqvist, K., and Niemelä, P. 1992. *Of mice and women: Aspects of female aggression.* Orlando, Fla.: Academic Press.

Bly, R. 1996. *The sibling society: An impassioned call for the rediscovery of adulthood.* New York: Vintage.

Bosma, H. A. 1985. *Identity development in adolescents: Coping with commitments.* Groningen, Netherlands: University of Groningen Press.

Brady, D. 1991. Saving the boomers: Churches shun tradition to attract young adults. *MacLeans,* June 3, 50–51.

Brake, M. 1985. *Comparative youth culture: The sociology of youth culture and youth subculture in America, Britain, and Canada.* London: Routledge and Kegan Paul.

Bronfenbrenner, U., McClelland, P., Wethington, E., et al. 1996. *The state of Americans: This generation and the next.* New York: Free Press.

Buchmann, M. 1989. *The script of life in modern society: Entry into adulthood in a changing world.* Chicago: University of Chicago Press.

Cadello, J. P. 1990. The coming of the submass and the dis-integration of personality. *Canadian Journal of Political and Social Theory* 14:34–46.

Caldicott, H. 1992. *If you love this planet: A plan to heal the earth.* New York: Norton.

Caplow, T., Bahr, H. M., Modell, J., et al. 1991. *Recent trends in the United States, 1960–1990.* Montreal: McGill-Queen's University Press.

Cavalli, A. 1995. "Prolonging youth in Italy: 'Being in no hurry.'" In *Youth in Europe,* ed. A. Cavalli and O. Galland, 23–32. London: Pinter.

Cavalli, A., and Galland, O., eds. 1995. *Youth in Europe.* London: Pinter.

Chadwick, B. A., Gauthier, M., Hourmant, L., et al. 1994. "Trends in religion and secularization." In *Convergence or divergence? Comparing recent social trends in industrial societies,* ed. S. Langlois, T. Caplow, H. Mendras, et al., 173–214. Montreal and Kingston: McGill-Queen's University Press.

Chisholm, L. 1995. "Conclusion: Europe, Europeanization and young people:

A triad of confusing images." In *Youth in Europe*, ed. A. Cavalli and O. Galland, 127–140. London: Pinter.

Chisholm, P. 1999. Teens under siege. *MacLeans,* May 3, 22–24.

Clark, W. 1998. Religious observance: Marriage and family. *Canadian Social Trends* (Autumn): 2–7.

Coles, B. 1995. *Youth and social policy: Youth citizenship and young careers.* London: UCL Press.

Collins, R. 1979. *The credential society: A historical sociology of education and stratification.* New York: Academic Press.

Conger, J., and Galambos, N. L. 1997. *Adolescence and youth.* 5th ed. New York: Addison Wesley Longman.

Côté, J. E. 1984. *The identity crisis: A formulation and empirical test of Erikson's theory of ego identity formation.* Ph.D. diss., York University.

———. 1986. Identity crisis modality: A technique for assessing the structure of the identity crisis. *Journal of Adolescence* 9:321–335.

———. 1993. Foundations of a psychoanalytic social psychology: Neo-Eriksonian propositions regarding the relationship between psychic structure and cultural institutions. *Developmental Review* 13:31–53.

———. 1994. *Adolescent storm and stress: An evaluation of the Mead/Freeman controversy.* Hillsdale, N.J.: Lawrence Erlbaum.

———. 1996a. Sociological perspectives on identity formation: The culture-identity link and identity capital. *Journal of Adolescence* 19:417–428.

———. 1996b. "Identity: A multidimensional analysis." In *Psychosocial development during adolescence: Progress in developmental contextualism,* ed. G. R. Adams, R. Montemayor, and T. P Gullotta, 130–180. Thousand Oaks, Calif.: Sage.

———. 1997. An empirical test of the identity capital model. *Journal of Adolescence* 20:577–597.

Côté, J. E., and Allahar, A. L. 1996. *Generation on hold: Coming of age in the late twentieth century.* New York: New York University Press.

Côté, J. E., and Levine, C. 1987. A formulation of Erikson's theory of ego identity formation. *Developmental Review* 7:273–325.

———. 1988. A critical examination of the ego identity status paradigm. *Developmental Review* 8:147–184.

———. 1989. An empirical test of Erikson's theory of ego identity formation. *Youth and Society* 20:388–415.

Crain, W. 1992. *Theories of development: Concepts and applications.* Englewood Cliffs, N.J.: Prentice-Hall.

Crompton, S., and Geran, L. 1995. Women as main wage-earners. *Perspectives on Labour and Income* 7 (4):26–29.

Cutler, B. 1990. Where does the free time go? *American Demographics* (November): 36–39.

Danesi, M. 1994. *The signs and meanings of adolescence.* Toronto: University of Toronto Press.

Davis, J. 1990. *Youth and the condition of Britain: Images of adolescent conflict.* London: Athlone Press.

*Diagnostic and statistical manual for mental disorders (DSM-III).* 1977. 3rd ed. Washington: American Psychiatric Association.

*Diagnostic and statistical manual for mental disorders (DSM-IV).* 1994. 4th ed. Washington: American Psychiatric Association.

Dreyer, P. 1994. "Designing curricular identity interventions for secondary schools." In *Interventions for adolescent identity development,* ed. S. L. Archer, 121–140. Thousand Oaks, Calif.: Sage.

Eisenstein, Z. 1998. *Global obscenities: Patriarchy, capitalism, and the lure of cyberfantasy.* New York: New York University Press.

Elshtain, J. B. 1993. *Democracy on trial.* Toronto: House of Anansi Press.

*Equality between women and men.* 1997. Stockholm: Swedish Institute.

Erikson, E. H. 1958. *Young man Luther.* Norton: New York.

———. 1959. "Late adolescence." In *The student and mental health: An international view,* ed. D. H. Funkenstein, 66–106. Cambridge, U.K.: Riverside Press.

———. 1963. *Childhood and society.* 2nd ed. New York: Norton.

———. 1964. *Insight and responsibiity.* New York: Norton.

———. 1968. *Identity: Youth and crisis.* New York: Norton.

———. 1979. "Report from Vikram: Further perspectives on the life cycle." In *Identity and adulthood,* ed. S. Kakar, 13–34. Bombay: Oxford University Press.

Ewen, S. 1976. *Captains of consciousness: Advertising and the social roots of the consumer culture.* New York: McGraw-Hill.

Ewen, S., and Ewen, E. 1982. *Channels of desire: Mass images and the shaping of American consciousness.* New York: McGraw-Hill.

Farnsworth Riche, M. 1990. The boomerang age: Don't assume 18-to-24-year-olds are adults. *American Demographics* (May): 25–30, 52–53.

Feinstein, S. C. 1985. "Identity and adjustment disorders of adolescence." In *Comprehensive textbook of psychiatry,* 4th ed., ed. H. I. Kaplan and B. J. Sadock, 1760–1765. Baltimore: Williams and Wilkins.

Fishman, S. 1997. The d generation. *Details* (April): 90–97, 170.

*The forgotten half: Non-college youth in America.* 1988. Washington: William T. Grant Foundation.

Frank, T. 1997a. *The conquest of cool: Business culture, counterculture, and the rise of hip consumerism.* Chicago: University of Chicago Press.

———. 1997b. Let them eat lifestyle: From hip to hype—the ultimate corporate takeover. *Utne Reader* (November–December): 43–47.

Fromm, E. 1955. *The sane society.* Greenwich, Conn.: Fawcett Publications.

Furlong, A., and Cartmel, F. 1997. *Young people and social change: Individualization and risk in late modernity.* Buckingham, U.K.: Open University Press.

Galland, O. 1995. "What is youth?" In *Youth in Europe,* ed. A. Cavalli and O. Galland, 1–23. London: Pinter.

Gecas, V. 1981. "Contexts of socialization." In *Social psychology: Sociological perspectives,* 165–199. New York: Basic Books.

Gecas, V., and Burke, P. J. 1995. "Self and identity." In *Sociological perspectives on social psychology,* ed. K. S. Cook, G. A. Fine, and J. S. House, 41–67. Boston: Allyn and Bacon.

Gerbner, G., Gross, L., Morgan, M., et al. 1980. The "mainstreaming of America": Violence profile no. 11. *Journal of Communication* 30:10–29.

Gergen, K. J. 1991. *The saturated self: Dilemmas of identity in contemporary life.* New York: Basic Books.

———. 1994. *Realities and relationships: Soundings in social construction.* Cambridge, Mass.: Harvard University Press.

———. 1996. "Technology and the self: From the essential to the sublime." In *Constructing the self in a mediated world,* ed. D. Grodin and T. R. Lindlof, 127–140. Thousand Oaks, Calif.: Sage.

Giddens, A. 1990. *The consequences of modernity.* Stanford, Calif.: Stanford University Press.

———. 1991. *Modernity and self-identity: Self and society in the late modern age.* Stanford, Calif.: Stanford University Press.

———. 1994. *Beyond left and right: The future of radical politics.* Cambridge, U.K.: Polity Press.

Gilligan, C. 1982. *In a different voice: Psychological theory and women's development.* Cambridge, Mass.: Harvard University Press.

Gilligan, C., and Attanucci, J. 1988. Two moral orientations: Gender differences and similarities. *Merrill-Palmer Quarterly* 34:223–237.

Glass, J. M. 1993. Multiplicity, identity, and the horrors of selfhood: Failures in the postmodern position. *Political Psychology* 14 (2): 255–278.

Glasser, W. 1972. *The identity society.* New York: Harper and Row.

Hardwick, D. A. 1984. College students' concept of adulthood. *Psychological Reports* 54:967–968.

Hareven, T. K. 1994. Aging and generational relations: A historical and life course perspective. *Annual Review of Sociology* 20:437–461.

Herrnstein, R. J., and Murray, C. 1994. *The bell curve: Intelligence and class structure in American life.* New York: Free Press.

Hollinger, R. 1994. *Postmodernism and the social sciences: A thematic approach.* Thousand Oaks, Calif.: Sage.

Hulbert, K. D. 1993. "Reflections on the lives of educated women." In *Women's lives through time: Educated American women of the twentieth century,* ed. K. D. Hulbert and D. T. Schuster, 417–443. San Francisco: Jossey-Bass.

Huxley, A. 1932. *Brave New World.* London: Triad Grafton.

Jacobsson, R., and Alfredsson, K. 1993. *Equal worth: The status of men and women in Sweden.* Stockholm: Swedish Institute.

Jhally, S. 1997. *Advertising and the end of the world.* Northampton, Mass.: Media Education Foundation. Videocassette.

Jones, G., and Wallace, C. 1992. *Youth, family, and citizenship.* Buckingham, U.K.: Open University Press.

Jonsson, B. 1994. Youth life projects and modernization in Sweden: A crosssectional study. Paper presented at Fifth Biennial Meeting of the Society for Research on Adolescence, San Diego, Calif.

Jordan, J. V. 1997. "A relational perspective for understanding women's development." In *Women's growth in diversity: More writings from the Stone Center,* ed. J. V. Jordan, 9–24. New York: Guilford Press.

Jordan, W. D. 1978. "Searching for adulthood in America." In *Adulthood,* ed. E. H. Erikson, 189–199. New York: Norton.

Josselson, R. 1996. *Revising herself: The story of women's identity from college to midlife.* New York: Oxford University Press.

Kegan, R. 1994. *In over our heads: The mental demands of modern life.* Cambridge, Mass.: Harvard University Press.

Keniston, K. 1975. "Prologue: Youth as a stage of life." In *Youth,* ed. R. J. Havighurst and P. H. Dreyer, 1–12. Chicago: University of Chicago Press.

Kerckhoff, A. C. 1990. *Getting started: Transition to adulthood in Great Britain.* Boulder, Colo.: Westview Press.

Klein, H. 1990. Adolescence, youth, and young adulthood: Rethinking current conceptualizations of life stage. *Youth and Society* 21:446–471.

Kohlberg, L. 1979. *Measuring moral judgment.* Worcester, Mass.: Clark University Press.

Kohlberg, L., Levine, C., and Hewer, A. 1983. *Moral stages: A current formulation and a response to critics.* Basel, Switz.: S. Karger.

Koth de Paredes, M. 1993. "Debt swaps for education in Latin America." In *Is there life after debt?* ed. A. Allahar and R. Cecil, 127–134. Conference Proceedings. London, Ontario: Inter-American Organization for Higher Education.

Kreisman, J. J., and Straus, H. 1989. *I hate you—don't leave me: Understanding the borderline personality.* New York: Avon Books.

Kroger, J. 1989. *Identity in adolescence: The balance between self and other.* London: Routledge.

Kroger, J., and Haslett, S. J. 1991. A comparison of ego identity status transition pathways and change rates across five identity domains. *International Journal of Aging and Human Development* 32:303–330.

Kuhn, D. 1979. The significance of Piaget's formal operations stage in education. *Journal of Education* 161:34–50.

Lacayo, R. 1994. If everyone is hip . . . is anyone hip? *Time,* August 8, 48–55.

Langlois, S., Caplow, T., Mendras, H., et al., eds. 1994. *Convergence or divergence? Comparing recent social trends in industrial societies*. Montreal and Kingston: McGill-Queens University Press.

Lasch, C. 1979. *The culture of narcissism: American life in an age of diminishing expectations*. New York: Warner Books.

LaVoie, J. C. 1994. Identity in adolescence: Issues of theory, structure, and transition. *Journal of Adolescence* 17:17–28.

Lengerman, P. M., and Wallace, R. A. 1985. *Gender in America: Social control and social change*. Englewood Cliffs, N.J.: Prentice-Hall.

Lerner, R. M. 1995. *America's youth in crisis: Challenges and options for programs and policies*. Thousand Oaks, Calif.: Sage.

Levinson, D. J. 1996. *The seasons of a woman's life*. New York: Alfred A. Knopf.

Lindsay, C., Devereaux, M. S., and Bergob, M. 1994. *Youth in Canada*. 2nd ed. Ottawa: Statistics Canada.

Lunt, P. K., and Livingstone, S. M. 1992. *Mass consumption and personal identity*. Buckingham, U.K.: Open University Press.

Maffesoli, M. 1996. *The time of tribes: The decline of individualism in mass society*. London: Sage.

Males, M. A. 1996. *The scapegoat generation: America's war on adolescents*. Monroe, Maine: Common Courage Press.

Marcia, J. E. 1989. "Identity diffusion differentiated." In *Psychological development: Perspectives across the life-span*, ed. M. A. Luszcz and T. Nettlebeck, 289–294. New York: Elsevier Science Publishers B.V.

Marcia, J. E., Waterman, A. S., Matteson, D. R., et al. 1993. *Ego identity: A handbook for psychosocial research*. New York: Springer-Verlag.

McGee, T. 1997. Getting inside kids' heads. *American Demographics* (January): 21–24.

Mead, M. 1928. *Coming of age in Samoa: A psychological study of primitive youth for Western civilization*. New York: Morrow Quill Paperbacks.

———. 1970. *Culture and commitment: A study of the generation gap*. Garden City, N.Y.: Doubleday.

*Men and equality*. 1999. Stockholm: Ministry of Industry, Employment, and Communications.

Merser, C. 1987. *"Grown-ups": A generation in search of adulthood*. New York: G. P. Putnam's.

Meštrović, S. G. 1997. *Postemotional society*. London: Sage.

Michener, H. A., and DeLamater, J. D. 1999. *Social psychology*. 4th ed. Fort Worth: Harcourt Brace.

Mintz, S. 1993. "Life stages." In *Encyclopedia of American social history*, vol. 3, ed. M. K. Cayton, E. J. Gorn, and P. W. Williams, 2011–2022. New York: Scribner's.

Modell, J., Furstenberg, F. F., and Hershberg, T. 1976. Social change and transitions to adulthood in historical perspective. *Journal of Family History* 1:7–31.

Mogelonsky, M. 1996. The rocky road to adulthood. *American Demographics* (May): 26–35, 56.

Montgomery, M. J., and Sorell, G. T. 1997. Difference in love attitudes across family life stages. *Family Relations* 46:55–61.

Mørch, S. 1995. Culture and the challenge of adaptation: Foreign youth in Denmark. *International Journal of Comparative Race and Ethnic Studies* 2 (1): 102–115.

Moses, B. 1997. *Career intelligence: Mastering the new work and personal realities.* Toronto: Stoddart.

Mumford, L. 1944. *The condition of man.* New York: Harcourt, Brace, and World.

Muuss, R. 1996. *Theories of adolescence.* 6th ed. New York: McGraw-Hill.

Myles, J., Picot, W. G., and Wannell, T. 1988. *Wages and jobs in the 1980s: Changing youth wages and the declining middle.* Ottawa: Statistics Canada: Social and Economic Studies Division.

Nobert, L., and McDowell, R. 1994. *Profile of post-secondary education in Canada.* 1993 ed. Ottawa: Education Support Branch, Human Resources Development Canada.

O'Neill, J. 1994. *The missing child in liberal theory.* Toronto: University of Toronto Press.

Owram, D. 1996. *Born at the right time: A history of the Baby Boom generation.* Toronto: University of Toronto Press.

Palladino, G. 1996. *Teenagers: An American history.* New York: Basic Books.

Petersen, A. C. 1993. Creating adolescents: The role of context and process in developmental trajectories. *Journal of Research on Adolescence* 3:1–18.

Piaget, J. 1954. *The construction of reality in the child.* New York: Basic Books.

Pleck, E. H. 1993. "Gender roles and relations." In *Encyclopedia of American social history,* vol. 3, ed. M. K. Cayton, E. J. Gorn, and P. W. Williams, 1945–1960. New York: Scribner's.

Proefrock, D. W. 1981. Adolescence: Social fact and psychological concept. *Adolescence* 26 (64): 851–858.

Pulkkinen, L., and Kokko, K. 1998. Stability of identity status from age 27 to 36. Paper presented at Society for Research on Adolescence Biennial Meeting, San Diego, Calif.

Putnam, R. D. 1995a. Tuning in, tuning out: The strange disappearance of social capital in America. *PS: Political Science and Politics* (December): 664–683.

———. 1995b. Bowling alone: America's declining social capital. *Journal of Democracy* 6:65–78.

————. 1996. The decline of civil society: How come? So what? *Journal of Public Sector Management* 27:27–36.

Rice, F. P. 1998. *Human development: A life-span approach.* 3rd ed. Upper Saddle River, N.J.: Prentice-Hall.

Riesman, D. 1950. *The lonely crowd: A study of the changing American character.* New Haven, Conn.: Yale University Press.

Rifkin, J. 1995. *The end of work.* New York: G. P. Putnam's.

Ritchie, K. 1995. Marketing to Generation X. *American Demographics* (April): 34–39.

Robinson, J. P. 1990a. Thanks for reading this. *American Demographics* (May): 6–7.

————. 1990b. I love my TV. *American Demographics* (September): 24–27.

Rogers, D. 1982. *The adult years: An introduction to aging.* 2nd ed. Englewood Cliffs, N.J.: Prentice-Hall.

Schlegel, A., and Barry, H. 1991. *Adolescence: An anthropological inquiry.* New York: Free Press.

Schnall, M. 1981. *Limits: A search for new values.* New York: Clarkson N. Potter.

Schultze, Q. J., Anker, R. M., Bratt, J. D., et al. 1990. *Dancing in the dark: Youth, popular culture, and the electronic media.* Grand Rapids, Mich.: William B. Eerdmans.

Smart, B. 1993. *Postmodernity.* London: Routledge.

Speer, T. L. 1998. College come-ons. *American Demographics* (March): 41–45.

Spiegler, M. 1996. Marketing street culture: Bringing hip-hop style to the mainstream. *American Demographics* (November): 29–34.

Sprinthall, N. A., and Collins, W. A. 1995. *Adolescent psychology: A developmental view.* 3rd ed. New York: McGraw-Hill.

Stafseng, O. 1994. A critique of slippery theories on postmodernity and youth. *Udkast* 22:190–210.

Stein, J. A., Newcomb, M. D., and Bentler, P. M. 1992. The effect of agency and communality on self-esteem: Gender differences in longitudinal data. *Sex Roles* 26:465–483.

Steinberg, L. 1990. "Pubertal maturation and parent-adolescent distance: An evolutionary perspective." In *Biology of adolescent behavior and development,* ed. G. R. Adams, R. Montemayor, and T. P. Gullotta, 71–97. Newbury Park, Calif.: Sage.

Strasburger, V. C., and Donnerstein, E. 1999. Children, adolescents, and the media: Issues and solutions. *Pediatrics* 103:129–139.

Tanner, J. 1996. *Teenage troubles: Youth and deviance in Canada.* Toronto: Nelson Canada.

Taras, D. 1999. *Power and betrayal in the Canadian media.* Toronto: Broadview Press.

Tavris, C. 1992. *The mismeasure of woman: Why women are not the better sex, the inferior sex, or the opposite sex.* New York: Touchstone.

Teeple, G. 1995. *Globalization and the decline of social reform.* Toronto: Garamond Press.

Tönnies, F. 1980. "Gemeinschaft und gesellschaft." In *The pleasures of sociology,* ed. L. A. Coser, 169–171. New York: New American Library.

Tronto, J. C. 1987. Beyond gender difference to a theory of care. *Journal of Women in Culture and Society* 12:644–663.

Turner, J. S. 1996. *Encyclopedia of relationships across the lifespan.* Westport, Conn.: Greenwood Press.

Turner, J. S., and Helms, D. B. 1982. *Contemporary adulthood.* 2nd ed. New York: Holt, Rinehart and Winston.

Unger, R., Draper, R. D., and Pendergrass, M. L. 1986. Personal epistemology and personal experience. *Journal of Social Issues* 42:67–79.

Vallacher, R. R., and Wegner, D. M. 1989. Levels of personal agency: Individual variation in action identification. *Journal of Personality and Social Psychology* 57:660–671.

Walker, L. J. 1991. "Sex differences in moral reasoning." In *Handbook of moral behavior and development,* vol. 2, ed. W. M. Kurtines and J. L. Gewirtz, 333–364. Hillsdale, N.J.: Lawrence Erlbaum.

Wallace, C. 1995. How old is young and young is old? The restructuring of age and the life-course in Europe. Paper presented at Youth 2000: An International Conference, Middlesborough, U.K.

Walsh, P. B. 1983. *Growing through time: An introduction to adult development.* Monterey, Calif.: Brooks/Cole.

Wannell, T., and Caron, N. 1994. *The gender earnings gap among recent postsecondary graduates, 1984–92.* Analytic studies branch research paper series, no. 68. Ottawa: Statistics Canada.

Weigert, A. J., Teitge, J. S., and Teitge, D. W. 1986. *Society and identity: Toward a sociological psychology.* Cambridge, U.K.: Cambridge University Press.

Wheelis, A. 1958. *The quest for identity.* New York: Norton.

White, L. 1994. Coresidence and leaving home: Young adults and their parents. *Annual Review of Sociology* 20:81–102.

White, M. S. 1979. Measuring androgyny in adulthood. *Psychology of Women Quarterly* 3:293–307.

Wink, P., and Donahue, K. 1995. Implications of college-age narcissism for psychosocial functioning at midlife: Findings from a longitudinal study of women. *Journal of Adult Development* 2:73–85.

Wirth, L. 1938. Urbanism as a way of life. *American Journal of Sociology* 44:1–24.

Wrightsman, L. S. 1988. *Personality development in adulthood.* Newbury Park, Calif.: Sage.

*Young Sweden.* 1998. Stockholm: National Board for Youth Affairs.

Zollo, P. 1995. Talking to teens: The teenage market is free-spending and loaded with untapped potential. *American Demographics* (November): 22–28.

# Index

# About the Author

James E. Côté, Ph.D. is a professor of sociology and has taught for the past fifteen years in the Department of Sociology, University of Western Ontario, Canada. He has authored or co-authored three books, including *Generation on Hold: Coming of Age in the Late Twentieth Century,* and two dozen journal articles, including titles like "A Social History of Youth in Samoa: Religion, Capitalism, and Cultural Disenfranchisement," and "The Discovery and Conquest of Youth: The Genesis of the New Reserve of Cheap Labor." He is the founding editor of *Identity: An International Journal of Theory and Research* and is active in learned associations like the Society for Research on Identity Formation and the Society for Research on Adolescence.

Professor Côté teaches courses in Social Psychology, the Sociology of Youth, Socialization, and Mass Society. His research interests include: Socialization, Human Development, and the Life Course; Cross-cultural and Historical Studies of Adolescence and Adulthood; Psychological and Sociology Approaches to Identity; The Social Psychology of Education and Personal Development; The Mead-Freeman Controversy in Anthropology.

Printed in the United States
64147LVS00006B/225

9 780814 715987